# ASTROLOGICAL AGES AND THE GALACTIC CENTER

## ANCIENT WISDOM FOR THIS TIME OF TRANSITION

HEATHER M. ENSWORTH, PhD

BEAR & COMPANY
ROCHESTER, VERMONT

Bear & Company
One Park Street
Rochester, Vermont 05767
www.BearandCompanyBooks.com

Bear & Company is a division of Inner Traditions International



First edition published in 2009 by iUniverse under the title *Finding Our Center: Wisdom from the Stars and Planets in Times of Change*
Revised edition published in 2026 by Bear & Company under the title *Astrological Ages and the Galactic Center: Ancient Wisdom for This Time of Transition.*



Cataloging-in-Publication Data for this title is available from the Library of Congress

ISBN 978-1-59143-555-6 (print)
ISBN 978-1-59143-556-3 (ebook)

Printed and bound in the United States by Lake Book Manufacturing, LLC
10 9 8 7 6 5 4 3 2

Text design by Priscilla Harris Baker and layout by Debbie Glogover
This book was typeset in Garamond Premier Pro with Avenir Next, Gill Sans MT Pro, ITC Legacy Sans, and Nobel used as display typefaces



To send correspondence to the author of this book, mail a first-class letter to the author c/o Inner Traditions, One Park Street, Rochester, VT 05767, and we will forward the communication, or contact the author directly at **risingmoonhealingcenter.com**.

# ASTROLOGICAL AGES AND THE GALACTIC CENTER

"This is a magisterial, revelatory work—a brilliant manual of instruction that offers us a long historical perspective, showing us where we have come from and where we are going. With profound scholarship, the author explains the path of the precessional cycle, showing how the mythology of ancient civilizations is woven into this cycle and how we can use this to understand our present time and respond to its challenge. There is so much wisdom in this book—wisdom that would help us to orient ourselves in this time of transition, connecting with the deep ground of the universe through our hearts, even to the galactic center of the cosmos itself."

Anne Baring PhD (hons), author of *The Dream of the Cosmos* and *Divine Wisdom and The Holy Spirit*

"Heather Ensworth has produced a masterpiece and, in doing so, has established herself as the authority on the shifts of the ages—the great cycles of time. As a shaman, she reminds us of the importance of remembering the magic of ancient indigenous wisdom and connection. Her magnum opus has a great purpose: to guide us back into co-creation with an interconnected Cosmos. This book is exquisitely written and vast in scope but also infused with deep love for all of creation. I do not doubt that it will become a defining classic and a guide for these times of profound transformation. It is the call from a wise, loving heart for humanity to wake up and remember who we truly are. An impressively beautiful work."

Pam Gregory, astrologer and author of *You Don't Really Believe in Astrology, Do You?*

"A fast-paced and engrossing read that simultaneously informs, enlightens, and inspires. Weaving together archetypal legends and symbols, astrological lore, archaeological discoveries, and ancient concepts of cyclical time, Heather Ensworth has skillfully charted the journey of human civilization through the ages, culminating in our time of profound transformation. The book resonates with much-needed esoteric wisdom and guidance for navigating the shift out of this age of darkness and into the ascending cycle of consciousness."

Bibhu Dev Misra, author of *Yuga Shift*

"In her captivating work, Heather Ensworth guides readers through an astonishing 12,000-year cycle, exploring the intricacies of seven astrological ages. Emerging from this evolutionary journey progression are exquisite patterns and inherent instructions, offering evidence of how deeply our human experience is connected to cosmic and galactic protocol. Heather skillfully weaves these potential complexities into a clear, practical framework, enabling readers to track their own personal journey out of, and back into, a Golden Age. Through her work we can feel and intuitively sense how purposeful the turbulence of our current times has been, opening our eyes to a broader, more divine perspective on the complete cycle of humanity and our universe—revealing that love remains the only sure and enduring force accompanying us through it all."

Ke'oni Hanalei, founder of Pohala Botanicals and author of *'ULU Mu Hawaiian Spinal Technology*

"Heather Ensworth has created a masterpiece that takes us through vast ages and cycles of time to examine the rise and fall of human consciousness and civilizations and the archetypal cosmic energies guiding each stage of our evolution. Her research into each Great Age on the precessional wheel is remarkable. She identifies major world-changing events from approximately 12,000 years ago to the present, showing how these events mirror dominant cosmic archetypes. This is a book of remembrance, honoring the ever-cycling 24,000-year journey of humanity. I am deeply grateful to Heather for writing it, helping us understand the profound meaning and importance of the times we now live in."

Jocelyn Star Feather, astrologer and founder of Sacred Planet, LLC

*Awareness of an archetypal dimension of reality and its intimate participation in human affairs has over the centuries received perhaps its most sustained and precisely articulated expression in astrology.*

RICHARD TARNAS,
*PROMETHEUS THE AWAKENER*

*Ah, not to be cut off,*
*not through the slightest partition*
*shut out from the law of the stars.*
*The inner—what is it?*
*if not the intensified sky,*
*hurled through with birds and deep*
*with the winds of homecoming.*

RAINER MARIA RILKE

# Contents

**PART THREE**

## UNDERSTANDING THIS TIME OF TRANSFORMATION AND MOVEMENT INTO HIGHER CONSCIOUSNESS

# Foreword

## *by Barbara Hand Clow*

The publication of Heather Ensworth's *Astrological Ages and the Galactic Center* integrates the influence of the Great Ages and the Vedic Yuga cycles. This concise and complex book is a page-turner. It delivers the long records of time, a data bank that inspired humanity until a few thousand years ago when it was forgotten during the nebulous Piscean Age. This is the guidance we need for the Age of Aquarius.

The precession of the equinoxes, the movement of cultures through twelve Great Ages that are each around 2,000 years, has been an arcane background topic in astrology. The classical Greeks described twelve Ages in a 24,000-year long "Great Year." The Great Year came into historical discourse in the 1970s in the West with *Hamlet's Mill: An Essay Investigating the Origins of Human Knowledge and Its Transmission Through Myth* by esteemed science historians Giorgio de Santillana and Hertha von Dechend. As an astrologer and student of Vedic literature when *Hamlet's Mill* was published, I was delighted, because I believe these astrological cycles describe phases of cultural evolution. Also in the 1970s, the Vedic master Swami Sri Yukteswar compared the Yuga cycles to the precessional ages. His book *The Holy Science* inspired my own deep study of these cycles in the 1980s, then a lonely journey because few astrologers thought much about precession, and the mythology in *Hamlet's Mill* is very confusing and obtuse. But by trusting my inner voice and astrology, I found the shifting Great Ages to be a way to peer into the past.

I missed Heather's 2009 edition of *Finding Our Center*. Luckily, our paths finally crossed a few years ago when she interviewed me. I was stunned by her mythological and astrological knowledge, and we immediately became kindred souls. I was really excited when I read *Finding Our Center*, because it features a brilliant synopsis of the most recent six Great Ages—Leo, Cancer, Gemini, Taurus, Aries, and Pisces—phases I'd explored in 2001 in *Catastrophobia* (retitled *Awakening the Planetary Mind* in 2011). I'd delved into the evidence for a great cataclysm during the Age of Leo 12,000 years ago and discussed human cultural recovery after it. We're now completing the half cycle, because the Age of Aquarius is opposite the Age of Leo in the 24,000-year-long Great Year. Heather and I believe we are remembering floating cataclysmic trauma buried in our psyches from 12,000 years ago. This is healing our fear from the Fall of Atlantis, the end of a dimly recalled Golden Age. Our meeting of minds is significant because recovering the story of the last six Great Ages is a critical phase of our healing, especially after the Kali Yuga ended in 2025. This yuga is the most unenlightened cycle in the 24,000-year Indian Vedic wheel of time that is forcing us to remember our story.

As Heather points out based on Bibhu Dev Misra's *The Yuga Shift*, the ending of the Kali Yuga corresponds to the timing of the Great Ages. Significantly for us in the West, Vedic wisdom about the yugas offers more clear information than the Greek Great Ages. The yugas inform us about the *meaning* of the timing: Human cultures ascend for around 12,000 years and then a cataclysm occurs because change is part of life. After the cataclysm 12,000 years ago, culture descended until 2025, when ascension returned to build cosmic consciousness. The profoundly time-conscious Vedic culture saved this precious knowledge.

This has been giving hope to the people in India inspired by Swami Sri Yukteswar and other Vedic scholars who also inspired the West during the 1970s, when, also, the memory of the Great Ages was revived. We have hope and courage as the long descent is ending. We *will* attain high consciousness again after losing it during the great cataclysm. We *will* find the courage to save our planet from shocking ignorance. We *will* ascend in joy and balance our needs with Gaia's creative matrix.

I love this book because of how it is arranged. Part One orients our solar system within the Milky Way galaxy. We've been struggling with blind confusions because astronomers have not described how Earth's precession affects the star cycles. For example, the ancient Egyptians seemed to believe our Sun is a binary star system orbiting with a star in the Sirius system. It is time for astronomers to describe our solar system's binary structure now that new and powerful telescopes have revealed most stars are binary. Walter Cruttenden of the Binary Research Institute in Newport Beach, California, has been arguing our Sun is a binary system, but most astronomers ignore him.

The ancient Egyptians probably knew we are binary, which is probably why they were obsessed with Sirius. Ancient cultures knew about precession and probably discovered some of the Kuiper Belt objects and Oort cloud bodies found since 2000. The ancients seemed to have known about many things we are "discovering," because there are so many traces of precessional knowledge in mythology. Also, I think it is compelling that astronomers have been consulting with astrologers about their extensive mythological knowledge as they name newly discovered objects in the solar system. I leave that discussion to Heather's voluminous data on these recent discoveries. As you will see in the Part Three of this book, the appearance of many previously unseen bodies in recent times is involved with our awakening now. Part One reorients our Sun, the direction that astronomy will have to take as we ascend back through the yugas and Great Ages. Once upon a time, astrologers were the astronomers.

In Part Two, we sink into the deep narrative—the core analysis of the six Great Ages since Leo 12,000 years ago. Heather examines ancient symbols that describe the Great Ages, the archaeology of remnants from precataclysmic advanced cultures, and the mythology that awakens our deep minds. Her core study of the six Great Ages is very deep and thoughtful, yet so simply and clearly expressed that you *see* into the lenses of time. Heather is a great mythologist and storyteller, a time machine with eyes. Her mind resonates so profoundly with past cycles that you may remember things you've always known. In Part Three, she describes the mythology of recently discovered Kuiper Belt objects such as Quaoar, and Oort cloud bodies such as Sedna. Note that Pluto was sighted in 1930, just when the Bomb was created with plutonium. When bodies are found, often they resonate with newly emerging things. The story of Sedna's dissolution in the sea reminds us how to dissolve in cosmic consciousness.

Nothing is ever really lost, just forgotten for a while, as my Cherokee Grandfather Hand, a great storyteller, taught me as a child. Until the Age of Pisces and the advent of Christianity, Indigenous people were inspired by the great stories of time. Because Heather is a great storyteller like my grandfather, I think her book will seize our culture's mind. A materialistic science like astronomy is a desert at the end of the disintegration of mythic awareness. Enjoy this wonderful book during your ascension through the yugas of Vedic tradition and the Great Years of the Greeks.

Barbara Hand Clow is an internationally acclaimed astrologer, ceremonial teacher, author, and Mayan Calendar researcher. Her numerous books include *Revelations of the Aquarian Age*, *Revelations from the Source*, *The Pleiadian Agenda*, *Alchemy of Nine Dimensions*, *Awakening the Planetary Mind*, and *The Mayan Code*.

INTRODUCTION

# The Meaning of Our World in Transformation

Since the beginning of human history and the development of conscious thinking, dating back hundreds of thousands of years, cultures have questioned the meaning of life and formed an understanding of our relationship with the Earth and the Universe. The forms of these cosmologies have changed across time and across cultures. How are we to decipher these ways of understanding life and the meaning of our existence? How do we become more consciously aware of the beliefs and values that shape our world in this time? How do we find a deeper purpose and meaning that can guide us in how to live our lives?

We currently live in an intense time of transition and transformation. Many of us feel the increasing pace of time and the escalating tensions in our world. We are faced with ever-erupting global conflicts and wars related to militant forces of nationalism and fundamentalism. We confront an increasing environmental crisis as we push our own and the Earth's survival to the brink of disaster. Hunger and famine are more widespread, and the gap between the world's wealthy and the poor is widening. Conflicts about nationality, ethnicity, gender, and religious beliefs are rampant.

The current world systems and social structures that we have relied on for our sense of stability and security are increasingly dysfunctional or are disintegrating. We feel the collapse of the paradigms of the past, and this in turn evokes widespread anxiety, anger, confusion, and polarization across the globe. This has led to uprisings, revolts, and chaos in many countries, as well as the rise of dictators or totalitarian and authoritarian leaders who seize power and control either through fueling people's fear or by presenting an illusion of being the one who can bring order out of chaos.

Individually, many of us feel that our lives need to change, yet we do not know how to do that or what that might mean. How do we make sense of this period of change and turmoil? How do we find our way in the increasing chaos and confusion of these times? Is there some larger meaning or purpose that lies beneath these crises? Where do we turn for answers?

In the midst of individual and collective turbulence, the religious institutions that have been a source of solace and of beliefs defining our sense of reality are showing signs of stress, fragmentation, and collapse. The Catholic Church has been fraught with accusations of sexual abuse and corruption in the United States and Europe, and this has led to a significant reduction in membership. In most modern Western countries, there has been a significant decline in religious belief as well as attendance in religious institutions.

We also see religious and political conflicts around the globe—in the Middle East, in Russia and Ukraine, in Sudan, and in Myanmar. These are just a few examples of what is happening around the globe. How do we understand the increasing violence, destruction, and polarization that is occurring in our world? Where do we turn to find solace and spiritual guidance? Why are we experiencing such turbulent times?

Perhaps, if we view our current experience in the larger context of human history, we can gain clues as to what we are experiencing and how to navigate these intense times. In ancient cultures, there was a deep understanding that our lives are guided and mirrored by the movements of the stars and planets as well as by changes here on Earth. Across human history, the Great Year, the precessional cycle of approximately 24,000 years in which the pole stars and constellations of the ecliptic gradually shift in the sky, has given us guidance regarding the evolution and shifts of our consciousness as well as cultural and Earth changes. Since ancient times, spiritual teachers and guides have known that the transitions from one astrological age to the next are times of turmoil. Part of the turbulence of our current time relates to the shifts in consciousness that we are experiencing in this transition from the Age of Pisces to the Age of Aquarius. Our ways of knowing, thinking, and formulating reality are being called into transformation and transmutation.

As we move through this shift, we are becoming more aware of the destructiveness of the paradigms of the past five thousand years. During this time, we moved into the patriarchal period, with an increasing suppression of the wisdom of the Sacred Feminine, an increasing disconnection from the Earth, and increasing division in our relationships with each other. These paradigms have valued power-over—conquest and control versus compassion, collaboration, and community. They idealize individuality, competition, and the accumulation of wealth rather than living in balance and harmony with each other and with the natural environment. We have seen the effects of the dominance of scientific materialism, linear thinking, and disconnection from Spirit and from a sense of interconnectedness with the life around us.

This has led to increasing polarization and division between self and other, spirit and nature, and the Sacred Masculine and Sacred Feminine. We see this polarization exemplified in the philosophies of Plato and Aristotle and further refined by the work of René Descartes and the scientific revolution. This destructive dualism and polarization have been codified in religious systems of thought that view the body as separate from spirit, and humans as set apart from nature. Nature is devalued in these patriarchal paradigms and seen as a resource to be exploited and controlled. Women, in their intrinsic connection with nature in their monthly cycles and childbearing, have also been devalued in patriarchal society. But as we will see, this split has not always been evident in human history.

In addition, we see the ongoing devaluation or active destruction of Indigenous cultures and other voices in the world that hold a different perspective and could guide us in coming back into balance with each other and the world around us. Despite the increasing cultural and environmental devastation surrounding us, those who dominate the world see this as a time when humanity is at its pinnacle of advancement.

The dualism in the world and the power-over paradigms, and the way they have impacted our sense of self and relationships with each other, is also evident in the history of our understanding of the human mind and in the development of psychology across the past one hundred years. Much of early psychological theory has been about the development of an individuated self (i.e., consider the theories of Freud and Jung as well as much of psychoanalytic theory). Psychological health was described as the capacity to separate from merger (usually in relationship with the mother) and to develop an autonomous sense of self. To be a fully functioning person also meant the capacity to contain and control one's feelings and impulses, to separate the mind from the body and emotions. Discrimination, analytical thinking, productivity, and many of the facets of left-brain functioning have been emphasized in modern Western culture. Intuition, imagination, holistic thinking, and empathic attunement (aspects more of right-brain functioning) have been devalued.

In recent years, with new developments in psychology and physics, we have begun to see a shift in this way of thinking. Recent psychological theories (such as the Stone Center's self-in-relation work and developments in self psychology and ecopsychology) have emphasized the importance of relationship in the formulation and maintenance of healthy human functioning. Dr. Allan Schore, who has written a seminal book, *Affect Regulation and the Origin of the Self,* links the effects of early emotional attunement and relationship to the neurobiology of early development and the subsequent development of the child's emotional and social functioning. Dan Pink, in his book *A Whole New Mind: Moving from the Information Age to the Conceptual Age*, states that effective functioning in our current time of change requires the skills, creativity, and flexibility of right-brain thinking that incorporate a more holistic way of being and knowing.

Developments in quantum physics are asserting what mystics have always known—that there is no clear demarcation between the observer and the observed, that there is no objective reality in the Universe, but rather that everything is interconnected. In her recent books, including *The Cosmic Hologram* and *The Story of Gaia*, cosmologist Jude Currivan has written brilliantly and beautifully about how we live in a holographic reality and are a part of and co-creators with this Cosmic consciousness. This sense of interconnectedness is also inherent in our increasing awareness that a butterfly's wings may trigger a hurricane on the other side of the globe. All of life is interwoven. We cannot separate ourselves from the larger whole, whether we are speaking of the global community, the fabric of nature, or our galaxy.

Environmentalists are calling us back to that awareness and reminding us that if we do not begin to live in more dynamic, respectful relationship with the plants and animals and landscape around us, we will destroy ourselves as well as our planet. Thomas Berry, among many others, passionately speaks of this in his book *The Dream of the Earth*. He has spoken of our need to understand this current time as the dawn of an Ecozoic age when all of our political and environmental policies need to reflect the awareness that we are only one species among many inhabiting this planet. Evolution biologist Elisabet Sahtouris has written brilliantly about this in her book *EarthDance: Living Systems in Evolution*, in which she describes how, as species mature, they learn to move from competition and "survival of the fittest" to an understanding of the importance of interdependence and interconnectedness. It is time, as she asserts, for our human species to learn from these other species and to grow up. It is time for an evolutionary leap for humanity.

Our increasing global interconnectedness, with the rise of the internet and social media, and our awareness of events around the world and of being part of a global community also bring this point home. We are profoundly affected by world events. We may try to isolate ourselves with nationalistic ideology and national boundaries or, more locally, in gated communities, but there is no real separation from the realities of the world that we live in. This is also becoming more and more apparent economically. We may strive to foster and secure our own wealth and material comfort, but we find that we reap the consequences when we deprive others to better ourselves. We see this in the instability of world markets and in the rise in terrorism in response to global injustice. We are becoming increasingly aware through compassion or through the consequences of our actions that we are not alone in this world. We are part of the global human community and part of nature. Each of us is one thread in the web of life of the Universe.

Our bodies and our psyches speak to us of this larger truth. Our bodies mirror our relationship to the natural world around us. As we overpopulate the globe, we find that cancer is on the rise. Cancer is the out-of-control multiplication of aberrant cells that spread through our bodies, bringing destruction to our organ systems. We have recently come out of a global pandemic that spread like wildfire around the globe due to our interconnectedness. As we pollute our air and rivers, we find ourselves experiencing disorders of the immune system. Our cells turn against us as we have turned against the Earth. The more that we respond with increasing efforts to exert control (through lockdowns, warfare, consumerism, or massive overdevelopment), the more we find ourselves faced with disease and the destabilization of our internal and external environments.

Psychologically, we have to wonder what it means that loneliness, anxiety, depression, and suicide are so rampant in modern Western cultures? Are these not, in part, a response to our increasing sense of disconnection from each other and from our natural environment and to the turbulence of these times? They are also a manifestation of our growing sense of confusion, despair, and disillusionment with our current ways of thinking and being. Perhaps some spiritual or subconscious part of us remembers that this is not the way that life has always been. We hear the faint whispering of our ancestral lineage reminding us of what it means to live in communion and in wonder, to be part of the larger whole. We remember what it was like to be in tune with the cycles of the seasons and the phases of the Moon. We remember when the movement of the stars and planets had meaning. We remember when we were a part of the fabric of life and knew the creative and loving energy that moves throughout the Universe. We remember when all was One, and we were held in that knowing, in that fierce embrace.

How then do we find our way back into balance? Or is it even possible to go back? Perhaps, like the prodigal child, we need to return with the knowledge of what it means to experience ruptured relationship, the angst of separation and the despair of disconnection. Like the adolescent who defiantly asserts separation, we are needing to mature in the awareness that we are only truly unique and whole when we remember what it means to come back into right relationship—now with more respect and awareness of the profundity of our interconnectedness and the damaging results of defiance, illusory control, and separation. Perhaps, analogous to our individual psychological development, we have needed to move through this phase in our collective cultural evolution. But, like the acting-out adolescent, if we remain locked in this developmental stage, we will become increasingly destructive to ourselves and to all of life around us. We are being asked to engage in a profound shift in consciousness. We are called to move into more conscious communion and co-creation with each other and with the natural world.

But how do we return? How do we make this shift? Ironically, in recent years, as we have become more aware of our increasingly fragile situation globally and environmentally, Western cultures have attempted to manage the problems through escalating efforts at control. We mandate vaccines and lockdowns to control against disease; we go to war preemptively to fend off the violence of terrorists. We declare "war" against cancer, drugs, "illegal" immigration, or poverty. We increasingly use antibiotics ("antilife" pills) and toxic chemicals (chemotherapy) to "fight" illness. While these approaches can be part of the path to health and survival for many who are ill, they also reflect our dominant mentality of separation, aggression, and power-over. More and more, we are realizing that there are more holistic and natural options to recover our health and well-being. We are seeing that war, power-over, and dominance are not effective paths to world peace and stability.

We need to look deeper into ourselves and reflect on our current paradigms. We need to learn to listen. The increasing illnesses are giving us a message about our imbalance with nature and disconnection from our own bodies. The spread of violence and despair is speaking to us of global injustice and inequity. The rising greenhouse gases in our atmosphere are showing us that we are violating the very air that we breathe. The answer is not to try harder to assert control and dominance but to pause and listen and remember what it means to be in right relationship. We need to return to attunement, to respect, to compassion, and to an awareness of the interconnectedness of all of life. What we do to the rivers, we do to our own bloodstreams. What we do to our sisters and brothers in other countries, we do to ourselves. What we do to the trees of the rainforests, we do to our own lungs. There is no separation. We live in a sentient Universe, and we are a part of a unified Cosmos.

In ancient times, our ancestors were more in tune with the meaning and wonder of the Universe. They had an intrinsic understanding of natural law, and they lived in intimate relationship with the plants that they ate and used for medicines and with the animals that they hunted for food. They knew that their survival was dependent on being in right relationship, on interacting with other species with honor and gratitude. Indigenous cultures continue to understand that their actions in the present affect the seven generations to follow. For thousands of years, they have known how to listen to the pulse of the Earth and the songs of the stars. How then do we find our way back to that knowledge, not forgetting where we have been and who we have become, but coming back into relationship with the Earth, each other, and all of life with more consciousness, compassion, wisdom, and respect?

Throughout human history, our cultural development has been shaped by the world around us and our relationship to it. This is evident in archaeology and in mythology across the ages. What we have forgotten is how much our ancestors understood themselves as part of a larger whole. They knew that the currents that shape the Universe also coursed through their veins and affected their lives. They looked to the patterns in nature and in the sky to guide them into more awareness of and attunement with the creative intelligence of the Universe. They glimpsed the signature of the Divine in the cycles of nature, in the color or shape of plants, and in the movement of the stars.

Since the development of Newtonian physics and the industrial age, we have attempted to remove ourselves from that web of connection and have tried to analyze ourselves and nature as separate "objects" for study, dissection, and mastery. We have learned a great deal about the Universe in this manner, but we have lost touch with a deeper sense of meaning and wisdom in the process. Our challenge is to begin to reweave our scientific understanding back into a cosmology, a sense of the meaning of who we are in relation to the Cosmos.

Perhaps, we can be guided by our ancestors in that effort. If we trace human history across the millennia, we will see that the patterns of culture and mythology were shaped by the movement of the stars in the sky, not in a deterministic sense but in a relational context. This is the art and science of astrology, which has been in existence for thousands of years. In recent history, astrology has been devalued. We no longer seek meaning and wisdom from the sky but have focused on seeing the planets as bodies of matter to be explored and measured. It is time to reweave our collection of factual data with our ancestors' attunement to patterns, cycles, and a context of meaning. While we have blinded ourselves to the sky with our artificial light in our cities, the patterns of the stars and planets remain in the firmament above us. It is time to move beyond the analysis of our minds and open our hearts to the messages that the Universe is trying to convey to us. The communication is there if we are willing to listen.

As we reconnect with this ancient wisdom, astrology supports us in the remembrance of the hermetic principle "as above, so below." Astrology is the understanding that the energies of the sky are mirrored in the energies on the Earth. I do not view astrology as deterministic or predictive but rather as a guide to us in seeing these patterns and in understanding the energies of the times that we are in and how to work with them in the most conscious way. Astrology supports us in reconnecting with the wisdom of the Cosmos and coming back into relationship with the consciousness of the Cosmos that is within us and all around us. The themes of the precessional cycle and of the astrological ages help us to chart our evolutionary journey of collective consciousness as humanity. This cycle guides us in a spiral journey of exploration and transformation as we move through different lessons and experiences on the planet in our evolutionary process individually and collectively.

In this book, we will trace some of the themes of the ages of human history through looking at the precession of the equinoxes and how the shifting of the constellations was reflected in the beliefs and developments of human culture. These themes will be presented in broad strokes. This is not meant to be a detailed historical or archaeological analysis. Rather, it is an effort to begin to reweave that web of connection, to see how shifts in the patterns of the Earth and sky are mirrored in our human consciousness and cosmology.

The Great Year or full circle of the precessional cycle through the signs of the zodiac (approximately 24,000 years) is similar to the ancient medicine wheel. We learn through going through the cycle and integrating the energies and wisdom of each of the signs. Eventually, we learn to step off the wheel and integrate the meaning of the whole. When we come to that awareness, we are able to disidentify from whatever age we are in and come to the center, holding the diversity of who we are and of our collective consciousness. In listening to the wisdom of the ages, we can be guided toward that more whole and centered way of being, and in so doing, move into higher consciousness and become conscious collaborators and co-creators of our destiny with Cosmic consciousness.

PART ONE

# SETTING THE STAGE

CHAPTER 1

# Living in a Time of Transition

We are currently in a transition between ages. We are leaving the Age of Pisces and are on the cusp of a new age, the Age of Aquarius. Ancient myths and modern science teach us that such periods of transition are marked by global and social turmoil. These times are stressful for the planet from a geological standpoint and also from a cultural or sociological perspective and involve significant shifts in human consciousness.

The cycle of astrological ages is related to the precession of the equinoxes. Our Earth revolves around the Sun and rotates on its axis. However, our view of the sky gradually shifts over time (currently, 1 degree every seventy-two years) due to the precessional cycle. The traditional understanding of this gradual movement of the Earth's axis in relation to the sky is that the Earth has a slow, wobbling movement due to the gravitational pull of the Sun and Moon, resulting in the shifting of the Earth's axis over time. This is the lunisolar theory of precession first advocated by Isaac Newton. However, Newton's mathematical formulas could not account for why the Sun's movement appeared to change in speed over time.

The visible manifestation of this precessional cycle that has been tracked across thousands of years is in the gradual changing of the celestial pole and the slow shifting of the constellations in the sky. For example, in 3000 BCE, the pole star was Alpha Draconis, but now our pole star is Polaris. (See Figure 1.1 and Figure 1.2 below.)

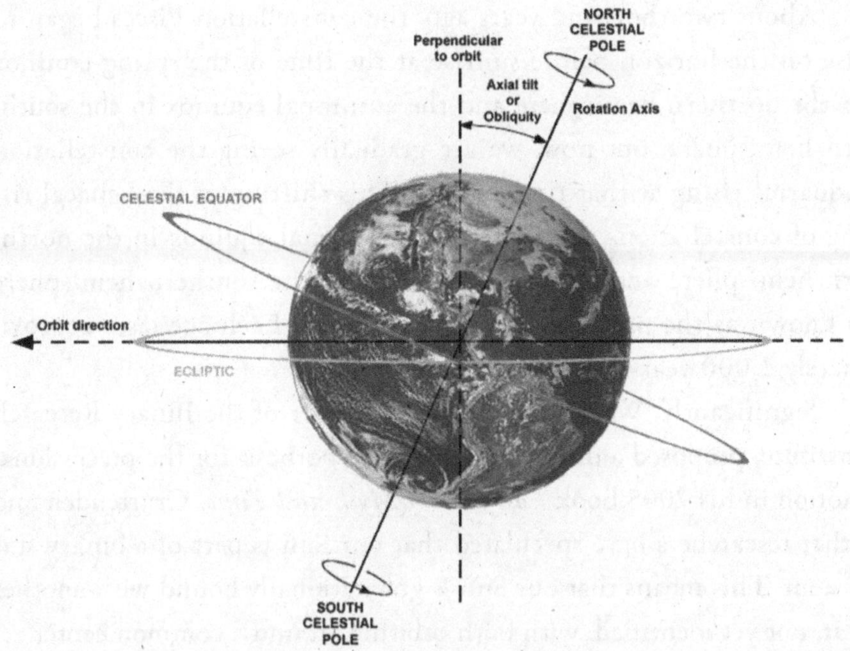


Fig. 1.1. The tilt of the Earth's axis and the movement of the celestial pole.
Illustration by Dennis Nilsson

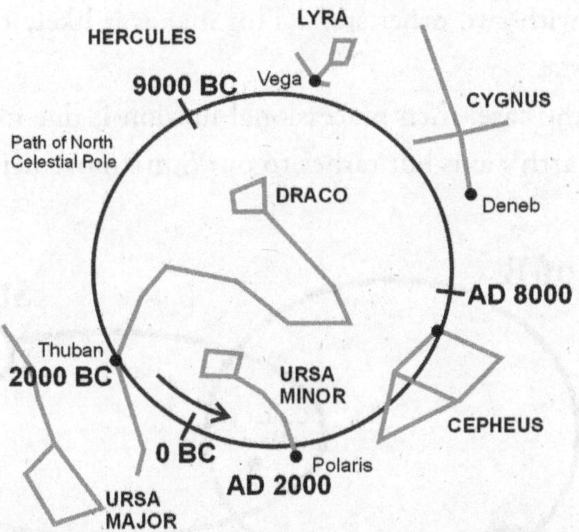


Fig. 1.2. The change in the pole star with the movement of the celestial pole.
Illustration by Miraceti

About two thousand years ago, the constellation Pisces began to rise on the horizon before sunrise at the time of the spring equinox in the northern hemisphere and the autumnal equinox in the southern hemisphere, but now, we are gradually seeing the constellation Aquarius rising at that time of year. This shifting of the heliacal rising of constellations at the time of the vernal equinox in the northern hemisphere and autumnal equinox in the southern hemisphere is known as the precession of the equinoxes. Each age lasts approximately 2,000 years.

Significantly, Walter Cruttenden, founder of the Binary Research Institute, proposed a different scientific hypothesis for the precessional motion in his 2005 book *Lost Star of Myth and Time.* Cruttenden and other researchers have speculated that our Sun is part of a binary star system. This means that our Sun is gravitationally bound with another star, not yet identified, with both orbiting around a common center.

Astronomers have noted in the past several years that binary star systems are common in the Milky Way galaxy. In fact, there are scientific estimates that up to 80 percent of all stars are binary stars or are in a star system with two other stars. This makes it likely that our Sun is also a binary star.

If this is the case, then precessional motion is due not to the wobbling of the Earth's axis but rather to our Sun's movement, which pulls

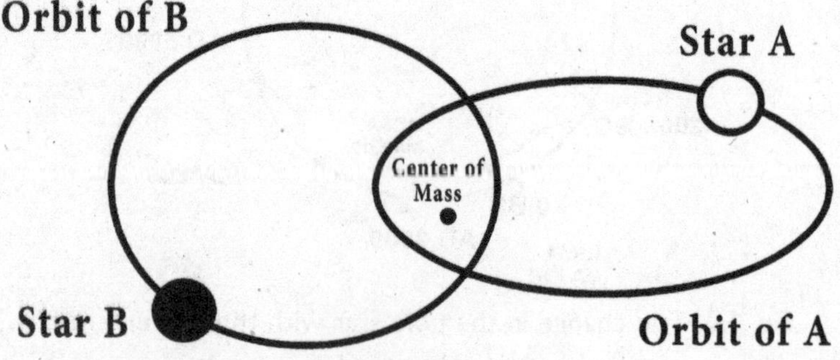


Fig. 1.3. A binary star orbit.

our solar system in a gentle arc through space. Our Sun and this binary star would move in a figure-eight motion around each other. As our Sun moves closer to the binary star, the speed of the cycle accelerates. As our Sun is more distant from its binary star, the cycle slows down. Robert Edward Grant has calculated that the length of precession ranges between 21,600 and 25,920 years depending on the Sun's distance from its binary star. However, according to Grant, if you find the mean time of the cycle, it totals 24,000 years.[1]

As Cruttenden explains the movement of this binary star orbit:

> Just as the spinning motion of the Earth causes the cycle of day and night, and just as the orbital motion of the Earth around the Sun causes the cycle of the seasons, so too does the binary motion cause a cycle of rising and falling ages over long periods of time, due to increasing and decreasing electromagnetic effects generated by our Sun and nearby stars.[2]

If, in fact, we are part of a binary star system, think how this would affect our understanding of the Universe and ourselves. Our overemphasis in modern Western culture on separation and individuation would be called into question, and in a deep and profound way we would need to understand ourselves, our solar system, and our Universe in a relational context. Rather than seeing our Sun as a solo solar hero, our Sun becomes a partner, dancing in a relationship with another star that is guiding us through our evolutionary process.

Some of the researchers advocating the binary star theory believe that the star we are orbiting as our binary star is Sirius. It is noteworthy that this star has been sacred in many ancient cultures. The Dogon culture in West Africa has honored Sirius for over five thousand years. Interestingly, long before the modern scientific discovery that Sirius is a twin star, with Sirius A orbited by its invisible twin, Sirius B, the Dogon tribe worshiped both and were able to describe Sirius B as an invisible, heavy, but very powerful star. They believe that Sirius is the axis of the Universe and the source of all life.

Lenie Reedijk has done extensive research on the temples of Malta and has realized that all of the intact temples have a clear alignment to the star Sirius. The temple builders changed the angle of the entryways slightly over time to shift with the movement of the precession and maintain alignment with Sirius. With these alignments, she has determined that some of these temples date back to 11,000 years ago.[3]

In ancient Egypt, Sirius was worshiped for thousands of years as the primary Great Mother and life-giving goddess Isis, who was seen as the source of life and as the one who helped souls to incarnate on this planet. The Egyptians also honored the rising of Sirius, as it heralded the flooding of the Nile, bringing life to people. Many other ancient cultures honored Sirius as a primary deity. Perhaps these ancient cultures had knowledge that was subsequently forgotten in more recent times.

Sirius is in the constellation Canis Major and is the brightest star in our sky. It is visible in both hemispheres and is slightly more than twice the mass of our Sun and slightly less than twice the diameter of our Sun. It is interesting that the number two recurs with this star in its relationship with our Sun. Also, it is 8.6 light years from our Earth and so is within the parameter of ten light years needed to fit with the possibility of being our binary star, and it is moving toward the Earth. It also has the greatest mass of any nearby star, and its companion star Sirius B is a highly dense white dwarf star.

According to Cruttenden, research into the possibility of our Sun being a binary star has increased in recent years, particularly with the discovery of the trans-Neptunian dwarf planets. Scientists at Caltech in California, including Michael Brown and Konstantin Batygin, have been searching for a massive planet ("Planet Nine") or even a binary star for our solar system due to the way in which these dwarf planets, including Pluto, have elongated orbits with their perihelions (closest point in their orbits to the Sun) all configured close together on one side of the Sun. They also have orbits that are tilted in relation to those of the other planets in our solar system, indicating that they may be influenced by the gravitational pull of a star or large planetary body.[4]

It is also noteworthy that the speed of the Sun's movement through its precessional cycle has accelerated significantly, according to measurements across the last two hundred years, reducing the length of the precessional cycle by one hundred years. So, again, this would indicate that our Sun may speed up in its movement as it approaches its binary star.

Cruttenden has explored this research about the possibility of our being part of a binary star system for over twenty years.[5] He states that a significant reference for our being part of a binary star system comes from the 1894 book *The Holy Science* by Indian astronomer and philosopher Swami Sri Yukteswar, in which Yukteswar writes:

> We learn from Oriental astronomy that moons revolve around their planets, and planets turning on their axes revolve with their moons round the sun; and the sun with its planets and their moons takes some star for its dual and revolves round it in about 24,000 years of our earth—a celestial phenomenon that causes the backward motion of the equinoctial points around the zodiac.[6]

Yukteswar also accurately indicated that the dates of the last aphelion and perihelion in relationship with the binary star, which are the furthest and nearest points from our Sun in the orbit, were 500 CE and 11,500 BCE, respectively. As we will see later, this correlates with the low point and high point of the Yuga cycle, which is the Hindu understanding of the precessional cycle.

Cruttenden's research indicates that the formulas related to the binary model are far more accurate in predicting the movement of precession as well as the changing speed of the Sun. Currently, he is exploring the possibility of Barnard's Star as our binary star. This star was discovered in 1915 by E. E. Barnard. It is a red dwarf star and, at

5.96 light years from our Sun, it is our second-closest star (with the three-star system of Alpha Centauri being the closest). Barnard's Star is located in the constellation Ophiuchus. Cruttenden believes that this may be our binary star in that it fits with what he sees as the necessary requirements for this star:

1. This star would be one of our closest stars.
2. It would need to have a high rate of motion (seen to move rapidly).
3. It would need to appear to be coming directly toward us.
4. The mid-gravitational point between our Sun and this star would need to be less than one light-year away to meet the parameters of the length of the precessional orbit period.[7]

According to Cruttenden, Barnard's Star meets all of these criteria. However, if we honor the increasing evidence that ancient cultures had advanced mathematics and astronomy beyond our current understanding, then we also need to factor in the many ancient cultures that viewed Sirius as an important star (and deity) in relationship to our Earth and Sun and as critical to our origins.

In addition, Hugh Evans has done extensive research on the star maps of Wales that were built into the landscape across 1,500 square miles in Neolithic times (dating back five thousand years). He believes that these star maps not only show the positions of the constellations of the zodiac but also incorporate an observatory of the movement of Sirius in relation to the precessional cycle. Again, we see that many advanced ancient cultures seemed to understand the profound association of the shifts of the precessional cycle with our relationship with the star Sirius.[8]

What is most significant is that this movement of the precessional cycle has been studied by humans for millennia and is encoded in many ancient sacred sites and temples around the globe. Initially, it may have been charted through the movements of the stars, particularly the pole stars, and then also the heliacal rising stars (those rising before the Sun) at different times of the year. Later, the constellations that are on the path of the ecliptic were viewed as important markers of the seasonal cycle of the year and the larger precessional cycle. Many ancients referred to the planets as the "wandering stars," moving against the backdrop of the constellations of the zodiac.

While Hipparchus, a Greek astronomer who lived around 147 BCE has been credited with the discovery of precessional motion, many scholars (in addition to the researchers cited above) believe that this knowledge was much more ancient in origin. Giorgio de Santillana and Hertha von Dechend, in their seminal book *Hamlet's Mill*, describe how cultures around the globe and across human history have understood this slow, gradual process of the precession of the equinoxes. These ancient cultures' astronomical knowledge of this phenomenon was embedded in their mythology, and these authors cite over two hundred myths from thirty different cultures around the globe, some dating back to the Neolithic (early prehistoric) period, that encoded numbers and references pertaining to the precessional cycle.

Many myths speak of this process as the "grinding of a mill," with the axis of the mill as the line reaching outward toward the pole star in the sky. These cultures often referred to the "four corners of the Earth," which are the world "pillars" or equinox and solstice points marking the framework of their world in that time. With the precessional motion, the framework of the world (i.e., the solstice and equinox points and the pole star) gradually shifts. Many myths from around the globe describe this shifting of the equinoxes and the times of transition between ages as fraught with danger. They associate images of "floods," "deluges," or cataclysmic disasters with these precessional changes.

In recent years, through scientific research, we have come to understand that the precession of equinoxes is also related to patterns of glaciation, deglaciation, and climate change. These periods of transition between ages have been associated with natural disasters that the ancients were attempting to warn us about. Scientists now know that the onset and retreat of ice ages are related to three factors in the Earth's orbital geometry: the obliquity of the ecliptic (which is the angle of the Earth's axis of rotation as well as the angle between the celestial equator and the ecliptic), the eccentricity of the Earth's orbit (i.e., the elongation of the Earth's path around the Sun), and the axial precession.[9] These factors affect the amount and intensity of sunlight and the patterns of cooling and global warming that can lead to entry into or the ending of ice age (fig. 1.4).

What is important to note here is ancient cultures' sophisticated understanding of the gradual movements of the stars and how these movements had a profound effect on the world. Their myths were attuned to these patterns in the sky and their meaning for us on Earth in a way that we in modern times seem to have forgotten. Ancient cultures not only understood that shifts in consciousness and Earth changes occur with the changes of the ages of the precessional cycle, but they were also aware of the times of massive reset that occurred on

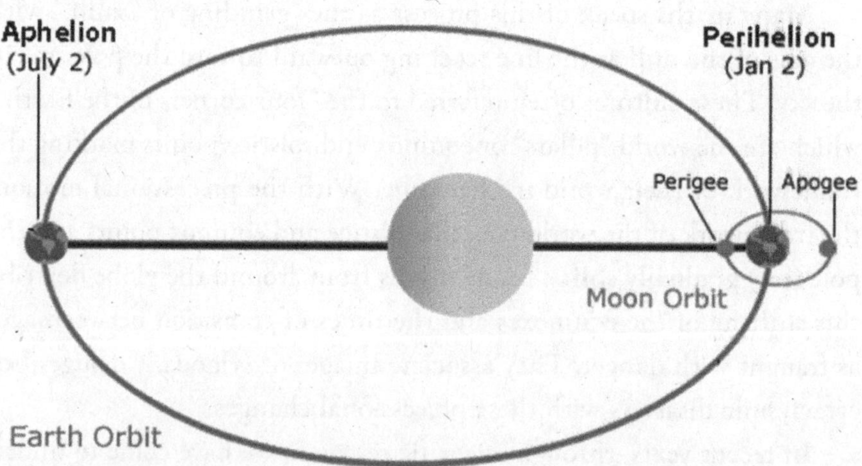


Fig. 1.4. Earth's elliptical orbit around the Sun.
National Oceanic and Atmospheric Administration

the Earth as part of this cycle. In particular, ancient cultures had an advanced understanding of astronomy and the cycle of cataclysms that occur due to our movement through the galactic plane approximately every 12,000 years that can lead to major solar flares and micronovas as well as comet impacts, causing pole shifts and cataclysmic changes on the planet.[10] This cycle relates to the midpoint and ending of a precessional cycle and the beginning of a new one, which is where we are now. Ancient cultures and our current modern science also indicate that other less extreme crises or Earth changes happen every 6,000 years as well.

The records and oral traditions of ancient cultures show their understanding of these major times of upheaval on the planet. Graham Hancock has recounted this scientific research in his book *Magicians of the Gods,* in which he describes how a series of comet strikes caused the massive Earth changes, flooding, and extinction of species from 12,800 to 11,600 years ago known as the Younger Dryas period. In his book *Yuga Shift,* Bibhu Dev Misra relates how that cataclysmic time and others related to comet strikes are cited in ancient Sanskrit texts as well as in the mythology and oral traditions of many ancient cultures.[11] We will examine how this information was also encoded in some of the monuments built in ancient times that may have been left as messages in stone for us, in that we are now in the 12,000-year transition time in the precessional cycle when these cataclysmic events are most likely to occur.

Not only does the precession of equinoxes cause major Earth changes, it also relates to shifts in our consciousness and in our social, political, and religious paradigms. Ancient cultures viewed the development of human consciousness as cyclical rather than linear. They understood that we move through periods of advance and decline in our consciousness as we move through the precessional cycle. If, in fact, the precessional cycle is related to our being a part of a binary star system, Cruttenden and others speculate that these cycles may relate to the electromagnetic fields that our Earth moves through in space as we engage in this approximately 24,000-year orbit. Perhaps we advance in our consciousness and development as we move closer to the gravitational center of that orbit and our binary star and decline as we move away.

In the Hindu cosmology, the precessional cycle is understood as the Yuga cycle, with a period of 12,000 years of ascending consciousness as humanity and then a descending cycle of 12,000 years. This is also seen in the ancient Greek understanding of the Great Year, with the different periods known as the Iron Age, Bronze Age, Silver Age, and Golden Age. These correlate with the more ancient Hindu understanding of the yugas, moving from the lowest level of consciousness in the Kali Yuga through levels of increasing consciousness with the Dwapara, Treta, and Satya Yugas.

In the time of the Satya Yuga, approximately 16,000 to 10,000 BCE, we held a higher level of intelligence and morality, lived longer, knew life without disease, and were in alignment with Cosmic consciousness

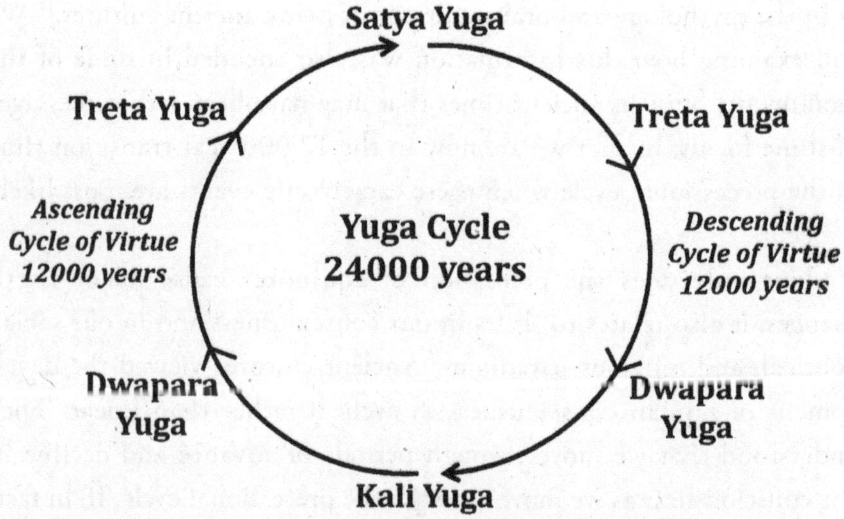


Fig. 1.5. The Yuga cycle.

Courtesy of Bibhu Dev Misra, *Yuga Shift* (White Falcon Publishing, 2023) and in balance and right relationship with each other and all of life. This was a time of expansive spiritual awareness, virtue, and the ability to communicate telepathically. There is also evidence that we had ongoing interaction with other galactic beings during this yuga. At that time, we were at our highest level of consciousness and knew the unity of metaphysical and physical reality. We were not bound in linear time or form but knew that we were spiritual and energy beings, able to shape-shift and enjoy the dance of co-creation with the Cosmos.

In the Treta Yuga, it is thought, our consciousness and virtue diminished by one-fourth and people began to practice religions rather than living in full intuitive alignment with the energies of the Earth and sky and Cosmos. Yet truth and being in right relationship were still primary. Due to our high level of consciousness in this time, it is likely that we were aware of the nature of the precessional cycle and that our consciousness would diminish over time. It is significant that the advanced civilizations of the Treta Yuga, or Silver Age, dating back 12,000 years, left messages in stone to help remind us in the later ages of this cycle how to come back into remembrance and alignment with the wisdom of the Cosmos.

As we moved into the Dwapara Yuga or Bronze Age, human virtue, consciousness, and intelligence decreased by another fourth, and there was increasing conflict, disease, discord, and disconnection from natural law and the consciousness of the Cosmos. We became more bound in the realm of duality and linear time.

Then, by the Kali Yuga or Iron Age, we have only one-fourth of our consciousness and virtue remaining. We experience our lowest level of consciousness, decreased intelligence and lifespan, and increased disease, discord, wars, immorality, and chaos. More and more, our lives are dominated by ego, greed, destruction, violence, disorder, disease, and disconnection from each other and from the Earth and Cosmos. We become mired in linear time and in our identification with material reality and lose our connection with the wisdom and intelligence of the

Cosmos. This is where we are now and have been for the past five thousand years.[12]

In *Yuga Shift*, Dev Misra details his extensive research on the Yuga cycle and his belief that we exited the Kali Yuga in March 2025. From his perspective, we have been in the ascending part of the Kali Yuga since 676 BCE, and this has been characterized by an increase in material wealth, while not including an increase in consciousness. He believes that we will see major shifts in our cultural paradigms and in our consciousness as we move out of the Kali Yuga and go through a profound time of transition and transformation.

This understanding of the precessional cycle and its correlation with the Hindu Yuga cycle is a profound reminder that our human evolution is not a linear path but rather a cyclical and spiral one. We are not now at the pinnacle of modern human consciousness but emerging from being at its nadir. Because we have been in the advancing phase of the Kali Yuga across the past three thousand years, our intelligence and technological inventions have increased, but we are still bound in scientific materialism, polarization, and the limited paradigms of this modern, third-dimensional reality.

Barbara Hand Clow in her book *Alchemy of Nine Dimensions* describes how, in ancient times, we were able to attune to all nine dimensions of consciousness, but that in more modern times, we have lost these capacities. She believes that now, as our consciousness is increasing, we may be able to open to these other levels of consciousness again.[13] We might correlate these nine dimensions to the shifts that occur with the ascending and descending phases of the Yuga and precessional cycles.

As described in Hand Clow's book, the first dimension of consciousness relates to our connection with the iron crystal core of the Earth and the way in which this resonates with energies from the galactic center, which is the first dimension of our galaxy. The crystal core of the Earth activates and emanates electromagnetic waves that vibrate through the

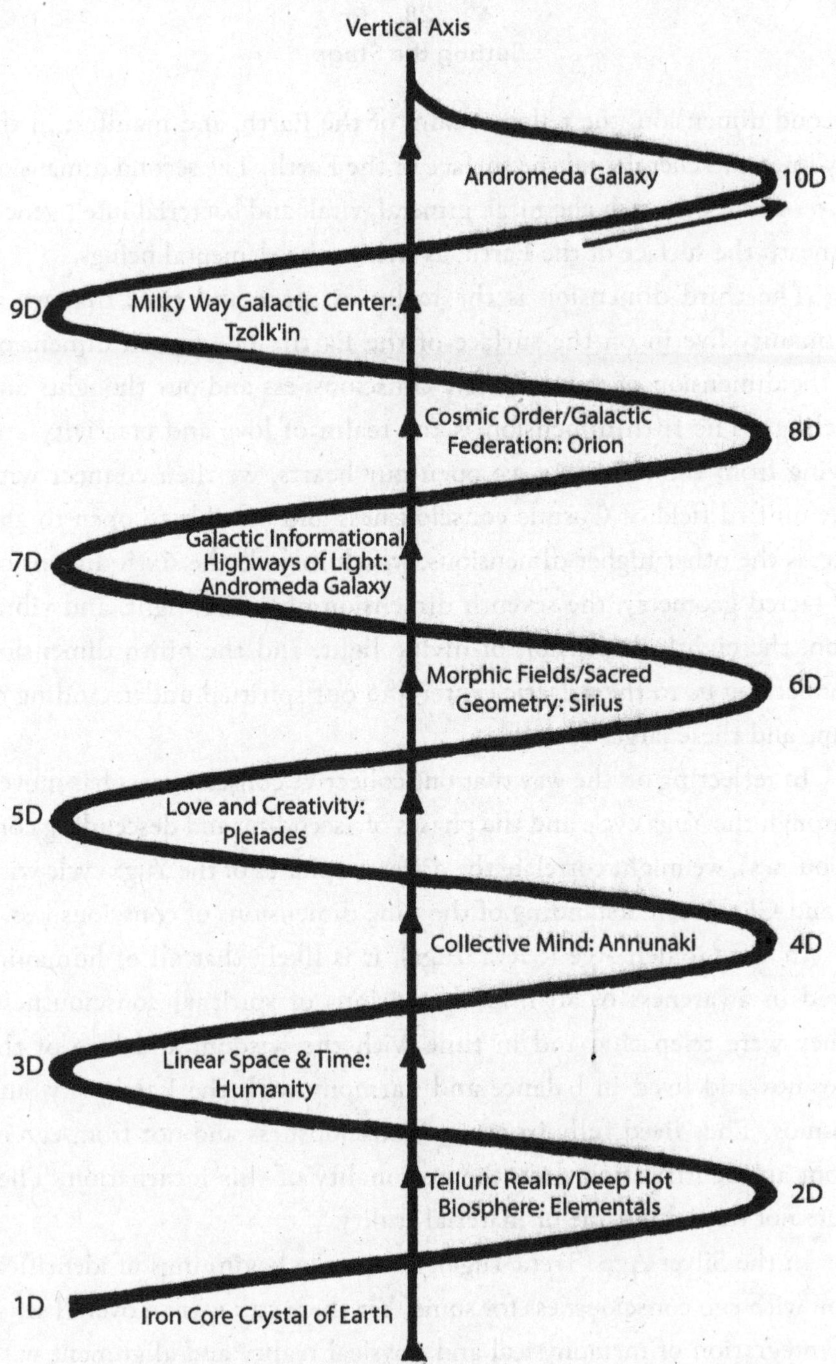


Fig. 1.6. The nine dimensions of consciousness.
Courtesy of Barbara Hand Clow with Gerry Clow,
*Alchemy of Nine Dimensions* (Bear & Company, 2024)[14]

second dimension, the telluric realm of the Earth, and manifest in the ley lines and energies on the surface of the Earth. The second dimension also includes the rich chemical, mineral, viral, and bacterial intelligences beneath the surface of the Earth, as well as the elemental beings.

The third dimension is the realm of space and time that we as humanity live in on the surface of the Earth. The fourth dimension is the dimension of our collective consciousness and our thoughts and feelings. The fifth dimension is the realm of love and creativity and living from the heart. As we open our hearts, we then connect with the unified field of Cosmic consciousness and are able to open to and access the other higher dimensions, which include the sixth dimension of sacred geometry, the seventh dimension of sound, light, and vibration, the eighth dimension of divine light, and the ninth dimension connecting us to the galactic center and our spiritual understanding of time and these larger cycles.[15]

In reflecting on the way that our collective consciousness has moved through the Yuga cycle and the phases of ascending and descending consciousness, we might correlate the different phases of the Yuga cycle with Hand Clow's understanding of the nine dimensions of consciousness.

In the Golden Age (Satya Yuga), it is likely that all of humanity lived in awareness of all nine dimensions of spiritual consciousness. They were telepathic and in tune with the wisdom and love of the Cosmos and lived in balance and harmony with the Earth, sky, and cosmos. They lived fully from soul consciousness and not from ego or from an identification with the personality of this incarnation. They were not bound in time or material reality.

In the Silver Age (Treta Yuga), we see the beginnings of identification with ego consciousness for some. Yet there still was an overall sense of integration of metaphysical and physical reality and alignment with soul consciousness and with living in balance with natural law and the consciousness of the Cosmos. This understanding permeated the sense of community and the awareness that each person is a fractal expression of Cosmic consciousness and a part of the diversity and unity of sacred community. There continued to be an awareness of the energies of sound, light, and sacred geometry (of the sixth and seventh dimensions) and how to co-create with them, but less connection with the eighth and ninth dimensions.

As we moved then into the Bronze Age (Dwapara Yuga), ego consciousness continued to increase and became more dominant. There was a reduction in spiritual consciousness in communities. Spiritual guidance and authority became more externalized, with spiritual leaders holding the ancient spiritual wisdom and authority. There was increasing discord and disharmony in the collective consciousness. While some continued to live from the heart and in the fifth dimension of consciousness, there was an increasing reduction in higher states of consciousness and more immersion in the fourth and third dimensions.

When we moved into the Iron Age or Kali Yuga, there was an increasing identification with physical reality and linear time and a focus on living only from third-dimensional consciousness. At first, there continued to be an honoring of the Earth and the first and second dimensions and the understanding of the Earth as sacred. However, as the time in this phase continued, there was an increasing disconnection from the Earth and from the honoring of the Earth's spiritual consciousness (and from the first and second dimensions).

We have reached a low point in spiritual consciousness in this age. While some remain committed to a path of soul consciousness, even many religious authorities now operate out of ego, greed, and a longing for power. Spirituality is now often institutionalized into religions and is more a form of social control than a path to spiritual enlightenment. We see increasing war, violence, conflict, greed, patriarchal power-over dynamics, and destruction of the Earth. Our ways of knowing are now dominated by left-brain linear thought and scientific materialism and a disconnection from our interconnectedness with the life around us and from the Earth and Cosmos. In this age, the consciousness of the collective is now mired in the third dimension and an identification with material reality and a sense of time as linear.

It is only by ignoring the evidence of the advanced technologies and architecture of ancient cultures dating back 12,000 years and their wisdom and high levels of consciousness encoded in myth and stone and in the remnants of their oral traditions that we can cling to the illusion that we are at the culmination of our linear advancement as humanity. As we observe and reflect on our modern cultures and the way in which our collective consciousness is increasingly dominated by greed, lies, violence, hatred, polarization, exploitation of natural resources, the destruction of the Earth, and disconnection from each other and from the sacredness of all of life, we realize that we are in fact at a low ebb in our virtue and consciousness as humanity.

We are now at the end of the Kali Yuga and the end of a precessional cycle. This means that we are in a time of major transformation and transmutation. As we experience this shift from one astrological age to the next and this critical threshold point in the cycle, we are all experiencing the increasing chaos, confusion, and conflict in our collective consciousness.

These periods of shifting between ages are times of tumult, as we let go of current patterns of social, political, and religious organization and move toward new ways of being. Such periods are often characterized by a significant degree of backlash, or reassertion of the old forms in a more rigid and exaggerated manner in reaction or resistance to the process of dissolution and change. The forms that the backlash takes are shaped by the themes of the age that is ending. In our current time, for example, we are seeing an increase in terrorism arising from fundamentalist religious groups. These terrorists are often sacrificing themselves in a form of martyrdom for their religious cause. We also see an increase in addictions, escapism, suicide, and psychosis, and in collective illusions or delusions. These are exaggerated and distorted expressions of the archetypes of the Piscean Age.

In addition, we see increasing fears of apocalypse around the globe. As Hand Clow writes in her book *Awakening the Planetary Mind* (formerly entitled *Catastrophobia*), we hold in our cellular memory the awareness of these profound times of cataclysm every 12,000 years. Yet rather than addressing this consciously and remembering the ancient wisdom about these cycles on our planet, we are caught in fear and are then in danger of unconsciously reenacting this trauma from the past through our destructive actions, with increasing environmental destruction and warfare. We need to awaken to the reality of the cycle that we are in and come back into alignment with the energies of the Earth and sky.

In this book, we will examine in more depth the archetypal patterns of the astrological ages across human history and seek to understand the themes of these ages. We will look in depth at the Piscean Age of the past two thousand years and seek to understand the new ways of being that we are moving into in the Age of Aquarius. We will explore in depth how we experience these cycles of ascending and descending consciousness and these times of cataclysmic change. We will also explore how we can raise our consciousness and move into a higher-dimensional reality, so that we are not bound by and entrapped in this cycle of ascending and descending consciousness.

As we have seen, this understanding of the precessional cycle and times of transition is very ancient. Yet we are beginning to see this awareness resurface in our modern times. Richard Tarnas in *Cosmos and Psyche* traces the way in which this ancient attunement to archetypal patterns and to our sense of living in a creative and intelligent Cosmos was gradually lost following the Copernican revolution and the Enlightenment over five hundred years ago. He describes the way in which we now live in a narrowly defined world of "science" and a "disenchanted" Universe.[16] With amazing hubris, we assume that our capacity for creativity, consciousness, and symbolism are uniquely our own rather than being an extension and reflection of those qualities in the Cosmos. He argues convincingly that we live in a sentient and meaningful Universe, and that it is to our own peril for us to continue to blind ourselves to that deeper reality.

I would posit that the conflict between these worldviews, the one of the Universe as a mechanistic "other" to be analyzed versus the Cosmos as a relational context of meaning, purpose, and vast intelligence, began as we moved into the patriarchal era (around 3000 BCE) and into the time of the Kali Yuga, also known as the Age of Ignorance, when we forgot what we once knew. This loss of connection with the sentient nature of the Universe may also relate to the cycles of advance and decline that are related to the binary orbit of our Sun with its companion star.

We will explore these shifts in consciousness in more depth in the coming chapters. As Tarnas notes, our understanding of this ancient wisdom and our increasing spiritual awareness began to resurface in modern times through Jung's depth psychology and his depiction of archetypes as principles embedded in our individual and collective unconscious. According to Jung:

> . . . the content of the collective unconscious is made up essentially of archetypes. The concept of the archetype . . . indicates the existence of definite forms in the psyche which seem to be present always and everywhere. Mythological research calls them "motifs." . . . This collective unconscious does not develop individually but is inherited. It consists of pre-existent forms, the archetypes, which can only become conscious secondarily and which give definite form to certain psychic contents.[17]

This calls into question the Cartesian notion of "I think therefore I am" and the postmodern notion that all of our theories and understandings of the Universe are based on the projections of our own thoughts and beliefs, or that we have the capacity as individuals to shape our own reality. While we have conscious choice in our lives, we are also part of larger cosmic currents of change. The Jungian archetypes harken back to the ancient wisdom that we are, in fact, formed and shaped by the currents of an archetypal field that is beyond our control and beyond our full conscious comprehension. In attuning to that field and aligning ourselves with those larger forces and patterns, we not only come back into balance and right relationship with the life around us but also step into a greater sense of our own wholeness. As we face this crisis of transition, it is more critical than ever before that we see the nature of the Universe and our own lives in a clearer and more holistic way, rather than remaining blinded by our false presuppositions and by our disconnection from the world around us.

As we move through this time of change, we need to be aware of the phases inherent in such global and personal transformations. The anthropologist Arnold van Gennep in his classic book *The Rites of Passage* stresses how major developmental shifts (whether individual or collective) are marked by certain phases of separation, transition, and then incorporation. Rites of passage parallel a death-rebirth process. We leave the old state, go through a transitional period, and then move into the new state or way of being. Ancient rituals and ceremonies celebrated these rites of passage and helped people through this transformational process. In modern Western cultures today, unfortunately, we have neglected this process and these types of transitional rites or ceremonies. In particular, we have minimized or repressed the critical importance of the liminal period, that time between the old and the new. This is a critical phase for releasing old patterns and preparing for or receiving initiation into a new form. In our movement away from a cyclical developmental view toward a more linear, exponential one, we have neglected this rich and important part of the change process.

The importance of the liminal period in cultural rites of passage is a reflection of the transitional phase that is a part of biological and cosmic rhythms. As Van Gennep notes, it is a part of all biological and physical movement and activity, in which you have periods of energy expression followed by exhaustion and regeneration, leading to a new phase of energy or movement.[18] These cycles are also mirrored in the phases of the Moon and planetary movements and even in the daily cycle of the Sun. They are also reflected in the seasons of the year and of plant and animal life. As Van Gennep writes:

> . . . life itself means to separate and to be reunited, to change form and condition, to die and be reborn. It is to act and to cease, to wait and rest, and then to begin acting again, but in a different way. And there are always new thresholds to cross: the thresholds of summer and winter, of a season or a year, of a month or a night; the thresholds of birth, adolescence, maturity and old age; the threshold of death and that of the afterlife.[19]

What does it mean then for us to be on the threshold of this new age? How can we mark this rite of passage and move through it with consciousness rather than reactivity? What information can we garner from the patterns of the sky about what the themes of this new age might be? How do we honor the lessons of the former age, but prepare ourselves for the new forms, beliefs, and paradigms of the new age?

Rites of passage are ceremonial celebrations of transitions but are also acts of protection due to an awareness of the vulnerability of the individual or group during the tumult of the change process. Honoring the transitional or liminal period of unknowing, undoing, and dissolution (paralleling death) is a critical part of that protective process. This book will look at ways in which we can honor this liminal period and learn its critical lessons while we prepare for the changes that lie ahead. We will honor the importance of being in a time of mystery as we move through this transition, yet we will also honor the guidance from the Earth and sky in how to navigate this shift and see the way how we are being called more fully into being co-creators of our own destiny with the consciousness of the Cosmos.

CHAPTER 2

# Seeking the Wisdom of the Past

*Homo sapiens*, modern humans, has been on the Earth for approximately 300,000 years. The historical period, in which we have written records of previous cultures and times, extends back approximately 5,000 years. Prior to written records, we have the art, archaeological evidence, and remnants of the oral traditions of prehistoric cultures to help us discern the traces of our past. We also have oral traditions honored and held across generations by current Indigenous cultures.

As we explore our ancient lineage, much remains in mystery. In this book, we will explore the wisdom of our ancient ancestors through mythology and what can be gleaned from the archaeological evidence. We will deepen our understanding of this ancient wisdom and of the cyclical process of our human evolution. It is important to realize that our current modern concept of linear time and history is a recent development of the past few thousand years and is an aberration in terms of our human understanding across the ages.

We will begin our exploration with a half turn of the precessional wheel, beginning in the Age of Leo (approximately 12,000 years ago). In part, we begin at this age because that is when human evolution and expansion increased significantly following the end of the last ice age and after the last major cataclysmic period on the planet. Also, as we will see in more depth later, this period has a significant relationship to the astrological age that we are moving into now.

From an astrological perspective, we can chart the phases of our past in ages lasting approximately two thousand years. These ages are named after the constellation of the zodiac that appears on the eastern horizon at the time of the vernal equinox in the northern hemisphere (and on the autumnal equinox in the southern hemisphere). These constellations, which mark the path of the ecliptic, have held meaning in cultures around the globe throughout human history. Ancient cultures believed that when stars touch the horizon, their energies incarnate and move among us.[1] While different cultures have perceived their meanings in various ways, certain underlying archetypal themes emerge from the images and stories told about them across cultures and time. These constellations of the zodiac carry meaning and wisdom that live in our collective consciousness even when we have forgotten their stories and even when we neglect to watch them move through the sky.

While we will trace these constellations and their meanings across the millennia, it is important to note that we do not have written historical and mythological records until approximately 3000 BCE. Prior to that time, we have to attempt to decipher the beliefs and lifestyles of earlier peoples from the archaeological record and remaining myths. We are able to find shards of these earlier beliefs embedded in the oral traditions and later mythologies emerging from subsequent cultures in those geographical areas. We also are able to use the archaeological record to gain insight into these earlier cultures.

A dramatic cultural shift occurred about 3000 BCE at the outset of our historical era. Archaeologist Marija Gimbutas, who has done extensive research on the prehistoric cultures of Old Europe, contends that this is when the ancient lineage of matrilineal and goddess-honoring cultures began to be supplanted by patriarchal culture. From the earliest archaeological evidence (dating back 35,000 years) up to approximately 3000 BCE, we find a predominance of goddess-worshiping cultures that used a lunar calendar for marking time. With the change into the patriarchal era (continuing up to the present), we moved from a focus on the Moon to the Sun and the development of a solar calendar.

In association with the prehistoric emphasis on the lunar calendar and Moon, Demetra George, in *Mysteries of the Dark Moon,* views the period of our human evolution as modern *Homo sapiens* across the past forty thousand years through the lens of the lunar cycle. In a complex and rich manner, she traces the shifts in our cultural and mythological patterns as correlated with the eight phases of the Moon (each equivalent to five thousand years of human history).

Within this model, she describes the past five thousand years of the patriarchal period as equivalent to the dark Moon phase. During this time, the connection with lunar (and Sacred Feminine) consciousness became repressed. However, we are now on the cusp of a new era analogous to the new crescent Moon phase when the understanding of the Sacred Feminine is reemerging. This is evident in the increasing interest in women's spirituality as well as the resurgence of ancient symbols from prehistory, such as the spiral, triskelion, and other ancient symbols seen in many advertisements and in social media. The images, symbols, and archetypal patterns of the ancient wisdom are resurfacing in our collective unconscious. This is a part of the larger transition that we are in at present.

As we explore the archetypal themes of the various ages and past cultures, we need to be careful not to project our own cultural assumptions and values back on those earlier times. In fact, it is possible that the precession of the equinoxes (and the constellations rising with the Sun at the vernal equinox in the northern hemisphere) is of more importance in more recent solar cultures than it was for prehistoric cultures.

Bernadette Brady has conjectured that earlier cultures may have been focused on the pole star, the still point in the sky, rather than on the movement of the constellations on the ecliptic with precession. She also has emphasized that in earlier times, the "canvas of the sky" was seen as having themes filling whole sections of the sky, "rather than as isolated images with isolated stories," as became more prevalent in later times (in particular, from the time of ancient Greece to the present).[2] While the images associated with the current zodiac find echoes in mythologies around the world and across thousands of years, we can only speculate as to how they were interpreted in the prehistorical period.

Also, it is important to differentiate between astronomy and astrology and our understanding of the signs of the zodiac versus the constellations in the sky. In that the tropical zodiac astrology chart was fixed in time, when Aries was on the horizon at the vernal equinox in the northern hemisphere, our tropical zodiac with 0 degrees of Aries as the beginning point was accurate during the Age of Aries but no longer reflects the placements of the planets and stars in the sky. With the movement of precession (and the current shift of 1 degree every seventy-two years), the difference between the tropical and the sidereal zodiac (which factors in the movement of precession) is now approximately 24 degrees. However, it also needs to be said that the sidereal zodiac astrology chart is also not an accurate reflection of the sky in that it assigns an arbitrary 30 degrees to each sign, while the constellations of the zodiac along the ecliptic in the sky vary significantly in length, with Virgo being the largest and Capricornus being the smallest.

This is where Bernadette Brady's emphasis on the importance of visual astrology is critical, in that she focuses on the actual movements of the Sun, Moon, and planets in the stars in the sky rather than what we see in our astrology charts. I strongly believe that one of the shifts that we will experience in astrology as we move into the Aquarian Age is the reconnection of our relationship with the sky and the actual movements of the luminaries and planets through the stars with visual astrology. I also believe that as we regain our understanding of the precessional cycle, we will see that it is a map, a blueprint, for remembering the archetypal wisdom of the Cosmos and of our journey of consciousness in order to come back to center, come into our wholeness and alignment with our soul selves to move into higher consciousness.

## THE WORLD TREE: THE MILKY WAY, GALACTIC CENTER, AND CELESTIAL POLE

Before we begin to explore the archetypal meanings of the astrological ages, it is important that we see this cycle in the larger context of our relationship with the Universe around us. We reside on a planet on the outer portion of the Milky Way, our galaxy. Our Milky Way is a spiral galaxy, one of many in the Universe. It is about 100,000 light years in diameter and contains approximately 100 billion stars. Our Sun lies about two-thirds of the way out from the center of this spiraling cloud of stars and gas in what is known as the Orion arm of the galaxy. We are about 25,000 light years from the galactic center, and it takes our Sun and solar system approximately 250 million years to complete one orbit around the galactic center.

When we look up into the sky, we can see the white band of countless stars of our Milky Way stretched across the sky. Many ancient cultures viewed the Milky Way as the "World Tree." Throughout the world's mythologies, the World Tree was seen as the connection and stabilizing bridge between the Earth and the sky. The World Tree or Tree of Life was thought to hold all of life in balance and alignment. We see references to this in the ancient Mayan culture, in the Hebrew Bible ("the tree of life"), and in the ancient Sumerian creation myth, among many others.

Other cultures, such as ancient Egypt, saw the Milky Way as a river and the life-giving milk of the Great Goddess, the Mother of all creation. For the ancient Egyptians, this river in the sky mirrored the life-giving river of the Nile on the Earth. For them as well as many other ancient cultures, the Milky Way was seen as the source of our life on Earth and as a spiritual path for souls to incarnate from and return to at the time of death.

With the naked eye, we can see a dark rift at the center of the Milky Way, which marks our galactic center. We now know through recent scientific investigations that this dark area is the black hole at the center of our galaxy. Many ancient cultures seemed to have understood in their own ways that this dark rift marked the source of life in the galaxy and on Earth. In this way, the human womb was seen as a mirror of the cosmic "womb." "As above, so below." As the procreative ability of women was honored on Earth, so it was also reflected in the sky, with the womb or vagina of the Goddess residing at the center of our Universe, giving birth to the stars and planets of the galaxy and all of life. Is it any wonder then that the yoni, the image and symbol of the vagina, is one of the earliest and most sacred symbols? We see this symbol appearing over and over again on the early goddess images found all over the world. The Milky Way was viewed both as the source of life and as the place that souls returned to at the time of death. As the Source and World Tree, it not only held the Earth and sky together but wove together the realms of life and death, of the visible world and the invisible realms.

It is also significant that while our black hole at the center of our galaxy (known as Sagittarius A*) has for thousands of years been quiet and inactive, it, like other black holes, has periods when it becomes an active galactic nucleus (or AGN). Our Sagittarius A* was highly active a few million years ago. At such times, the galactic center emits a vast amount of light, energy, and matter from its core. It becomes lit up in the night sky and may be the source of references to our "Second Sun" or "Central Sun."[3] It is therefore highly significant that beginning in 2024, our galactic center has shown signs of reactivation and is in the initial phases of the AGN as it is now daily emitting bursts and, at times, longer flares of light. This is a powerful indication of this time of shift that we are in.

The constellation Cygnus (seen as a vulture, bird, or swan in most cultures across time) is close to the midpoint of the Milky Way and is at the upper end of the dark rift, near the circumpolar stars. In his recent book *The Cygnus Mystery,* researcher Andrew Collins noted that the oldest known temple, Göbekli Tepe (meaning "hill of the navel"), built around 9500 BCE in what is now the southwestern part of Turkey, is in exact alignment with this constellation. He speculates that this temple may have harkened back to earlier cults honoring the time when Cygnus's brightest star, Deneb, was the celestial pole star (dating back 17,000 years). It is also significant that the Osirian temple in Egypt that most likely dates back at least 12,000 years also has a significant alignment to Deneb and to the constellation Cygnus. We see, then, that our ancient ancestors have been in tune with these critical markers in the sky for thousands of years.

We therefore find in ancient cultures a sophisticated understanding of astronomy, of the path of the Sun and planets, and of the critical solstice and equinox points. They also showed an awareness of the precession of the equinoxes as they tracked the shifting of the constellations in alignment with the solstices and equinoxes. As the planets and stars moved above them, the point of stillness, the celestial polar point, also became a sacred center. The World Tree was seen as extending from the Earth and rooted in this still point in the sky.

For many thousands of years prior to 4500 BCE (near the beginning of the Age of Taurus), there was no northern pole star. The still point around which the other stars circled was in darkness. From 4500 to 2000 BCE, Draco's stars were the pole stars, with Thuban as the focal point as the star that was brightest and closest to the celestial pole. As Brady notes, throughout the ages, Draco was seen as a "snake, a dragon or a serpent."[4] In the earliest times, this dragon image incorporated what we now know as Ursa Major and Ursa Minor and was seen as half bird and half snake.[5] This again correlates with the earliest known goddess images, which were the bird and serpent goddesses dating back as early as Upper Paleolithic cultures.

For these early prehistoric cultures, it is likely that the dark stillness at the celestial center of the circumpolar stars was (like the galactic center) seen as a source of the origins of life, the fertile void from which we come and to which we return at death, much like earthly caves were honored as womb and tomb. The color black in ancient times was the color of life and fertility, correlating with the fertile black soil as well as the darkness of the galactic center. For these cultures, the night was sacred and the Moon was honored as the primary sky deity, more so than the Sun. The ancient image of the triple goddess arose from the Moon in her phases as crescent, full, and waning or dark Moon. From 33,000 BCE on, we find archaeological evidence of bones marking the lunar phases and carvings correlating the Moon with the life cycle of plants and with women's menstruation and ovulation.

For ancient cultures, the pole star or celestial pole as well as the galactic center were seen as the sources of all of life. The shifting of the pole star as well as the constellations of the ecliptic signified our evolutionary process through time. The ecliptic, in particular, signified the realm of embodiment and our experience of coming into form and moving through cycles of consciousness on the earth plane. For these ancient cultures, honoring the alignments of the Earth and sky and the way in which the energies of the sky are mirrored on the Earth was part of how they integrated metaphysical and physical reality.

The Milky Way, the pole star, and the movement of the stars of the zodiac in alignment with the equinoxes and solstices (the four pillars or four directions) were the template for being in alignment with the energies of the Earth and sky. At times, the Milky Way was also viewed as a serpent. For example, the ancient Maya referred to the winter Milky Way as the "White Boned Serpent." They also viewed their bird deity "Itzam Ye" as residing at the top of the World Tree, which may be an allusion to the constellation Cygnus.

References to a bird and serpent in the World Tree can also be found in the Sumerian creation myth. It is also significant that in the symbolism of ancient Egypt, Isis is imagined as an integration of the ancient Neolithic vulture and serpent goddesses. In ancient Egypt, the vulture goddess ruled Upper Egypt, while the serpent goddess ruled Lower Egypt, and they were originally seen as aspects of one goddess. Isis was understood as the life force of the Universe and the one who held the soul at the time of incarnation and at the time of death. As the vulture goddess, she carried the soul through the death transition and was able to breathe life back into the dead.

We also see the centrality of the serpent in the biblical Genesis story. In archaeology, the most ancient goddess images are bird and serpent goddess figures, dating back to approximately 30,000 BCE. It is noteworthy to consider how this integration of the bird and the serpent portrays the unity and integration of the Earth and the sky as well as mirroring these themes in the images of the Milky Way.

The constellations of Sagittarius and Scorpius mark one end of the Milky Way and frame our view of the galactic center. On the opposite side of the sky, the Milky Way encloses and is framed by the constellations Gemini and Taurus. In many cultures, the constellation of Sagittarius was seen as a bow and arrow or an archer with the tip of the arrow pointed toward the galactic center. The tail of the scorpion, the image of the stars of Scorpius, also points to the galactic center. In many myths, we see references to the entryway to immortality being guarded by the "scorpion men" (for example, in the Mesopotamian epic of Gilgamesh). Perhaps this is also the source of the ancient association of the sign Scorpio with death and rebirth.

It is also significant, as will be described in more depth later in the book, that the constellations of Ophiuchus and Orion, both also on the ecliptic but not included in our traditional twelve constellations/signs of the zodiac, also mark the two ends of the Milky Way. Ophiuchus, the Serpent Bearer, stands above Scorpius, with one foot touching the stars of the scorpion. Orion is positioned between Gemini and Taurus and is opposite Ophiuchus.

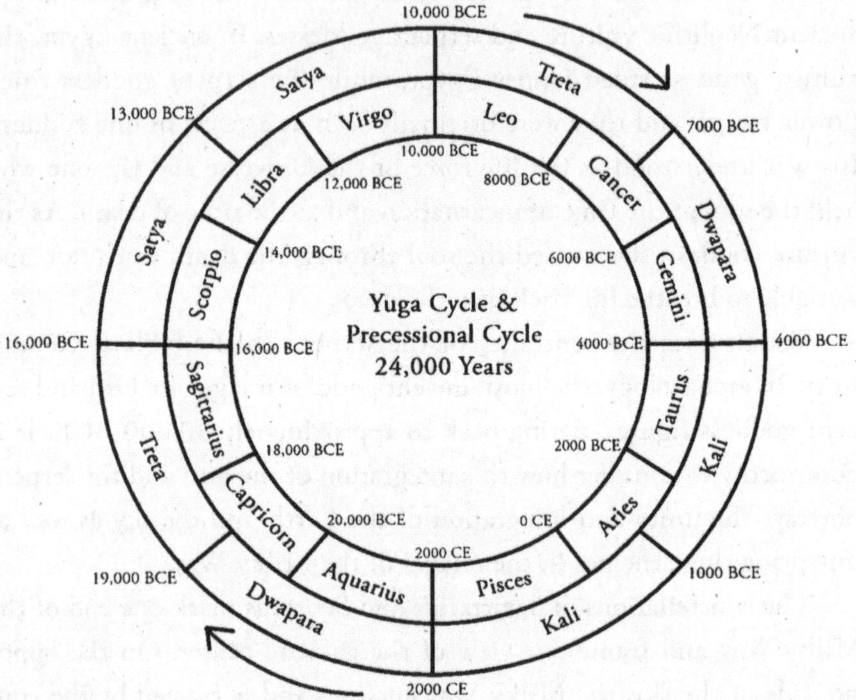


Fig 2.1. The phases of the Yuga cycle and the precessional cycle.
(courtesy of collaboration with Bibhu Dev Misra)

As we correlate the shifts in the ages of the precessional cycle (each approximately 2,000 years) with the phases of the Yuga cycle (approximately 3,000 years), it is highly significant to realize that the beginning of the Golden Age (the ascending Satya Yuga) is aligned with the Age of Scorpio. In that Ophiuchus is above the constellation Scorpius, this means that the Golden Age is also the Age of Ophiuchus. Libra is also in the Golden Age, with the first half of the age in the ascending cycle and the second half of the age (the sub-age of Aries) in the descending part of the Satya Yuga or Golden Age. The 2,000 years of the Age of Virgo then complete the remainder of the descending part of the Golden Age (Satya Yuga).

So, the Age of Leo marks the beginning of the Silver Age (Treta

Yuga). The next age, Cancer, straddles the ending of the Silver Age and beginning of the Bronze Age (or Dwapara Yuga). The Age of Gemini is fully in the Dwapara Yuga, followed by Taurus, which marks the beginning of the descending Kali Yuga phase. The first half of the Age of Aries is in the descending Kali Yuga, and then the second half marks the first 1,000 years of the ascending Kali Yuga. Our current Age of Pisces, now coming to an end, is the final 2,000 years of the ascending Kali Yuga phase.

Note that it is only the four fixed signs of the zodiac (Leo, Taurus, Aquarius, and Scorpio) that directly correlate with the shifts in the phases of the Yuga cycle. Perhaps this is why these four constellations and the four royal stars associated with them are seen as highly significant in so many ancient cultures. These stars were designated as royal stars in ancient Persia (dating back to approximately 550 BCE) and were seen as the guardians of the four directions. They include Regulus (the heart of Leo), Antares (the heart of the scorpion/Scorpius), Fomalhaut (the mouth of the fish below the stars of Aquarius), and Aldebaran (the eye of the bull of Taurus). We will explore these in more depth later in the book.

In addition, it is significant to reflect on the profound meaning of the Golden Age spanning the Ages of Scorpio, Libra, and Virgo. We will explore these signs of the zodiac more later in the book, but it is important to note here that Libra, marking the midpoint of the ascending and descending phases of the Golden Age, is associated with Ma'at, the ancient Egyptian archetypal principle or "neter." Ma'at is symbolic of the energy of right relationship and the awareness that everything is meant to be in right balance and right harmony with all that is. We are meant to live in balance and harmony with the sacredness of the life on Earth and with the energies of the sky and stars. It is when we are out of right relationship that chaos and destruction result. It is interesting to note that the root meaning of "disaster" is "disconnection from the stars."

Ma'at, in ancient Egypt, was the goddess with the ostrich feather, symbolizing truth and justice. All of those in ancient Egypt, and especially the pharaohs, were judged by whether they lived by the rules of Ma'at and were living in right harmony with others and with the Earth and Cosmos. How different our world would be if we required leaders to live by these principles of natural law and to be in right harmony and balance with all of life!

We will return to the meanings of these other phases in the precessional cycle and the Yuga cycle at the end of the book after exploring the meanings of the last 12,000 years, beginning with the Age of Leo. It will be important for us to track the shifts in consciousness as we explore the meaning of the different ages. This cycle of ages is not only a process for us as humanity to explore different themes as we work with the archetypes of the different constellations/signs of the zodiac, but it is the template for our evolutionary journey of consciousness. Our experience on the earth plane is a dance with duality, with the energies of consciousness and unconsciousness, light and dark, good and evil, and order and chaos. We humans are infinite beings having a finite experience as we incarnate here. We are eternal soul selves in an embodied experience, learning through the experience of mortality and duality. As we will explore in this book, we can move through this journey and cycle of precession, bound by this journey in time and space, or we can, at any time (at any point) in the cycle, remember who we truly are—infinite soul selves who are an expression of Cosmic consciousness—and reclaim this higher consciousness and no longer be bound by the wheel of karma (cyclical change) and entrapment in duality.

An archetypal template for understanding wholeness and alignment in ancient cultures from around the globe is the medicine wheel.

The medicine wheel incorporates the awareness that everything is interconnected. The circle symbolizes the wholeness and unity of all that is. The cross of the directions represents our connections to the East, West, South, and North as well as to the elements air, water, fire,

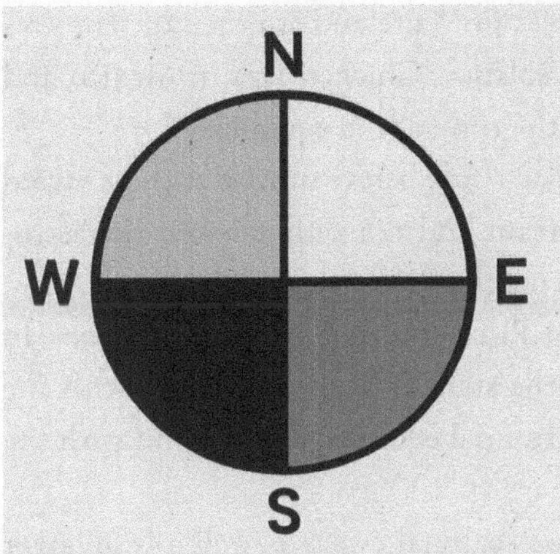


Fig. 2.2. The medicine wheel.

and earth, the energies that run through all of life. The medicine wheel is actually a sphere, representing our connection with the unity of Earth and sky. As we understand the interface of the ecliptic and the Milky Way in the sky, we realize that this mirrors the medicine wheel template on the earth plane. In honoring the directions and the alignment with Earth and sky, we are honoring our interconnectedness with all of life and that our physical reality and spiritual reality are interwoven and are part of the unified field of Cosmic consciousness. Ancient cultures oriented their sacred sites and communities in alignment with the four directions, and they also honored the four directions in the sky, in particular seeing the times of the equinoxes and solstices (as well as the cross-quarter holidays) as sacred times and as the pillars holding the framework of the sky. These times also mark the dance of light and darkness across the year and the seasonal cycle on Earth.

We see ancient sacred sites around the globe dating back thousands of years with meticulous alignments to sunrise at the times of the solstices and/or equinoxes. The temple of Karnak and two of the pyramids on the Giza plateau in ancient Egypt, Stonehenge in the United Kingdom, and many other ancient sacred sites were built to align with sunrise at the time of the summer solstice. Newgrange in Ireland,

Machu Picchu in Peru, and temples in Malta and at other ancient sites align with the sunrise at winter solstice. Chichen Itza in Mexico and other sites align with the Sun at the time of the equinoxes.

The constellations of the zodiac rising before sunrise at these sacred times of year became very important and not only marked the astrological age but also the seasonal energies of the year. For example, now, in the Age of Pisces, the stars of Pisces rise before spring equinox in the northern hemisphere, while the stars of Sagittarius align with the winter solstice, Virgo with the autumnal equinox, and Gemini with the summer solstice.

Ancient cultures tracked these seasonal cycles as well as the larger epochs of time and the movement of the stars in the precessional cycle. Of particular significance to many of these ancient cultures was when one of the equinox or solstice points of the ecliptic aligned with the galactic center, the black hole at the center of our galaxy, and therefore with the constellation of Sagittarius. In this way, it is significant in our time that, at the winter solstice, the Sun is in Sagittarius and in alignment with the galactic center. This has been true since 1998 and will continue for several more years.

In ancient times, this honoring of alignment with the energies of the Earth and sky and the center (the source of all of life) was critical in maintaining our sense of balance and integration of spiritual and physical reality. This is the meaning of the center of the medicine wheel as well as of the World Tree, both being seen as holding this unified field of the consciousness and of stability and balance. This is also related to the ancient Egyptian "djed," the pillar of Osiris (carrying much of the same meaning of the World Tree) that was raised in ceremony every year, symbolizing resurrection, the renewal of life on the Earth, and the time of fertility, as well as the victory of good over evil, of spiritual alignment and wisdom over disconnection and destruction. The djed also symbolized the spine, and in spiritual practices, as we raise our kundalini (serpent energy moving up the spine), we activate the pineal gland and move into expanded consciousness and into alignment with the energies of the Earth and sky. Another symbol of this for the ancient Egyptians was the image of the bird on top of a pillar or the stem of a papyrus. Often, it is also seen as a falcon on a post, symbolizing alignment with and the elevation of Horus (the son of Osiris), the enlightened one. This symbol of alignment, of higher consciousness, of resurrection, of victory over the energies of disconnection and chaos, can be seen throughout time and other cultures as well.

As far back as the paintings in the Lascaux cave, we see the image of the bird on a pillar. As Hugh Evans notes, this image is seen in many cultures, including in ancient Egypt, Nevali Cori (near Göbekli Tepe in Turkey), ancient Sumer, Babylon, and Africa, as well as in Native American images and in more modern times in symbols associated with political power (such as the symbol of power in the Roman Empire and in Prussia).[6] This is also an image associated with resurrection and order arising out of chaos after times of cataclysm, such as the biblical story of the bird landing on a post after the deluge, signifying a return of balance after the storm. This is a symbol, then, of our reclaiming our awareness of who we are, of moving into higher consciousness and back into alignment with our soul selves and with the consciousness of the Cosmos. We will see the significance of this in our own time as we look at the astronomical alignments of upcoming years in the final chapter.

The intention of this book and this exploration of the last 12,000 years of the precessional cycle is both to chart the shifting themes in our human evolution of cosmology through the ages—to track this process of descending and ascending consciousness—and to see how we can navigate this profound time of transition, move into the new paradigms of the Aquarian Age, and move out of this time of the Kali Yuga (of forgetting and disorder and disconnection). We will also reconnect with the ancient wisdom traditions of the advanced cultures to explore how we can understand this cycle of our evolutionary journey on the planet and step into higher consciousness. In this way, we move into spiritual enlightenment and into a higher-dimensional awareness rather than being entrapped unconsciously in the realm of cyclic change and being bound in our experience of time and mortality. We then remember who we truly are—fractal expressions of Cosmic consciousness—rather than repeatedly falling into periods of disconnection, dysfunction, disease, and disorder in the lowest phases of the precessional cycle (as we are in now). We then are also able to move into alignment with the energies of the Earth and sky, work our journey consciously, dance with the energies of duality, and co-create with the consciousness of the Cosmos within us and all around us. We then step off the karmic wheel and reclaim our capacity for higher consciousness and attunement with the Oneness of all that is.

PART TWO

# EXPLORING THE ARCHETYPAL THEMES OF THE AGES

# Overview of the Ages Across the Past 12,000 Years

In exploring the archetypal themes and patterns of the ages prior to our historical period, we need to rely on the archaeological record and what we know of those periods of human and cultural development. We also need to be aware that, while the archetypal patterns are analogous to energy fields that exist around us in the Universe and mirrored in the cycles of the stars and planets, our interpretations of them are also shaped by our cultural and psychological perceptions. These summaries of the ages, then, are not a definitive explanation but rather an exploration of correlations between our understanding of the archetypal themes and the cultural patterns of the times.

Evidence of images of the constellations date back as far as 17,000 years ago with the paintings in the Lascaux cave that depict a circle of animals in the sky, including the constellation Orion, the bull of Taurus, and the stars of the Pleiades. Another early astrological record that we know of, from ancient Mesopotamia around 2300 BCE, is the omen and divination lore of Enuma Anu Enlil that recorded the movements of the stars and planets and their meanings for the life of the community. The earliest Babylonian records indicate that their zodiac consisted of six signs (not twelve), each consisting of 60 degrees rather than the traditional 30 degrees. The constellation of Taurus, or the Bull, was much larger than our current configuration. The current signs of Pisces and Aquarius were seen as the Babylonian "Fish-Man," while Capricorn was seen as the "Goat-Fish." The stars of Libra were incorporated into the sign of Scorpius and were seen as the claws of the Scorpion.[1]

It is significant to note that across history, our conceptions of the sky have moved from a more holistic and integrated tapestry to an increasingly fragmented compilation of images. This reflects the shift from right-brain dominance in prehistoric cultures to the left-brain analytical way of thinking of the historical era. It also reflects our increasing sense of separation and fragmentation culturally.

We see in the Dendera zodiac of ancient Egypt (from the Ptolemaic period) many of the constellations of the ecliptic of our modern zodiac, as well as other circumpolar constellations such as Ursa Major. It was Ptolemy in ancient Greece in the second century CE who listed the forty-eight classical constellations, including the twelve constellations of the zodiac. These forty-eight constellations relate to the stars visible in the northern hemisphere, and the twelve constellations of the zodiac are on the ecliptic and locate the position of the Sun in its cycle through the year.[2] We currently have eighty-eight constellations recognized by the International Astronomical Union (IAU), with thirty-six constellations primarily in the northern hemisphere and fifty-two primarily in the southern hemisphere.

As we review the precession of the equinoxes and the past astrological ages, we will use the lens of our current zodiac to see how these themes manifested in those times. We will also explore how the themes of each constellation incorporate the meaning of the opposite sign in the wheel of the zodiac as the sub-age or second half of the precessional age. Jeffrey Wolf Green has proposed this format as a way of understanding the shifting themes during these astrological periods.[3] For example, he conjectured that the latter half of an age (or second sub-age) reflects the energy and archetypes of the opposing sign of the zodiac and is an effort of the collective consciousness to come to a more balanced integration of the meaning of each sign. We will also weave into our understanding of the signs of the zodiac the planets that are associated with them (as the rulers of the signs) dating from classical Greek culture to the present. The exact beginning and end dates of each astrological age vary among astrologers. What is most important are the themes of the larger time periods and not the exact dates, since these cannot be determined definitively. It is also important to note that we often experience a transitional period as one age shifts into the next.

For this exploration of the astrological ages, we will explore the last 12,000 years of the cycle, as we move from our experience of higher consciousness (the end of the Golden Age or Satya Yuga and beginning of the Silver Age or Treta Yuga) to our current time at the lowest level of consciousness, the Iron Age or Kali Yuga. We will use approximate dates for the beginning and end of each age, with the realization that the speed of the cycle changes over time, so that some ages may be somewhat longer than 2,000 years and others somewhat shorter. Also, it is important to remember that there is no clear, exact demarcation between the ages, in that it may take up to a few hundred years to fully transition from the energies and consciousness of one age to the next. Also, as Dev Misra notes in *Yuga Shift*, there is a transition period of 300 years between each yuga of the Yuga cycle. So, he sees each phase of the Yuga cycle as lasting 2,700 years, followed by a transition period of 300 years, for a total of 3,000 years for each yuga. It is also significant to note that he views the times of major Earth changes as occurring at the transitions every 3,000 years. However, the major crisis points occur every 6,000 years, and the most intense times of cataclysm occur every 12,000 years at the midpoint of the cycle and at the end of one precessional cycle and the beginning of the next, which is where we are now.

The ancient Sanskrit texts speak of these cataclysms as alternating between water and fire. The cataclysm 12,000 years ago was called the

Deluge or the great flood. The cataclysm prophesied for the time of the precessional cycle that we are now entering is called the Conflagration (cataclysm by fire), coming at the end of the Kali Yuga. We will incorporate these times of Earth changes from the Yuga cycle into our analysis of the energies of the astrological ages to discern how this has impacted our shifts in human consciousness and can guide us in navigating this profound time of transformation and transmutation.

CHAPTER 3

# The Age of Leo

*(approximately 10,000–8000 BCE)*

The Age of Leo began at the end of the Golden Age (the Satya Yuga) and marked the beginning of the Silver Age (Treta Yuga) around 10,000 BCE. This period in our prehistory was the transition from the Paleolithic (Old Stone) Age to the Mesolithic (Middle Stone) Age. During this time, Stone Age people began to domesticate animals and move toward settlement and away from the hunter-gatherer way of life. At the same time, there is increasing archaeological evidence that there were also advanced cultures in different parts of the world with a highly sophisticated understanding of astronomy, mathematics, technology, and spirituality. We see evidence of this dating back at least ten to twelve thousand years in ancient Egypt, Peru, Turkey, Malta, India, China, Australia, and in Mali, Niger, South Africa, and other locations in Africa as well as in other parts of the world. These advanced cultures showed the characteristics of the consciousness of the Silver Age and coexisted with the Stone Age people.

According to Graham Hancock, our Earth experienced a major comet impact approximately 12,800 years ago, leading to a sudden, drastic drop in temperature on the planet that caused ice age conditions. This led to the extinction of a massive number of animal and plant species as well as humans, and lasted for approximately 1,200 years until

11,600 years ago, or approximately 9600 BCE. This theory is called the Younger Dryas impact hypothesis, and despite an enormous amount of backlash to this view, there has been increasing scientific evidence confirming this global catastrophe.[1]

It is important to note that the evidence of advanced cultures dating back 12,000 years—seen in sites such as Göbekli Tepe in Turkey and the pyramids and Sphinx on Giza plateau in Egypt—is likely the remnants of advanced cultures that experienced this cataclysmic reset on the planet. As we explore their sites, it seems that they encoded in stone their wisdom about the precessional cycle as well as these times of major Earth changes on the planet.

Göbekli Tepe, which dates back to about 9500 BCE, was oriented toward particular stars. There has been speculation about orientations toward Orion and Sirius as well as the constellation of Cygnus and the star Deneb.[2] As we shall see later, Orion and Sirius were seen by advanced cultures in ancient times as critical markers of the precessional cycle. Deneb, in the constellation of Cygnus, was the pole star at the time of the Golden Age.

Interestingly, parts of this ancient Neolithic site were intentionally buried approximately one thousand years after its construction. Could the builders have been intentionally leaving a message buried in stone for later times—for this time? Were they reminding us of the cycle of precession, of ascending and descending consciousness, and that this is a critical time in the cycle?

In his book *The Star Mirror*, researcher Mark Vidler presents his view that these ancient cultures were aware of the astronomical cycles of precession and not only encoded specific star alignments in their sites but also left messages for the future. According to his research, sites such as Giza, Avebury, and Angkor Wat have mirror alignments with some of the brightest stars in the sky that are now coming into alignment. He has developed what he calls the Earth/Star mirror theory in which he asserts that the Earth's highest mountains as well as specific geographical and sacred sites align with the brightest stars in the sky and also form isosceles triangles. In this way, there is an Earth grid that mirrors the star grid, and he believes that some sacred sites were designed to show alignments that are coming into play in this time to alert us to this profound time in the precessional cycle and this time of potential cataclysmic crisis.[3]

Again, the astrological Age of Leo correlates with the shift from the Golden Age (or Satya Yuga) into the Silver Age (or Treta Yuga). Advanced cultures in that time retained the wisdom of the Golden Age and an advanced understanding of astronomy, mathematics, technology, and spirituality but also knew that they were at the beginning of a declining cycle with a decline in human consciousness, and most likely knew that future generations would increasingly forget the wisdom of the past. Perhaps, they have left us messages in stone to remind us and awaken us, knowing that we would then be at the lowest level of consciousness in the cycle.

Also during this age, 9000 BCE marked the recession of the most recent ice age, allowing an expansion of human population, yet it came with a dramatic increase in temperature on the planet. With this climatic change and the melting of the ice came a period of floods. The landmasses that now constitute our continents only began to take their current forms between 15,000 and 5000 BCE.[4] Floods are memorialized in the mythology of most ancient cultures. Most of the cataclysmic flooding caused by the melting ice occurred in three periods: around 13,000–12,000 BCE, 10,000–8000 BCE, and then 6000–4000 BCE. Accompanying the mass flooding were dramatic Earth changes, including earthquakes and volcanic eruptions.[5]

In *Underworld: The Mysterious Origins of Civilization*, Graham Hancock cites recent research that the massive floods destroyed some of the oldest and most ancient civilizations located in coastal regions that now are beneath the surface of the sea. Current undersea archaeological explorations are discovering ruins of ancient cities off the coasts of India, Malta, Japan, and China, among other regions. These recent discoveries raise profound questions. What if our modern civilizations are the outgrowth of the more inland and less advanced survivors of these ancient cataclysmic floods? This would seem to confirm the Hindu understanding of the Yuga cycle and that much of our historical period (of the past five thousand years) is actually an Age of Ignorance, the Kali Yuga (when we have lost awareness of the wisdom that we once knew) rather than the pinnacle of human development, as we like to imagine. This might also help explain the disjuncture between the more advanced ancient cultures, such as the one in ancient Egypt, and the other Neolithic cultures. Perhaps remnants of these advanced civilizations from the coastal regions survived and seeded the sites of ancient cultures such as that of ancient Egypt, while the surrounding cultures of people located in the inland regions were far less advanced.

It is significant that Dev Misra has analyzed the scientific data regarding human intelligence and has discovered that studies conducted on large samples from Europe, the Middle East, Japan, and Australia confirm that human cranial capacity has declined by approximately 10 percent across the past 12,000 years. This means that rather than adhering to the Darwinian notion of our linear evolutionary process, our intelligence as a species has actually declined significantly as we have experienced the descending phase of the precessional/Yuga cycle. To put this into perspective, the percentage difference in cranial capacity is close to the difference between the brains of *Homo erectus*, our earliest human ancestors, and modern *Homo sapiens*![6] According to his research, we see a sine curve of declining and then increasing intelligence (and cranial capacity) as we move through the descending and ascending phases of the Yuga cycle. As we are now in the beginning of the ascending phase, we see a significant increase in cognitive ability and technological advancements in the past few hundred years. Those in the Age of Leo would have been aware of these shifts related to the precessional cycle, and in their concern for future ages were leaving messages encoded in their sacred sites to guide us in this time in remembering the wisdom that we once knew but had since forgotten.

During this period, Leo was the constellation rising before the Sun at the time of the vernal equinox in the northern hemisphere. The constellation Leo has been perceived by cultures across time as a lion figure. This image was associated with these stars in ancient Babylon, Egypt, Persia, Syria, and then later by the Turks and Hebrews.[7] There is increasing evidence that the Sphinx (the half-human and half-lion figure) in Egypt was built during this period (approximately 10,500 BCE or earlier), facing due east at the time when the constellation Leo was rising at the time of the spring equinox.[8] Geological evidence indicates that erosion patterns on the Sphinx fit the weather conditions in 10,500 BCE at the beginning of the Age of Leo, when the weather there was temperate with significant rainfall, unlike later times after the desertification of the area.[9]

This is also the age when the earliest pyramids were constructed in Mexico and Egypt. While the conventional view of archaeologists is that the Great Pyramid in Egypt was constructed about 2700–2500 BCE, Graham Hancock and Robert Bauval cite recent research (particularly from the field of archaeoastronomy) positing that the Great Pyramid was most likely built much earlier, during the Age of Leo.

The pyramids on the Giza plateau in Egypt were placed in a formation patterned after the stars of Orion's belt as they appeared in the sky at the cusp of this age.[10] Interestingly, Robert Edward Grant has noted that many pyramids around the globe are also oriented in alignment with the stars of Orion.[11] The constellation of Orion was at its lowest point of declination in the sky in the Age of Leo. Currently, Orion is at its highest point in the sky in terms of its declination in relation to the horizon (and most removed from connection with the Earth). Perhaps this is symbolic of our journey across 12,000 years of shifting consciousness for us as humanity.[12]

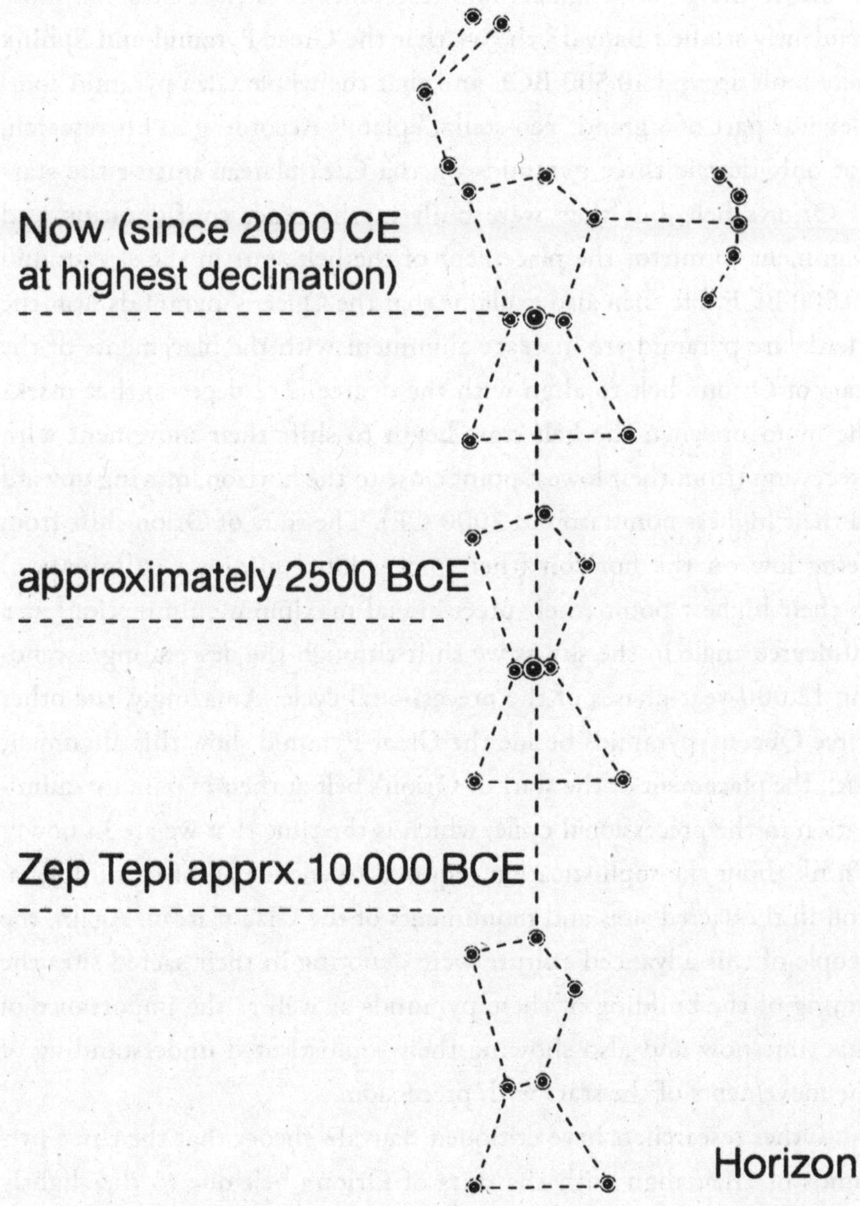


Fig. 3.1. The changing declination of Orion across the last 12,000 years

Scott Creighton, engineer and researcher of ancient sites, has independently studied Bauval's theory that the Great Pyramid and Sphinx were built around 10,500 BCE and that the whole Giza pyramid complex was part of a grand "geo-stellar" plan.[13] According to his research, not only do the three pyramids on the Giza plateau mirror the stars of Orion's belt, but they were built in the exact configuration and alignment to mirror the placement of the belt stars in the sky around 10,500 BCE. He then also explains that the Queens' pyramids near the Menkaure pyramid are in exact alignment with the placements of the stars of Orion's belt to align with the degree (212 degrees) that marks the moment when the belt stars begin to shift their movement with precession (from their lowest point close to the horizon, moving upward to their highest point around 2000 CE). The stars of Orion shift from being low on the horizon (their precessional minimal culmination) to their highest point (their precessional maximum culmination) at a 90-degree angle in the sky as we shift through the descending/ascending 12,000-year phases of the precessional cycle. Amazingly, the other three Queens' pyramids beside the Great Pyramid show this alignment with the placement of the stars of Orion's belt at their maximum culmination in the precessional cycle, which is the time that we are in now![14] Think about the sophistication required to encode all of this information in the sacred sites and monuments of the Giza plateau. Again, the people of this advanced culture were denoting in their sacred sites the timing of the building of these pyramids as well as the importance of this time now and also showing their sophisticated understanding of the movements of the stars with precession.

Other researchers have critiqued Bauval's theory that the three pyramids of Giza align with the stars of Orion's belt due to the slightly offset position of the center pyramid in relationship to the center star of Orion's belt (Alnilam). However, independent research by Scott Sacharczyk and Rob Miller[15] have found that the offset between the center of the Khafre pyramid and the center of the great Giza circle (including the six Queens' pyramids) is precisely 44 by 14 cubits, which creates a ratio of 44/14 or 22/7, which is essentially the ratio of pi (3.14285714), the ratio of the circumference of any circle to its diameter. This would indicate that the builders of this pyramid complex were also trying to point to the importance of the full great Giza circle complex as part of their message.

In addition, it is significant that the star shafts of the Great Pyramid are aligned to the star Sirius and the belt stars of Orion as well as the circumpolar stars Thuban and Beta (in Ursa Minor), again pointing to these significant markers of the precessional cycle. The pyramids were built in alignment to these stars to bring the land and rulers into right relationship with the energies of the sky and the Universe as well as to track the movement of precession. In our modern era, we continue to be baffled by this ancient culture's sophistication of technological and astronomical understanding. We are still unable to decipher the way in which the pyramids were built with such precision and accuracy.

For the ancient Egyptians, the Great Pyramid was not a burial site but a place of spiritual initiation. Through extensive training and ceremony, the initiate was guided in exiting the body to experience the spiritual realm and then return (in essence, experiencing a simulated death/rebirth process) with higher spiritual awareness to guide the initiate in living on the earth plane as a spiritual being in an incarnated form. In this way, the integration of metaphysical and physical reality was renewed.

For the ancient Egyptians, the constellation Orion was extremely important. It was the celestial counterpart of their deity Osiris and was known as "Sah," the "Far-Strider."[16] In ancient Egyptian culture, Orion's rising during the year was an important calendrical and spiritual marker across thousands of years and was incorporated in their celebration and honoring of Osiris. Osiris was the god of vegetation and was symbolic of the fertility of the land. In an ancient Egyptian myth dating back to about 4000 BCE, the ruler Osiris was slain by his jealous brother, Set, and then revived by Isis, his sister and wife and the Great Goddess and Mother of all of Life.

This myth encodes in a profound way the meaning of the precessional cycle, so I will recount the story in more depth. The myth features Isis, who we now understand as symbolic of the star Sirius, and Osiris, associated with the stars of Orion. For the ancient Egyptians, these deities were actually "neters" or archetypal energies of the Cosmos. Isis was understood as the life force of the Universe and the one who held the soul at the time of incarnation and at the time of death. Isis was the first of four children of Nut, the sky goddess, and Geb, the Earth god. The other children included Osiris, Nephthys, and Set. Isis was seen as the Great Mother Goddess of the Universe or the Creatrix. As the star Sirius, her appearance in the sky in their annual cycle heralded the coming of life-giving rains to the Nile River and the start of spring. For the ancient Egyptians, the Nile was their source of life. This river flowed north to the sea and mirrored on Earth the white river of stars, the Milky Way, in the sky.

In the myth, Isis married her brother Osiris, and the two became the first queen and king of Egypt. They were gentle and kind rulers who were much loved by their people. Osiris taught the ways of agriculture, while Isis showed the people how to weave, grind corn, and make bread. In the twenty-eighth year of their rule, Set, their brother, was filled with jealousy and sought to kill Osiris. He fashioned a beautiful box of cedar, ebony, and ivory made exactly to Osiris's proportions. At a feast, he offered the box as a gift to whoever could fit within it. All of the guests attempted the feat, but only Osiris fit perfectly. When he climbed into the box, Set and his seventy-two co-conspirators nailed the lid shut and sent the coffin down the Nile and out to sea. Note that this number, seventy-two, relates to the shifting of precession with the movement of the sky 1 degree every seventy-two years.

As the story continues, Isis mourned the loss of her beloved husband and went in search of his body. The coffin had traveled to

Phoenicia, where it lodged in the branches of a tamarisk tree. Isis heard of its whereabouts and traveled to that land. She was able to retrieve the box and return to Egypt, and she then revived Osiris by flying over him in the form of a kite (a bird). She fanned him with her wings and breathed life back into him long enough to become pregnant with their son, Horus. Isis then hid Osiris's body in the reeds along the river.

Set discovered the body while hunting and was enraged that he had been found and brought back by Isis, so he chopped Osiris into fourteen pieces and scattered them far and wide to be eaten by the crocodiles. Isis and her helpers searched and recovered thirteen of the pieces of his body. Isis fashioned the missing piece, his penis, from clay to complete his body. She then revived Osiris with the fanning of her wings. Osiris then chose to leave the earthly realm and become the god of the underworld, welcoming those at the time of death. Later, as an adult, Horus avenged his father and conquered Set, banishing him to the desert and reclaiming the rule of the land. In another version of the story, Horus defeats Set but then in his mercy allows him to go free.

For the ancient Egyptians, Set represented the energy of time and the cycle that we move through with precession. The root meaning of this word in ancient Egyptian is "chaos and disorder," and Set was viewed as the god or archetype of confusion, storms, war, deserts, violence, disorder, and chaos. This is a profound description of humanity's state as we move into the Kali Yuga. As we view the past five thousand years, we see increasing wars, violence, and disorder. Also, it is significant, as evolution biologist Elisabet Sahtouris has said, that if you viewed our planet, Earth, from the Moon across the past five thousand years, the primary visible change that you would see is the increasing desertification of the Earth.[17] We also see in our current times an increase in major storms and Earth changes. We are truly in the time of Set.

It is also significant to note that the reference in the story to seventy-two (the number of conspirators with Set) is the number of years that it currently takes for a shift of 1 degree in the sky with precession.

However, as noted earlier, the speed of our movement (the Sun, Earth, and solar system) changes as we move closer to and then farther away from our binary star. As Robert Edward Grant has noted, the speed of precession shifts from approximately 21,600 years for the full cycle at its fastest rate to 25,920 years at its slowest rate (with the average being 24,000 years, which then is the accurate measure of the full cycle). This explains the current view of many that the precessional cycle is 25,920 years (which is the result of taking our current speed and multiplying 72 by 360 for the full cycle). However, given Grant's estimates, precession actually shifts from the most rapid movement of 1 degree every sixty years to the slowest movement of 1 degree every seventy-two years. So, the reference in this Isis/Osiris story is to the slowest time in the precessional cycle, which is when the energy of Set becomes most active and dominant. This again reflects the advanced knowledge and wisdom of the ancient Egyptian wisdom tradition.

What is also significant is that the average rate of movement with this cycle is 1 degree every 66.6 years. Could it be that this is the number referred to in the biblical book of Revelation? Revelation 13:18 (New International Version) reads: "This calls for wisdom. Let the person who has insight calculate the number of the beast, for it is the number of man [humanity]. That number is 666." In the biblical account, this is when humanity will be dominated by the energies of Satan or disconnection from the divine, which is another description of Set and may signify the awareness of what happens to our consciousness as humanity when we are bound or entrapped in this precessional cycle and forget who we truly are, what we are capable of, and how we can (as so many ancient cultures and wisdom traditions have shown us) step "off the wheel" and move into higher consciousness.

For the ancient Egyptians, Horus (as the child of Isis and Osiris) symbolized order, the path of consciousness and living in right alignment with the energies of natural law and being in harmony with the intelligence of the Cosmos. He is the enlightened one who is not controlled by

Set or caught in the cycle of declining consciousness and disconnection from the energies of the Cosmos. Those who chose to be on a spiritual path, a path of enlightenment, were called the "followers of Horus." It is significant that in one version of the story, after he conquers Set, Horus allows Set to live, perhaps showing understanding that the duality of order and chaos, of consciousness and ignorance, and of good and evil are a part of the evolutionary journey of humanity on the planet.

Osiris (Orion) is the god who guides us in how to live in alignment, and his demise at the hands of Set is symbolic of our journey through the precessional cycle and of getting entrapped in these periods of disorder and chaos. Osiris demonstrated how we can live when we are at our highest level of consciousness and capacity to live in right relationship and harmony with all that is. It is noteworthy that after being revived for a second time by Isis, Osiris chooses to go to the lower world, to guide souls at the time of death, rather than remaining on the earth plane. Perhaps this is a reference to the fact that the constellation Orion sinks below the horizon as we move into the Age of Taurus (and into the time of the Kali Yuga).

The ancient Egyptians believed that stars that disappear below the horizon only to return later are symbolic of death/rebirth. Osiris is the archetype of the god who dies and is resurrected or reborn. His departure from the Earth and from our sky also parallels many ancient myths about the disappearance of the wise ones (perhaps galactic beings with higher consciousness) that occurs as humanity moves into the Kali Yuga and devolves into this period of lower consciousness. Our lower consciousness and lower frequency are no longer compatible with theirs. Perhaps this explains the mystery of the seemingly sudden disappearance of many advanced cultures such as the Lemurians, Tuatha de Danaan, and others around the globe.

Isis is the archetype of the Creatrix, the great goddess, who watches over what unfolds and revives Osiris again and again after he is caught in the cycle of chaos and time (in interaction with Set). This story profoundly parallels our moving through the precessional cycle and Sirius, as our binary star, holding us in this profound process of evolution and reviving us again and again after the times of cataclysm and our becoming entrapped in the bonds of chaos and time.

It is significant in the story that Osiris was cut into fourteen pieces. If we see this myth as a depiction of the precessional cycle, then twelve of the pieces may relate to the constellations of the zodiac. The final two pieces (including the one that was missing) may relate to the other two constellations on the ecliptic: Orion and Ophiuchus. We have seen how Orion (Osiris) relates to the evolutionary shifts in our consciousness on the planet throughout the precessional cycle. Interestingly, Ophiuchus, the fourteenth constellation, is directly opposite Orion in the sky and is located close to the galactic center. This constellation (the Serpent Bearer) is symbolic of the great healer, the enlightened one, and the one who has fully integrated the energies of the Sacred Feminine and Sacred Masculine. This is symbolized in how Ophiuchus, the healer, is holding the serpent, the most ancient image of the Sacred Feminine and also the symbol of life/death/rebirth. Perhaps, this represents the "lost piece" that needed to be reshaped by Isis to bring Orion (and us as humanity) back into wholeness.

It is also significant that at the time of the movement into the Golden Age (Satya Yuga), we moved into the Age of Scorpio (16,000–14,000 BCE), and Ophiuchus is the constellation directly over the constellation Scorpius. Perhaps then, we could also call the Golden Age the Age of Ophiuchus. This great healer was associated with Asclepius in Greek mythology, the wise healer trained by Chiron who knew how to heal others and how to raise the dead. He guides us in how to heal and be "resurrected" from entrapment in the third-dimensional energies of time and chaos. It is also significant that Ophiuchus is the Serpent Bearer, who holds the head of the serpent in one hand and the tail of the serpent in the other. Not only is the serpent the most ancient symbol of the Great Goddess/Creatrix, aligning Ophiuchus with Sirius/Isis, but the serpent is also an image of the lunar nodes (known as the head and tail of the dragon or serpent). The lunar nodes mark the times when the Sun and Moon meet at the ecliptic. They signify eclipses, and they have been associated since ancient times with our experience of karma, our journey in working the consequences of our actions and choices across our lifetimes. Ophiuchus has mastered the challenges of karma and is in full alignment with the energies of Cosmic consciousness, of Isis and Osiris, guiding us in how we too can move into higher consciousness.

As we now see, in a profound way, this myth is encoding information about our movement through the precessional cycle. It describes how we get entrapped in periods of chaos and mired in time (Set) and in paradigms of struggle for power and control. These are times of being out of alignment with the Earth and sky and ancient wisdom. Isis/Sirius heals us (as she did Osiris) and revives us. Yet, as we stay caught in the precessional cycle and phases of ascending and descending consciousness and intelligence, we continue to be bound in the struggle and "torn apart," only to rely on Isis/Sirius to piece us back together again. The positions of Orion and Ophiuchus opposite each other in the sky are showing us the challenges of this cyclical journey through the precessional cycles and are calling us to awaken, to move into a higher state of consciousness and see our capacity to "step off the wheel" or step out of samsara (the cycle of change, the round of death/rebirth), as the Buddhists have called it.

Later, when Leo was rising at the time of the summer solstice (approximate 6000 to 4000 BCE), the ancient Egyptians encoded in their annual ceremonies an honoring of Orion/Osiris as the constellation of Orion rose above the horizon just before the rising of Sirius (Isis). This marked the time of the summer flooding of the Nile bringing life-giving water to the desert and was the celebration of Osiris's resurrection. The ceremony included the raising of the djed, a pillar that was symbolic of the spine of Osiris as well as of a tree, the World Tree, holding the Earth and Sky and four cardinal points. "Djed" means "to be stable, to be firmly established," and this annual ritual was a way to come back into alignment with the energies of the Earth and Sky and to ensure that the pharaoh was in right relationship with Ma'at, the energies of the Universe. Perhaps, these later myths and rituals harken back to earlier practices dating from the Age of Leo. In ancient Egypt, being in alignment, in right relationship, with the stars was a critical part of their cosmology. The pharaohs also believed that after death they traveled to Osiris (Orion) to be reborn as a star.[18]

Thus, in this period (6000–4000 BCE) in the Age of Gemini and the beginning of the Age of Taurus, when Leo rose with the summer solstice, it also came to represent the deity or guardian protecting the sacred waters of life, fertilizing the dry land. In this way, we frequently see in ancient and modern times a lion's head sculpture on fountains, symbolizing the lion's role in protecting the flowing water. This also brings us to an interesting correlation between the constellation of Leo and its polarity constellation Aquarius, which has been viewed in most cultures as the Water Bearer holding and pouring the urn of life-giving water to the Earth.

The archetypal themes of Aquarius color the second half of the Age of Leo. In this sub-age (approximately 9000–8000 BCE), we see an increasing expansion and development of social culture, which is associated with one of the archetypal themes of Aquarius, valuing community. This sign's traditional astrological planetary ruler is Saturn. Saturn is about form and structure and, in its association with Aquarius, provides the capacity to manifest the creative impulses of Leo in concrete form. This is certainly evident in the construction of some of the ancient monuments of this period as well as the development of human settlements across the Middle East and Old Europe.

It is also significant that our associations of Leo in our modern times relate to the energies of fire and the heat of the summer and the Sun. Bernadette Brady notes that an important myth related to lions that dates back to the end of the Age of Taurus and is the ancient

Egyptian myth of the lion goddess, Sekhmet. She was the daughter of Ra (the Sun god) and used fire to scorch and consume her father's enemies, reflecting the association of Leo with the fierce light and heat of the Sun during the longest days of the summer but also with the theme of revenge against those who were defying the gods. According to Brady, she was known as the "Lady of Flame" or "great lady, holy one, powerful one."[19]

As we have examined the recurring cataclysmic crises on Earth that occur during the precessional cycle, Sekhmet may also represent the archetypal energy of the action of the Cosmos to set things right on the Earth when we have been caught up in chaos and become out of balance with each other and with our relationship to the Earth and sky. Sekhmet, with her fiery energy, brings justice to the land and may relate to the energies of the solar flares or the solar micronovas that bring change and restitution to the Earth and also serve as wake-up calls for humanity.

In traditional astrology, the sign Leo is also known as a fixed fire sign associated with the inspiration and fire of spirit manifesting in creativity. It is associated with the heart in medical astrology. At the heart of the lion in the constellation is the star Regulus. This is one of the royal stars of Persia and the guardian of the north. Historically, it has been associated with leadership and with the importance of ruling from the heart rather than seeking power or success through revenge.

The traditional astrological ruler of the sign Leo is the Sun, our star. It is interesting that many of the hieroglyphic images from ancient Egypt show the orb of the Sun over the head; for example, in images of Isis. Also, many ancient cultures dating back to the Age of Leo, such as the pre-Incan sites in Peru, seem to reflect an understanding of ways in which the life-giving energy of the Sun could be harnessed, not only for harvesting the land, but also for increasing human health and consciousness. Interestingly, in our modern times, Hira Ratan Manek has re-discovered an ancient Hindu ritual of sun-gazing that significantly enhances the functioning of the pineal gland and allows a person to use the Sun's energy for nutrition, healing, and increased consciousness and well-being.

Hira Ratan Manek, who was studied by many medical centers around the world, was able to use solar energy to provide his nutrition, fasting from food for prolonged periods of time while thriving through the integration of energy from the Sun. Manek contended that the Sun's energy has physical, mental, and spiritual benefits for us that have been forgotten in modern times. He established the Solar Healing Center in Florida to continue to conduct research on this ancient practice.

In integrating the wisdom of the Age of Leo, perhaps we can remember and begin to work again with the power and healing effects of the Sun. This age also reminds us of the wisdom of the lion, of living with courage from the heart, and of finding our power through being in right relationship with all of life rather than seeking the illusion of power through manipulation and control. And as we have seen, the advanced cultures of the Age of Leo left us messages in stone to support us in awakening and coming back into connection with the wisdom of the Sun and stars, to guide us back into remembering who we are, why we are here, and the meaning of the time that we are in now. In a profound way, they knew that we would fall into a period of forgetting and that this would be a time of transformation, a critical choice point, in the precessional cycle. They have given us a map, a template, for how to navigate this time and awaken, heal, and move into higher consciousness.

## CHAPTER 4

# The Age of Cancer

### *(approximately 8000–6000 BCE)*

Historically, this age marked a shift from the Mesolithic to the Neolithic period (New Stone Age). In that time, Cancer was rising at the time of the vernal equinox. As temperatures increased and sea levels rose, agricultural communities began to develop more fully and the domestication of animals increased. Some of the earliest settlements (in Catal Huyuk circa 6500 BCE and southeastern Europe circa 7000 BCE) date from this time. It is also the time of the Fertile Crescent cultures that were established on the banks of the Nile in Egypt, on the Tigris and Euphrates Rivers in Mesopotamia, and on the Indus River in India. As we move into this age, the first half of the Age of Cancer was still in the Silver Age (or Treta Yuga), but by around 7000 BCE there was a transition period and movement into the Bronze Age (Dwapara Yuga), which then continued through the Age of Gemini.

As these shifts occurred, there was enough wisdom and awareness of the past for these ancient cultures to realize that they were in times of diminishing consciousness and psychic attunement to the energies of the Earth and sky. Graham Hancock has explored in his book *Supernatural* how ancient cultures dating back thirty thousand years used psychoactive plants to seek guidance and open their consciousness to higher spiritual realms. It is noteworthy that historical research on the use of psychoactive plants in prehistoric times shows an increase in their use as we move into the end of the Age of Cancer and beginning of the Age of Gemini. There is evidence of the use of psychoactive plants such as cannabis in Japan (dating back to 8000 BCE), betel in Thailand and Indonesia (7000 BCE), henbane, waterlilies, and possibly blue lotus in ancient Egypt (6000 BCE), and psilocybin in Algeria (6000 BCE).[1] Could it be that as our consciousness and intelligence continued to diminish, there was a realization that we were losing our access to divine consciousness, to the intelligence of the Cosmos? Perhaps, the increasing use of these plants was to help people reconnect with wisdom and guidance from higher-dimensional realms in ways that they had known naturally in previous ages.

As we move into this age, there is an increasing understanding of our reliance on the Earth for nurturance, and these ancient cultures demonstrated an honoring of the Sacred Feminine. Ruins from ancient sites show the predominance of worship of the goddess, with the architecture of settlements being built in feminine shapes.[2] The Neolithic people had a strong association with the Earth as a fertile mother giving birth to plants and to all of life, and the Grain Goddess was a dominant deity in the cultures of Old Europe. With Cancer rising at the time of spring, these stars may have been associated with the life-giving Earth Mother.

In ancient Egypt, the constellation Cancer was associated with the scarab beetle, a symbol of life after death. Perhaps this related, in part, to the resurgence of life in this age following the cataclysm and period of recovery in the Age of Leo. This was also the time when the floodwaters had receded and the waters on the Earth were now in balance, allowing the seeding and fertilizing of new life on the planet.

Since classical Greece, Cancer has been associated with the water element. It is noteworthy that during the Age of Cancer, images of goddesses with breasts marked by V's and chevrons were prevalent in Old Europe. Archaeologist Marija Gimbutas indicates that breasts marked with these lines symbolize "the Bird Goddess as the divine Source of Nourishment—milk/rain—or as the Giver of Life in general."[3] According to Gimbutas, in the iconography of prehistoric times throughout the world, water was depicted in zig-zag or serpentine images. The M sign is an abbreviated zig-zag. "In Magdalenian times (approx. 15,000–9000 BCE) and later in Old Europe, zig-zags and M's are found engraved or painted within uterine and lens (vulva) shapes, suggesting the symbolic affinity between the zig-zag, M, female moisture, and amniotic fluid."[4] The M sign is later seen in the Egyptian hieroglyph M, "mu," meaning water, and in the ancient Greek letter M, "mu."[5]

The Moon, which is the planetary ruler of Cancer, in ancient cultures was also linked with the rain and life-giving waters. Jules Cashford writes in *The Moon: Myth and Image* that:

> When the thin curve of the Crescent Moon rose as new out of the black night, it appeared to many people to be a cup which held all the waters of life: rain, dew, the moisture of air and cloud, the water of springs, rivers, seas, the sap of plants and trees, and the blood and milk of animals and human beings.[6]

The Moon is also associated with the waters of our feelings or emotions, another core aspect of the meaning of the sign of Cancer. The Moon affects the tides of our oceans as well as our bodies and also affects our melatonin levels and our sleep-wake cycles. As we attune to the energies and phases of the Moon, it guides us to be in balance with our bodies and emotions and to be aware of our interconnectedness with the rhythms of the lunar cycle and of the Earth.

Through researcher Veda Austin's work *The Living Language of Water*, we now understand that water holds consciousness and retains the memories of our Earth and our history. Perhaps ancient peoples understood not only how critical water is for all forms of life, but that it retains the memories of our history on the planet and is a source of consciousness beyond its physical properties. This is supported by our increasing awareness that ancient sacred sites were intentionally built over the locations of subterranean waters. Biogeometry expert Doreya Karim, in her article "Biogeometry: A New Science to Understand Ancient Sacred Sites," has noted that "regardless of changes in beliefs, civilizations still chose the same sacred locations for their rituals. These marked sacred sites were commonly located over underground streams that ran through rocky strata with revered water on which many rituals were practiced."[7] Karim believes that ancient cultures that were more right-brain dominant were able to sense the subtle energies of the currents of subterranean waters at these sacred sites. Geobiologist Rory Duff has also discovered in his research that sacred sites were often positioned at critical intersections of energy ley lines over underground water.

In later ages, in the historical era, Cancer was first linked with the image of the crab by the Chaldeans, due to the Sun's apparent sideways movement through this constellation. At about 2000 BCE (at the beginning of the Age of Aries), Cancer was positioned to rise at the summer solstice in the northern hemisphere. In this period we see the most evidence in ancient Egypt of this constellation being seen as the scarab beetle, the symbol of immortality, and being the place where the Sun god was fully reborn at the time of the summer solstice and of the most light during the year.[8] Later, the belief developed in ancient Egypt that the constellation of Cancer was the place where human souls entered into the Earth's material realms, the place of the soul's incarnation, while the stars of Capricorn (rising at the winter solstice) were seen as the place of the soul's departure at death.[9] For the ancient Egyptians, the scarab beetle was associated with the third form of the Sun god Ra, Khepera, who, in their creation myths, was the force rising from the primeval water and was the source of all life.[10] Here in this later time, we see a shift from the association of Cancer with the Moon to the Sun, as Egypt was moving into the Age of Aries and these stars were rising at the summer solstice, yet the stars of Cancer were still associated with the source of life and the primeval waters.

In traditional astrology, the sign Cancer is known as a cardinal water sign, and in medical astrology it is associated with breasts and the womb. Again, there is a strong association of Cancer throughout mythology with the Great Goddess and the source of all life. As mentioned before, the traditional astrological ruler of this sign is the Moon, which makes sense given the strong link between the Moon and the Sacred Feminine and the prominence of lunar calendars in the Age of Cancer. The cycles of the Moon were also very much correlated with times of planting and harvesting the crops, and monitoring these phases was critical for ancient agricultural cultures.

Up to the beginning of the patriarchal period (and the Age of Aries), ancient cultures used the lunar calendar for tracking time, and the night was seen as more sacred than the day. There was also a deep understanding of the Moon and how its phases correlated with ovulation and menstruation for women. Engraved bones dating back to 25,000 BCE. show observations and notations of the phases of the Moon.[11] The goddess of Laussel from the Dordogne, France (circa 22,000–18,000 BCE), clearly demonstrates the early associations between lunar phases and women's fertility. In this way, from the Upper Paleolithic period on, we see the intimate relationship between the Moon and the life-giving womb of women. For thousands of years, caves, representative of the womb of the Earth, were sites of sacred ceremony and of honoring the goddess.

The origin of the triple goddess (dating back to Paleolithic times) comes from the waxing, full, and waning phases of the Moon. These in turn are related to the phases of women's lives as "maiden," "mother," and "crone." For women in ancient times living in close relationship with the Earth and sky, their pineal glands and melatonin levels were affected by moonlight, which is what caused women's menstrual cycles to be in relationship with the phases of the Moon. Women would ovulate at the time of the full Moon and menstruate at the time of the dark

Moon. Today, there is evidence that as women attune to the energies and rhythms of the lunar cycle, our hormones come into balance, and we are able to more fully honor the sacredness of the cycles of our bodies and of menstruation.[12]

For many ancient cultures (and among many Indigenous cultures currently), women retreated together at the dark of the Moon to menstruate, meditate, and bring back visions for the community. The time of the dark of the Moon was the time of deep transformation and the final day of the lunar cycle. The Moon is invisible each month for three days that include the dark of the Moon, the time of the new Moon (when the Moon merges with the Sun in sacred marriage), and then the first day after the new Moon. In this way, the Moon and lunar cycle guide us in honoring the cycle of life/death/rebirth as it goes through its death, its rebirth and coming into fullness at the time of the full moon, and then its waning as it brings the cycle to a close. This monthly lunar cycle therefore is another template for the cycle of ascending and descending consciousness that we experience with the Great Year, the precessional cycle.

The dark-Moon period of the lunar cycle was also when sacred sexual ceremonies took place in many ancient cultures. Women's sexuality was understood as bipolar in nature, with periods of intense sexual energy at both ovulation and menstruation. Ovulation related to the life-giving, birthing force of sexuality resulting in childbearing. The time of bleeding was a time of deep power and healing, of connection with the energies of life, death, and rebirth. To engage in the sexual act at this time was to encounter the power of the life-giving and death-bringing Goddess. This also relates to the deep ancient understanding of the sacredness of menstrual blood. Yet later, in the patriarchal period and in the time of the Age of Aries, menstrual blood was seen in many cultures and religions as "unclean," as indicated in Hebrew, Islamic, and Hindu texts from this period. Again, we see how paradigms and the meaning of symbols shift as we move through the ages.

Another example of this relates to shifts across the ages in the understanding of women's sexuality. In prepatriarchal cultures, we see evidence in many ancient myths of the sacredness of sexuality and of the dark of the Moon. For example, the first known written myth from Sumer (from the Age of Taurus) describes Lilith, who was the handmaiden of Inanna (child of the Moon god) who brought men from the fields to the sacred temple for sexual rites at the the time of the dark Moon. These sacred rites honored the power of female sexuality and the ability of sacred sexuality to heal and open people to higher consciousness. However, in the Age of Aries, this understanding changed, as Lilith in mythology began to represent the image of a "harlot," a destructive seductress who came at night to torment men and endanger infants and pregnant women. In Hebrew mythology, Lilith was seen as the first wife of Adam and was banished for refusing to submit to his dominance. A view of sexuality as "ungodly" pervades ancient Hebrew legends about Lilith, and she is replaced by the more accommodating Eve.[13] Across the historical and patriarchal period, Lilith became associated more and more with a view of women's sexuality as dangerous or evil, and darkness (like the dark of the Moon) was seen as a punishment and was associated with death rather than an entrance to the transformative power of the goddess and sacred times of ceremony.

As the shift into patriarchy occurred, this free and independent expression of women's power and sexuality became seen as a threat and had to be subverted and repressed. "In both orthodox and apocryphal literature, Lilith's shadow falls on women as far forward in time as the fifteenth century AD, when in the same imagery as was employed for Lilith, thousands were accused of copulating with demons, killing infants and seducing men—of being . . . witches."[14] During the burning times in Europe (approximately 1300–1700 CE), many of the women accused of being witches were, in fact, called "liliths."

This more ancient, prepatriarchal interweaving of the power and healing nature of women's sexuality (separate from procreation) was also apparent in the early mythology of Medusa. The name Medusa comes from the Sanskrit word "Medha," meaning "sovereign female wisdom." She was associated with the dark of the Moon, and she was worshiped as a primary goddess in ancient Egypt and by the Libyan Amazons in North Africa and was later incorporated into Cretan and Greek mythology. The origin of gorgon masks was that these were worn by women during sacred ceremonies, such as the sexual rites, to indicate their deep connection with the goddess and as a form of protection.

The goddess Medusa was also connected with the power of menstrual blood. In the later Greek version, her blood was given to the healer, Asclepius, and it had the power to heal or to destroy. Interestingly, the blood from the right side of her body (associated with the movement of the waxing Moon) was healing, while the blood from her left side (symbolic of the waning Moon) had the power to kill. While, in earlier times, menstrual blood and the sacred sexual rites were about the life/death transformative nature of the goddess and a deep connection with Sacred Feminine power, in the patriarchal period, they became associated primarily with death, with "uncleanness" and destruction. In Greek mythology, Medusa's stare turns men to stone. In Hebrew beliefs and practices, menstruating women were "unclean" and needed to be kept separate from the community during the time of bleeding. The power of women's menstrual blood and of these early sacred sexual ceremonies that were originally about healing and merging with the energy of the goddess became denigrated into being agents of death and destruction. During the patriarchal period, as male dominance became the cultural norm, it was necessary to undermine and repress this deep power of the female body and of women's sexuality.

In the Age of Cancer, when the Moon was honored, sexuality and women's bodies were viewed as sacred and as symbolic of the creativity and fertility of the Goddess. There was a deep understanding of the life-giving nature of women's menstrual blood, mothers' milk, and the waters of the Earth. All of life was a part of the "Great Round." Death was not to be feared but was only one aspect of a larger cycle. As the waning Moon gave birth to the new Moon, so the tomb was also the womb, death emerging in new life. The goddess as life-giver and death-bringer was not split but was part of a unified whole.

As an example of this very different understanding of death in ancient times, there was no word in ancient Egypt for death until the Age of Taurus. Prior to this, death was understood as "westing." For the ancient Egyptians, as the Sun disappears in the west at sunset and reappears again in the east the following morning, as the Moon goes through its disappearance and then reappearance, and as stars sink below the horizon only to return again, they also saw death as a transition, a time of disappearance to return again in a new incarnation. Death was not seen as an ending but rather as a time of transition and transformation.

The sub-age of Cancer is Capricorn, traditionally ruled by Saturn. This sign of the zodiac relates to the development of structure and culture. In ancient Babylon and in many other ancient cultures, this constellation was seen as the "goat-fish" or the goat with a fish's tail. The sea-goat in Babylonian mythology was the god Ea, or "He of Vast Intellect." Ea was the protector of his people and the one who brought people the wisdom of agriculture and how to live in community. This sign of the sub-age signified wise teachers who were thought to come from the sea in the form of a fish and changed into the form of a goat to move on the land and teach the people, only to then return once again to the sea. Interestingly, these images may relate to extraterrestrial beings who visited the Earth and interacted with humanity in these more advanced ages but then withdrew as we moved further into the descending cycle.

Also, rising from the waters of Cancer, the energy of Capricorn brought the awareness of how to manifest visions in action and how to live in agricultural communities and in tune with the cycles of the seasons and nature. It was about bringing systems and structure into the life of the community.

While consciousness continued to diminish in the Age of Cancer, there was still a profound understanding of the interaction between and interweaving of metaphysical and physical reality. In that age, we understood the rhythms of our bodies, of the growth of plants, and of tides in attunement to the phases of the Moon. There was an honoring of the sentience of plants and animals, and how we could work with plants as well as with the cycles of the Moon to open us to higher states of consciousness.

As we reintegrate the meaning and wisdom of the Age of Cancer, we are able to reconnect with the lineage of the Sacred Feminine, with the sacredness of the life around us, and with the archetypal energies of the Moon and lunar cycle. We are also able to remember our deep connection with the natural cycles of the Moon and honor sacred sexuality as a path to healing and spiritual awakening. As we remember and reintegrate the gifts of the Age of Cancer, we are able to correct the imbalances of the modern patriarchal period and come back into right relationship with our bodies and with the natural world. Our understanding of Spirit and matter, of male and female, of light and dark no longer need to be polarized. We also are supported in releasing our fear of death and seeing it as a transition rather than an ending. With the energy of Capricorn, we are able to integrate this embodied wisdom and manifest it in our daily lives.

It is important to remember that even when we are bound in the cyclical changes of the precessional cycle and these phases of descending and ascending consciousness, each age also holds a key, an aspect of our consciousness and of the wisdom of the Cosmos, that we need to reclaim to move into wholeness. As we reflect on these ages, we can reclaim the gift, the archetypal meaning and wisdom of each of these signs of the zodiac. We can also see the shadow aspects of the ages that emerge as we move into more and more disconnection and lower consciousness with the descending phase of the cycle. As we attune to the journey of the precessional cycle, we can learn from these shadow aspects to clear the imbalances and distortions in our psyches and collective consciousness to come back into balance and alignment with our soul selves and with our interconnectedness with the Oneness of all that is.

## CHAPTER 5

# The Age of Gemini

*(approximately 6000–4000 BCE)*

The Age of Gemini (along with the sub-age of Cancer) is in the Bronze Age or Dwapara Yuga, a time of increasing decline in spiritual consciousness and increasing division and polarization among humanity. Historically, this is the later part of the Neolithic era and is characterized by the increasing settlement of communities focused on food production as well as the development of animal domestication and increased production of pottery and weaving. Stone tools were widely utilized, and we also see the development of metallurgy. In Mesopotamia, they began to use clay tokens to account for livestock and commodities. All of these activities involve communication, interaction, and learning, which are characteristics of the Gemini archetype.

In most ancient cultures, including the ancient Egyptians, Hebrews, and ancient Europeans, the two companion stars of Gemini (Castor and Pollux) and the constellation as a whole were seen as two figures or twins. In later Greek culture, the two stars were associated with the archetypes of light and dark. This was the case in other cultures as well. For example, in later Egyptian beliefs, these stars were seen as the struggle between Horus (god of the morning star) and Set (god of the evening star).[1] The twins thus became associated with the notion of polarity and with the struggle between good and evil or light and dark. This reflects the increasing polarization and sense of duality of the Dwapara Yuga and descending consciousness.

In the Age of Gemini, when the stars of this constellation rose at the time of the vernal equinox, images of the twin goddesses emerged in Old Europe. In *The Language of the Goddess,* Marija Gimbutas reported that "double-headed goddesses" or mother-daughter images appeared throughout the Neolithic and Copper Ages and were found in Catal Huyuk (circa 6500 BCE) as well as at the site of the Vinca culture. She noted that the heads of these figures often showed attributes of the bird goddess, with heads that were beaked and bodies that were covered with chevrons, meanders, and cross-bands.[2] These female double goddesses at times depict two adults (perhaps sisters) and, at other times, seemed to be the image of a mother and child. It also reminds us that the honoring of the Sacred Feminine and of the goddess was still prominent in this time.

In her book *The Double Goddess,* Vicki Noble explored the possible cultural meanings of the twin goddesses that have been found in ancient cultures from the Middle East to Central Asia, India, Tibet, Mexico, and Peru. She believed that these images across time and cultures may have represented the multifaceted archetypal patterns of women's relationships, including those of mother/daughter and female collaborative leadership as well as lovers. She also associates these twin goddesses with the dual nature of the Great Goddess in her lunar and solar aspects as well as in her being the Creatrix and Destroyer, bringer of both life and death. However, I think it is significant that this duality is now seen as separate figures (the double goddess) rather than as aspects of the one Great Goddess, as it was seen in earlier ages. We are beginning to see in this age an increasing sense of duality and an understanding of self and other, of the separation of life and death and of light and dark.

As stated previously, it was also during this age that the path of the ecliptic coincided with the Milky Way. At the end of this age, the movement of the Sun and planets in the sky began to separate from the Milky Way and may have been the impetus for the creation myths from the end of this age that refer to being cast out from Paradise. Throughout many ancient cultures, the Milky Way was seen as the path of the sacred and the source of life or the place of immortality. With the separation of the ecliptic from this path, the world of humanity was seemingly separated from the path of the divine. As in the Garden of Eden myth in the Old Testament of the Bible (from the Age of Aries), Adam and Eve become conscious of their identity as separate from God and were thrust out of the garden. As we move into these later ages, the sense of separation and polarization continues to increase.

Could the Age of Gemini have been a period when the first seeds of human duality consciousness, of self and other, and of polarization began? This also may be the time in which we began to have a sense of separation between Earth and Sky. Prior to that, there is evidence that the Cosmos was experienced as a unified whole. In fact, in ancient Sumer, the term for the world was "heaven-earth," the sphere above and beneath as the realm within which we reside.

Another important possible association with Gemini and the twin stars, Castor and Pollux, may be found in the creation story of the ancient Maya in the Popol Vuh (written and translated in the 1500s CE but dating back in oral tradition to a much earlier time). In his books *Maya Cosmogenesis 2012* and *Galactic Alignment,* John Major Jenkins did pioneering research into the astronomical configurations referenced in the Popol Vuh and in the Mayan Long Count calendar and the monuments at Izapa, Mexico, which is the central site of the classical Mayan civilization and the place where the Long Count calendar was created. The ancient Mayan Long Count calendar tracks the last world age (what they referred to as the Fourth World) from a start date of August 11, 3114 BCE to an end date on December 21, 2012. On this winter solstice date, the Sun was in conjunction with the galactic center. The Sun went into conjunction with the galactic center in 1998, and this ongoing alignment (across a few dozen years) marked the end of one precessional cycle and the beginning of a new one.

Jenkins examines the creation story of the Popol Vuh and shows how it is related to these astronomical events. He describes how, in the story, the Solar Lord, Hunahpu, is resurrected at this date. Previously, Hunahpu had been defeated and killed by the Lords of the underworld, Xibalba (the dark rift at the galactic center). His sons, the Hero Twins, rescue him after journeying to Xibalba, the lower world, and avenging their father. In the process, the Hero Twins also defeat the deity of the previous age, Seven Macaw, who then falls from the sky. Jenkins equates Seven Macaw with the stars of the Big Dipper (Ursa Major) and contends that the myth is describing Mayan cosmology's shift from a focus on the celestial pole (guarded by Ursa Major) to a focus on the galactic center as the primary source of life.

If we add to Jenkins's astronomical associations, we might see the Hero Twins as the twin stars of Gemini, Castor and Pollux, who throughout time and across cultures have been seen as sacred twins in world mythology. Toward the end of the Age of Gemini, when the stars of Gemini still rose with the Sun at the time of the vernal equinox, Thuban became the celestial pole star and was in this location from approximately 4500 BCE to 2000 BCE. The stars of the Big Dipper, Seven Macaw, circled around the celestial pole, marking this sacred portal. Around 2000 BCE, however, the celestial pole began to shift away from Thuban toward Polaris, our current celestial pole. At about the same time, the stars of Gemini had sunk below the horizon and no longer rose before the Sun at the vernal equinox and were now replaced by the stars of Taurus.

Polaris is at the tip of the constellation Ursa Minor and is much further from the stars of the Big Dipper. Perhaps this is the meaning of the fall of the Seven Macaw. As the Hero Twins, the stars of Gemini, descended into the lower world, they engaged with the Lords of the underworld and with Seven Macaw and eventually helped to revive their father. It must also be noted that the Sun aligns with the Milky Way only within the constellations of Scorpio and Sagittarius near the galactic center and with the stars of Taurus and Gemini at the other end of the sky. In this way, we can see how the Hero Twins, opposite the stars of Sagittarius, can easily be seen as the offspring of their father, the Solar Lord, the winter solstice Sun in Sagittarius.

The understanding of our profound relationship with the galactic center is significant in this story and in the archetypal meaning of the sign of Gemini. As anticipated in the Mayan Long Count, we are now in a critical time when our winter solstice Sun is in alignment with the galactic center, marking the end of a 24,000-year cycle. We will discuss this in more depth later in the book.

In traditional astrology, Gemini is a mutable air sign and is associated with the planet Mercury. Mercury is a small planet whose orbit is eighty-eight days, and it never moves more than 28 degrees from the Sun. Across history and cultures, it has been seen as a messenger. Mercury and the sign Gemini are symbolic of mental activity, learning and teaching, and a hunger for knowledge. It is during this age that we see the first experiments in writing, which then emerged more fully in the Age of Taurus.

In mythology, Mercury has a close relationship with the Sun and Moon. It is associated with the caduceus, the healing rod that now symbolizes the practice of medicine. The caduceus symbolizes the way in which Mercury represents the activation of the pineal gland and higher consciousness when kundalini awakens and travels up the spine, unifying the masculine and feminine channels around the spine. It therefore is able to guide us in moving out of the polarization of male and female and into unified consciousness and is seen as androgynous.

Mercury also represents the integration of the energies of the Moon and the Sun and the unity of mind, body, and spirit. Many ancient cultures (including ancient India and Egypt) believed that when Mercury (which is always close to the Sun) is also in union with the Moon, then mind and body (and memory) are unified. Mercury connects with the light and essence of the Sun and also is able to connect with our embodied selves (the Moon) and to see the dark side of the Moon that we on Earth never see. In this way, Mercury is able to integrate the light and the dark and what is conscious and unconscious for us.

Mercury moves in and out of visibility as it moves close to the Sun and then out to the farthest part of its orbit. In this way, we also see Mercury as the divine messenger, able to move between the worlds. As so many ancient cultures view the Sun as the Source of our soul's movement in and out of incarnation, Mercury is also seen (especially in ancient Egypt) as the transporter of souls at the time of birth and death. In ancient Sumer, Mercury was seen as Ninshubar, the handmaiden of Inanna who was able to assist her in moving into and out of the underworld.

In ancient Egypt, Mercury is associated with Thoth, god of wisdom and magic, who translates the language of Ra, the Sun god. In ancient Greece, Mercury was seen as Hermes, the messenger of the gods, who brings us wisdom, is able to move between the spiritual and earthly realms, and is the source of the Hermetic principles that describe ways of knowing and how we can deepen our wisdom and understanding of the Cosmos. As we moved deeper into patriarchal times, in ancient Rome, Mercury took on more of a trickster aspect. In that time, Mercury was seen as symbolizing luck and thievery and the ways that we can use our minds to try to control the world around us. This reflects how archetypes and understandings of the planets morph as we move through the ages and further into the descending aspect of the Yuga cycle.

The sign of Gemini is also associated with the arms, lungs, and nervous system. In ancient cultures, there was an awareness that the two sides of the body hold the energies of the Sacred Masculine (on the right side) and the Sacred Feminine (on the left side). We move in this period into an understanding of how these dualities live in our bodies as well as in our psyches.

The sub-age of Gemini is Sagittarius. Since ancient times, this constellation has been seen as an archer or a bow and arrow. In later ages, this sign was associated with the energy of war and the rise of archers, who were lethal in that they could kill from afar. However, in more ancient times, it was known that the tip of the archer's arrow pointed toward the rift in the Milky Way and the galactic center, guiding us to keep our focus on Source and to remember our origins from this cosmic womb.

In this way, the archetypal meaning of Sagittarius is about our being on a spiritual journey and our quest for Source, for the deeper meaning of life. As Gemini helps us to learn and gather knowledge, Sagittarius guides us in understanding wisdom and the meaning and purpose of this knowledge. Gemini represents more left-brain ways of thinking, while Sagittarius is associated with the more integrative and holistic ways of knowing associated with the right brain. Together, Gemini and Sagittarius integrate knowledge and wisdom, and it is significant that both of these constellations lie near the path of the Milky Way, from ancient times seen as the source of incarnation and life.

Perhaps the twin stars of Gemini remind us that our current dualistic thinking is only a phase in human consciousness and that with the return of the Sun to the galactic center, we will remember our underlying unity and common Source. Gemini and Sagittarius, in their alignment with the Milky Way, also remind us that our wisdom and knowledge need to be in alignment with the Tree of Life, with the mystery and energies of the Universe. When we detach ourselves and view the life around us as objects, rather than as parts of the unified web of life, we end up in distorted ways of thinking and being. Indeed, we then truly find ourselves expelled from the Garden and lost in our own sense of alienation and separation. When we look to the image of the twins, individual in their identity but intrinsically interconnected, facing the life-giving path of the Milky Way, we find our way back to the Garden of Paradise and to deep connection with all of life.

CHAPTER 6

# The Age of Taurus

## *(approximately 4000–2000 BCE)*

As we moved into the Age of Taurus, we entered the Kali Yuga, the time of forgetting and of increasing decline in spiritual consciousness. This period is known historically as the Chalcolithic period, in that there was increasing use of copper tools in addition to stone tools. It also evidenced the rise of city-states, particularly in Sumer and ancient Egypt. This is also the period in which written language was more fully developed. Prior to this, knowledge was retained and passed down primarily through oral tradition. In even more ancient times, the advanced cultures of the Golden Age dating back over 12,000 years ago had the capacity for telepathic communication and direct access to knowledge and wisdom through higher consciousness without need for written communication or retaining memories in oral traditions.

The stars of Taurus, the image of the Bull, began to rise at the time of the spring equinox about 4000 BCE and heralded a period in which the Bull was honored as sacred. In ancient Egypt, the cult of Hathor (the celestial cow goddess) was prominent.[1] The Phoenicians worshiped El, the bull god.[2] The cult of the Bull spread throughout ancient cultures, including Sumer, India, and Crete.

In classical astrology, Taurus is known as an earth sign. During this time, the use of agriculture spread and oxen were domesticated. This age marked the end of the Neolithic period and the movement into the Bronze Age (around 3500–3000 BCE), when metalworking became more prevalent. With the development of written language, according to Leonard Schlain, author of *The Alphabet Versus the Goddess*, we begin to shift into being more left-brain dominant after being more right-brain dominant. The left brain involves more analytical, linear thinking, while the right brain is more intuitive, holistic, and integrative in ways of knowing.

The Age of Taurus, at its outset, was a period when the Earth was viewed as sacred and goddess cultures continued to flourish in ancient Europe and throughout the Middle East. The sign Taurus is ruled by Venus, and many ancient cultures honored this planet as a primary deity. For example, in ancient Sumer, during the Age of Taurus, the principal deity was Inanna, later known in Babylonian times as Ishtar. Both relate to Venus and her cycle of movement in the sky from evening star to morning star.

Archetypally, in traditional astrology, Venus relates to what we value and to our relationships. It is about our deep connection with nature and with sexuality and procreation. Venus in ancient times was portrayed as a goddess of fertility and love. Interestingly, in some cultures—for example, among the Maya—Venus was also viewed as a goddess of war. The ancient Maya (dating from the Age of Aries) timed their battles with the heliacal rising of Venus (when Venus was first seen rising before the Sun). We will explore later how this may relate to the meaning of the Venus cycle and to the different cultural understandings of Venus as a morning and evening star.

Venus's association with war may be related, in part, to the nature of the sub-age of Taurus, Scorpio (3000–2000 BCE), which carries the energy of its traditional ruler, Mars. Interestingly, this sub-age correlates with the movement from the Neolithic Age into the Bronze Age, when metalworking, including the formation of weapons, became more prominent. The sign Scorpio relates to themes of death, passion, and deep transformation. While Taurus relates to what is tangible and seen, Scorpio relates to what is unseen, beneath the surface, culturally taboo. The polarity of Taurus and Scorpio also relates to the use or misuse of power as well as the increasing duality between life and death.

The themes of the Age of Taurus, related to this polarity, demonstrate a struggle that began to take place over how we would be in relationship with each other and with the natural world. At the beginning of the Age of Taurus, the Earth was honored as being sacred and was treated with respect, yet as we moved into the sub-age of Scorpio, there were increasing efforts to control, tame, and subdue the Earth and her resources. In this age, we also see a shift in the relationship between men and women from one of equality at the beginning of the age to the gradual shift into the power imbalance of patriarchy starting in the sub-age of Scorpio. War began to spread as the themes of power and dominance came to the fore.

As with all of the archetypal polarities that the signs and planets represent, they do not indicate predestination or fate but rather relate to the themes of the times. As humans, we are able to exert our free will and choose to live out the deeper meaning or manifest the shadow side of these archetypes.

At the outset of this period, the peaceful goddess cultures flourished. These cultures valued equality, cooperative relationships, and creativity (as is evident in the beauty of the art and monuments of this time). As the age unfolded, it also was a time of dramatic change. During this period, the Kurgan nomadic tribes began to invade the cultures of the Mediterranean and ancient Europe, bringing a radically different lifestyle. From about 4400–3000 BCE, they brought about a shift in focus from agriculture to nomadic herding and from a more egalitarian, peaceful form of society to the beginning of patriarchal culture.[3]

What happened that led to this profound cultural shift? How is it that the Old European cultures honoring the Earth Goddess were overtaken by patriarchal "sky god" cultures? One fascinating hypothesis put forward by two British astronomers, Victor Clube and William Napier, and Mike Baillie, an Irish paleoecologist, is that our planet has experienced profound catastrophic encounters with debris from comet activity (or "cosmic swarms") related, ironically enough, to the Taurid complex, the comet debris that the Earth passes through in late fall and early summer. The research conducted by these scientists as well as others indicates that several periods of catastrophic environmental and climactic change occurred across the past five thousand years. These dates include: 2911 BCE, 2345 BCE, 1628 BCE, 1159 BCE, 208 BCE, and 536 CE.

Evidence from tree rings, ice core samples, and historical and mythological records points to the probability of widespread destruction resulting from comet activity. When cometary debris explodes in our atmosphere or on the surface of the Earth, it results in massive destruction, including volcanic activity, earthquakes, flooding, poisonous ocean outgassing, dust clouds, and widespread famine and death. Baille, who has compiled the archaeological, climatological, and geological evidence for the period around 2300 BCE, has written that:

> The archaeological evidence sets forth two significant phenomena that took place at or about 2300 B.C. First, a large number of sites were destroyed by earthquake and conflagration, over a large land area encompassing all of the known advanced cultures at that time. Second, cultural changes occurred, not only in the areas of destroyed sites, but over the entire Earth.[4]

In the article "Comets and Disaster in the Bronze Age," published in *British Archaeology*, Benny Peiser writes:

> At some time around 2300 BC, give or take a century or two, a large number of major civilizations of the world collapse, simultaneously

> it seems. The Akkadian in Mesopotamia, the Old Kingdom of Egypt, the Early Bronze civilization in Israel, Anatolia and Greece, as well as the Indus Valley civilization in India, the Hilmand civilization in Afghanistan and the Hongshan culture in China—the first urban civilizations in the world—all fell into ruin at more or less the same time.[5]

Peiser goes on to note a similar collapse in world cultures around 1200 BCE (for example, the Mycenaeans of Greece, the Hittites of Anatolia, the Egyptian New Kingdom, Late Bronze Age Israel, and the Shang Dynasty of China).[6] Researchers have begun to realize only in the last fifteen years that the widespread destruction was due not to military or human activity but to dramatic climatic and environmental changes (for example, earthquakes, eruptions, tidal waves, fires, and famines), related to comet activity.[7] The catastrophic effects of comet activity led to periods of cultural destruction and dissolution and coincide with the shift of the Hindu Yuga cycle into the lowest point in human consciousness at the end of the descending Kali Yuga.

In addition, Baillie posits that the Exodus of the Hebrews from Egypt occurred in 1628 BCE and coincided with a period of comet activity and the concomitant eruption of the Santorini volcano. He equates the imagery depicting this event in 1 Chronicles (including the pestilence and death in Israel and Egypt, the parting of the sea, the "Angel of the Lord" appearing in the sky and the "pillar of cloud" guiding the Israelites) with the sight of the comet and subsequent earthquakes, death, and volcanic eruption in the region. He also notes that the name of the Israelites' God, Yahweh, traditionally interpreted as "I am that I am," can also mean "the storm god," the destroyer, or "he who causes to fall rain and thunder from the heavens."[8]

Baillie, Clube, and Napier also attribute the worldwide environmental and cultural crises of 540 CE and the Black Death in Europe in 1347 CE to comet activity. Shortly after the crisis period of 540 CE, there was a sudden shift in Ireland in religious orientation from pagan beliefs and practices to Christianity. Saint Patrick, either a real or mythological figure, is thought to have lived in this time and was seen as the one to drive out the "serpents" from Ireland. In that there are no snakes in Ireland, this is more likely a reference to comets, as these were frequently described in ancient cultures as "serpents." It is also significant to note that the death of Saint Brigid (who is associated with the more ancient fire goddess Brigid) is dated at 525 CE. Brigid was known as the "fiery dart" or "arrow of fire." Perhaps these references associate her with the appearance of fiery comet activity in the sky about this same time.[9]

Increasing evidence from astronomy, archaeology, dendrochronology, and geology points to these significant times of environmental and cultural crises. These climactic and global crises correlate with the period in prehistory (2911 BCE and 2345 BCE) when a dramatic shift from goddess cultures to "sky god" cultures took place. The "sky god" cultures were characterized by a shift from honoring the Earth to fearing a transcendent and punishing father god in the sky. This sky god required sacrifice, penance, and obedience in order to avoid his wrath and judgment. I believe that the fear evoked by these terrifying cometary impacts led to the cultural shift from matrilineal, Earth-honoring goddess cultures to the patriarchal "sky god" cultures.

Another major celestial event was also occurring during this age. Beginning about 2700 BCE, the celestial north pole star began to shift from Alpha Draconis in the Draco constellation to Polaris (which is our current celestial pole star in the northern hemisphere). As we shall see later, this change was reflected in myths of the time noting the uprooting of the cosmic tree holding Earth and sky together. This period in prehistory was a time of dramatic change, emanating from the sky and activating profound Earth changes.

Returning to the archetypal themes of this age, classically, the sign Taurus is associated with the throat and with creativity. So, it is significant that the first writing (cuneiform) appeared during this period in Sumer (around 2700 BCE) and then shortly after in the hieroglyphic writing of ancient Egypt. It is also the period in which the Egyptian Book of the Dead was compiled to address the journey through death to rebirth (Scorpio). It was also when the I Ching emerged in preliterate form in China, addressing issues of life, duality, and the origin of the world (Taurus). Due to the development of writing in this period, we have the benefit of written mythology to examine the themes of this age and later ones in more depth.

One of the first known written myths from the historical period is from ancient Sumer and is the story of the goddess Inanna. Inanna was Queen of Heaven, daughter of the Moon god, and was identified with the planet Venus. This myth chronicles the Venus cycle in which Venus appears as an evening star for approximately 260 days, then disappears beneath the horizon for about 3 to 7 days and then reemerges as a morning star for approximately 260 days. Venus returns to its point of origin after eight years (and five synodic cycles), making the numbers five and eight sacred to Venus. The image of the pentacle is associated with Venus, and in ancient times, Venus was often depicted as an eight-petalled flower.

The myth of Inanna depicts the Venus cycle and explores the meaning and mystery of this pattern of evolution, from being an evening star to her descent and subsequent return as a morning star. The themes of life, death, and rebirth reflect the meaning of the Taurus/Scorpio polarity. In addition, the myth also describes the changes that were occurring in the sky and the culture during that time. The oldest tablets of the myth date from 2000 BCE, but the story was thought to be a part of an oral tradition most likely dating back to about 3000 BCE. Within the Inanna cycle is the Sumerian creation story. In this tale, we see evidence of the increasing duality and division within the culture between men and women, the upper world and the lower world, and the Earth and Sky. Formerly, in the Sumerian language, the world was described as "heaven-earth," or the unified sphere of the dome of the sky and the earth below.[10] The myth of Inanna demonstrates the increasing separation between the two as well as a split in the formerly unified goddess, as seen in the passage below:

> In the first days, in the very first days,
> In the first nights, in the very first nights,
> In the first years, in the very first years,
> In the first days when everything needed was brought into being . . .
> When heaven had moved away from earth,
> And earth had separated from heaven . . .
> When the Sky God, An, had carried off the heavens,
> And the Air God, Enlil, had carried off the earth,
> When the Queen of the Great Below, Ereshkigal, was given
> The underworld for her domain . . .
> At that time, a tree, a single tree, a huluppu-tree
> Was planted by the banks of the Euphrates.
> The tree was nurtured by the waters of the Euphrates.
> The whirling South Wind arose, pulling at its roots
> And ripping at its branches
> Until the waters of the Euphrates carried it away.[11]

The story depicts the uprooting of the World Tree, the cosmic tree holding Earth and sky together. The still point in the heavens was shifting during this age as the celestial pole star was moving from Thuban to Polaris. The storm in the myth may also refer to the upheavals in 2911 BCE and 2345 BCE resulting from the cataclysmic effects of comet activity.

The story continues with Inanna taking the uprooted tree and planting it in her garden. "She settled the earth around the tree with her foot."[12] Inanna, the Queen of Heaven, was reestablishing stability in the world by replanting the cosmic tree. However, as the tree grew, Inanna was troubled about some creatures residing in the tree. There is "a serpent who could not be charmed," an Anzu bird, and the "dark maid Lilith," who built her home in the trunk.[13] As the story unfolds, Inanna calls on the aid of the warrior Gilgamesh, who banishes the unwanted inhabitants and forms a throne and bed for Inanna from the tree.

If we remember that these images (the serpent, bird, and Lilith) were strongly associated with the ancient Neolithic bird and serpent goddess traditions, we begin to see the significance of the events in the story. The myth described both the radical shift in the sky and what was occurring culturally. "As above, so below." The winged serpent (the constellation Draco), which had represented one of the most ancient images of the Goddess, was being uprooted from its stable point in the sky with the shifting of the pole star as, simultaneously, the ways of the Sacred Feminine began to be devalued culturally. The unified goddess holding the mystery of life and death and of order and chaos, was split into the Goddess of the Great Above and the Goddess of the Great Below in the same way that the Earth and Sky were increasingly seen as separate entities. Perhaps, as stated before, this split began with the transition from the Age of Gemini into the Age of Taurus and the separation of the ecliptic from the Milky Way, but in the Age of Taurus, this polarization intensified. The split also echoes the themes of the Taurus/Scorpio polarity of life and death, and of what is seen and unseen (i.e., the realm of the invisible, the repressed, and death).

As we move further into the Inanna story, we see more themes of the beginning of the Age of Taurus, including an honoring of nature and of sensuality. Inanna speaks with her brother Utu, the Sun god, about her longing to wed. The story demonstrates the passion and pleasure associated with sexuality that is a characteristic of the archetypal meaning of Taurus (associated with the energies of the Earth and embodied spirituality) as Inanna celebrated the desires of her body.

My vulva, the horn,
The Boat of Heaven,
Is full of eagerness like the young Moon.
My untilled land lies fallow.
As for me, Inanna,
Who will plow my vulva?
Who will plow my high field?
Who will plow my wet ground?[14]

Later in the story, Inanna and Utu argue about who would be her lover. Inanna wanted a farmer: "The man of my heart works the hoe. The farmer! He is the man of my heart!"[15] However, Utu convinced her to choose Dumuzi, the shepherd: "Sister, marry the shepherd. Why are you unwilling? His cream is good; his milk is good . . . Inanna, marry Dumuzi"[16] We see in this struggle the shift in Middle Eastern cultures (as we move into the sub-age of Scorpio) from the primacy of agriculture to the dominance of nomadic shepherds who were invading the land.

In the central part of the myth, Inanna hears the call from the "Great Below" and sets out on a journey to the underworld to visit her sister, Ereshkigal, who had been banished to the world below. In other myths, the banishment of Ereshkigal was attributed to her having been raped and abused. Ereshkigal originally represented the ancient Grain Goddess, the unified goddess of life and death and harvest. Now, she has become the underworld goddess separate from her sister, the Queen of Heaven, demonstrating the increasing split in the former ancient Great Goddess who was both Creator and Destroyer. In the story, Inanna was traveling to visit her sister because Gugalanna ("the Bull of Heaven") was dying. This signifies the Sumerians' awareness that the constellation Taurus, the Bull, was sinking below the horizon in the east at the time of the vernal equinox in this sub-age of Scorpio.

As the myth continues, Inanna is challenged at the entrance to the underworld and has to go through seven gates in her descent into the underworld, just as the planet Venus goes through seven conjunctions with the crescent new Moon in her evening star phase. When Inanna finally encounters her sister, Ereshkigal, in the depths of the underworld (which is associated with when Venus disappears from view in the sky and is in her interior conjunction with the Sun), Ereshkigal in her rage and jealousy "fastened on Inanna the eye of death. She spoke against her the word of wrath. She uttered against her the cry of guilt. She struck her. Inanna was turned into a corpse . . ."[17] In this interaction, Inanna faced the violence, rage, and death now attributed to the underworld.

This myth demonstrates that the formerly unified goddess in this sub-age had been split into Inanna, the Queen of Heaven and of fertility (Taurus) living in the upper world, and the Goddess of death and destruction, Ereshkigal (Scorpio), living in the lower world. It also shows the increasing disconnection with the sacredness of the Earth that is now more and more associated with mortality, suffering, and death. In addition, issues of power, violence, and domination (Scorpio) became important cultural themes in the sub-age, as the Kurgan invasions destroyed the goddess cultures and heralded the beginning of patriarchal culture.

In the Sumerian story, Inanna is rescued and resurrected by two androgynous earth creatures sent from the upper world by Enki, the god of wisdom. After being dead for three days, she is revived and returns to the upper world transformed (Scorpio). Again, she ascends through the seven gates (as, in the Venus cycle, the planet reemerges as a morning star and goes through seven conjunctions with the balsamic Moon). As she exits the underworld, the spirits of the underworld follow her and demand that someone take her place. This intense energy at the time of the emergence of Venus from her inferior conjunction with the Sun may be the reason that the Maya saw this as a time to go to war.

Back in her kingdom, Inanna encounters her consort, Dumuzi (Mars), who has usurped her throne in her absence. Dumuzi ends up being sent to the lower world for six months of the year as his punishment. He too has to undergo the death/rebirth transformation in the Great Below.

Some of the themes of this Sumerian myth are echoed in the Hebrew creation story (written between the fifth and tenth centuries BCE) in the book of Genesis, in which Adam and Eve are expelled from the Garden of Eden. In partaking of the Tree of the Knowledge of Good and Evil, Adam and Eve became self-conscious and experienced a rupture in their relationship with the Divine. In this story, a serpent was the catalyst for their downfall and was cursed along with them. Again, we see the serpent, an ancient image of female power and regeneration, being transformed into an image of evil, something to be feared and banished.

As the Earth and Sky began to be perceived as separate entities, so also enmity began to infect the relationships between men and women and between humans and the natural world. For the first time, the notion of nature as something to be tamed or controlled began to enter human consciousness. With the sign Scorpio (the sub-age of the Age of Taurus), the archetypal themes are those of power, its use and misuse, and issues of life and death. Again, it is significant that this age also marked the transition into the Kali Yuga and the time of declining consciousness and increasing war, division, and discord on the Earth. In addition, 3113 BCE is the starting point of the Mayan Long Count calendar's 5200-year cycle that ends in 2012 CE and was based on their intricate astronomical knowledge of the Venus cycle.

Another myth coming out of Sumer at the end of this age, which exemplifies these themes, is the Epic of Gilgamesh. Gilgamesh was a Sumerian king who lived sometime between 2800 and 2500 BCE. In the tale, he was a hero and a shepherd who was driven and overbearing with the men who worked under him. So the people called on the goddess Aruru, who fashioned a companion for Gilgamesh, someone who could match his strength and energy. She created the warrior, Enkidu, a natural man who lived in the wild and related more easily to animals than to humans. Again, we see the increasing split between culture and nature. Where once humans and the natural world were part of a unified whole, now there was an increasing sense of duality and division. In the story, Enkidu is lured into friendship with Gilgamesh (and into society) by being seduced by the harlot Shamhat. As he became more enculturated, he lost his intimate connection with the animals. After being with the "harlot":

> [Enkidu] set his face towards the open country of his cattle.
> The gazelles saw Enkidu and scattered,
> The cattle of open country kept away from his body . . .
> Enkidu had been diminished; he could not run as before.
> Yet he had acquired judgment, had become wiser.[18]

Echoing the themes of the creation story in Genesis, Enkidu became more self-conscious and entered into a new way of being in relation to nature, which was more separate and estranged.

Later in the story, Gilgamesh and Enkidu went on an adventure to destroy the monster, Huwawa, who guarded the great forest. Again, the theme of the intensifying struggle between humanity and nature is portrayed. After destroying Huwawa, Gilgamesh was asked by Ishtar (the later Babylonian version of the Sumerian goddess Inanna) to marry her. After Gilgamesh rejected her, Ishtar set the Bull of Heaven on the two companions. Enkidu slew the bull. Again, we have a reference to the death of the Bull, the shifting of the Taurus constellation from the vernal equinox. Enkidu was then sentenced to death by the gods.

Gilgamesh, overwhelmed with grief and his own fear of death, set off to find Utnapishtim, who dwelled at the entrance to the eternal realm and could tell him how to find the herb of immortality. In his quest, Gilgamesh arrived at the pass of the mountain of Mashu ("Twins"), "whose peaks reach as high as the banks of heaven—whose breast reaches down to the underworld—the scorpion people keep watch at its gate—those whose radiance is terrifying and whose look is death—whose frightful splendor overwhelms mountains—who at the rising and setting of the Sun keep watch over the Sun."[19]

De Santillana and von Dechend speculate that this description is a reference to the constellation Scorpius (Scorpio) and its twin stars, Lambda and Upsilon. Yet it might be equally valid to interpret this description as describing the arc of the Milky Way, from one end in Gemini (the "twins") to the other end at Sagittarius and near Scorpius. As stated earlier, the galactic center is located near the constellations of Sagittarius and Scorpius and is "guarded" by the scorpion people. The image of the scorpion (Scorpius) as the guardian of the gate to immortality is evident in many ancient cultures, including ancient Egypt (where it is known as Selket) and among the ancient Maya.[20]

While Gilgamesh eventually was aided in finding the immortal realm and diving deep into the dark waters to retrieve the herb of immortality, he lost it at the end of the story when it was snatched away by a serpent (literally translated as "earth-lion.")[21] Perhaps part of the moral of this tale was to remind people that, though society might increasingly strive to explore and know the realms of nature and the Cosmos, our efforts to be in control of life and death and the laws of the Universe ultimately end in futility.

At the same time, this tale clearly refers to the critical solstice and equinox points during the Age of Taurus—the vernal equinox in Taurus, the autumnal equinox in Scorpius, the winter solstice point in Aquarius, and the summer solstice in Leo. These formed the critical "poles" of this age (featuring the fixed signs) and will be important as we look at our current movement into the Age of Aquarius.

As we reflect on this age, it is noteworthy to see the intensity of this period's Earth changes and cultural shifts and the increasing polarization and separation of Earth and Sky, male and female, light and dark, life and death, and notions of good and evil. Yet when we remember that every age is a part of the larger cycle of the Great Year, we can honor the mystery of the learning that was unfolding in our human consciousness in this time of turmoil and increasing duality.

It is also significant that it is in the sub-age of Scorpio that we shift into the patriarchal period and see the manifestation of the shadow aspects of Mars (the traditional planetary ruler of Scorpio), including war and the rise in abuse of power as well as an increasing fear of death. Whereas in earlier ages death was seen as a transition and as a part of the cycle of life/death/rebirth, now death is feared and is seen as an ending, with an increasing need to strive for survival through conquest.

As we review this period, the early phase of this age teaches us the importance of honoring the sacredness of the Earth, of our bodies, of our sexuality, and of our attunement to the rhythms of the Earth and the Moon. It helps us to reconnect with the energies of the Sacred Feminine. Understanding the Venus cycle and myth of Inanna also supports us in understanding our journey of transformation and what we learn through our relationship experiences. It guides us in remembering that we need to reclaim the lost aspects of ourselves and heal in order to emerge in our lives in a more empowered way.

Also, as we see the shifts that happened after the Earth changes and the comet impacts as we moved into the sub-age of Scorpio, it guides us to face our fears, to see how trauma can activate our disconnection from the Earth and from each other and trigger our fear of death. We can also see from this sub-age that if we do not face these fears and heal from our trauma, it can lead to our being unconsciously controlled by trauma and fear and then becoming harbingers of death ourselves (through violence, war, and conquest). As we bring this more into our consciousness and the light of awareness, then we are able to heal and come back into wholeness.

CHAPTER 7

# The Age of Aries

## *(approximately 2000 BCE–0 CE)*

Aries is the constellation of the Ram and in traditional astrology is ruled by the planet Mars. Both the sub-age of Scorpio (ending the age of Taurus) and the beginning of the age of Aries are ruled by Mars. This is a period in human history in which warfare became a dominant aspect of culture. With the rise in patriarchy came an increase in warrior cultures and the increasing suppression of women and of the wisdom of the Sacred Feminine. It is also in this age that we move more fully into the Kali Yuga and the lowest point in terms of our spiritual consciousness at the collective level.

The sub-age of Aries is Libra (1000 BCE–0 CE) which is ruled by Venus. Across the two ages of Taurus and Aries, we see the interplay of Mars and Venus evidenced in the shifting nature of gender relationships and the tension between the valuing of connection (cooperative and collaborative relationship) versus that of dominance (power-over). This tension and dynamic were seen throughout different cultures in this age in social policy and practice, in interpersonal relationships. and in societal views of nature.

This theme is also a part of the polarity of archetypal meanings of the signs of Aries and Libra. In traditional astrology, Aries is a cardinal fire sign. It is the energy of assertion, the longing for independence, for experiencing the self as a separate entity. Libra, in contrast, is about balance, harmony, and mutuality in relationship. We see throughout the Age of Aries this tension between the increasing assertion of individuality and the effort to maintain a sense of harmonious relationships in society through the imposition of law and forms of justice. The themes of the Libra sub-age relate to how we engage in relationship and in interaction with each other, how we define justice and find a way of coexisting in order and harmony. These signs and their planetary rulers also relate to increasing conflicts between the genders and between the archetypal energies of the Sacred Feminine and Sacred Masculine.

In the Age of Aries, the cult of the bull of the former age was gradually replaced with that of the ram. The sacrifice of lambs and rams as ceremonial practice was prevalent throughout many cultures. In Egypt, there was a shift from the bull god, Montu, to the ram god, Amon. As is typical with the shifting of ages, the imagery and cultic practices of the past age were denigrated. In the Age of Aries, images of bull slayings became prominent, for example, in the Mithraic religion of Persia. In the Hebrew account of Moses descending from Mount Sinai with the Ten Commandments, he sternly criticized the people for their worship of the golden calf (a symbol of the previous Age of Taurus).[1]

In contrast to the more earth-centered spirituality of the Age of Taurus, in the Age of Aries (associated with a fire sign), fire ceremonies became a critical part of religious practice. For example, in the Hebrew Bible, Moses met Yahweh in the sacred fire. Also during this age, Zoroastrianism focused on the importance of fire rituals.

With the sign of Aries's traditional astrological association with the head (and mental activity) and with leadership, we see an increase in this age in the codification of culture with laws; for example, those established in the Hebrew Torah and the code of Hammurabi in Babylon (2081 BCE). The Vedic texts were also developed in this period by the Aryans invading India. These texts emphasize hierarchy and the class structure of society. These codified laws show a shift from an understanding of natural law to the imposition of human law.

In India, Indra, the war god, was a prominent deity. Toward the end of this age, the Hindu Upanishads emerged (650 BCE), as did the Chinese Taoist philosopher, Lao-Tzu (531 BCE), and the Buddha was born in 528 BCE. These seeded many of the spiritual ideas that flourished in the next age, Pisces.

Many empires arose during this age in Egypt, Greece, China, and Rome. Alexander the Great in Greece was depicted with ram's horns on his head.[2] The rise of the Roman Empire came at the end of this age (around 510 BCE). These empires reflect the Aries archetype of the warrior and the need for conquest and control.

It is also in this age that we see a fuller shift from right-brain dominance to more left-brain ways of thinking and knowing. With this, there was an increase in written language and in self-conscious and separatist ways of thought and of being. Prior to this, with more right-brain dominance, humans experienced themselves as part of the larger whole of life around them, relating to other life-forms in an intuitive, empathic, and even telepathic manner. The shift into the Age of Aries brought an increase in self-assertion and individualism, and the left-brain way of defining reality in a more detail-oriented and linear manner became more prominent. Individual consciousness increased as did efforts to structure the laws and social mores of society. This also led to an increase in power struggles and efforts by leaders to dominate, rather than the more egalitarian modes of governance that characterized earlier prepatriarchal communities.

In part, this shift from right-brain dominance to left-brain dominance may have been due to the development and use of written language. As Leonard Shlain has written in *The Alphabet Versus the Goddess,* written language led to the increasing dominance of the left hemisphere, which controls the speech and language sections of the brain. Interestingly, the most ancient written languages were pictorial, such as the cuneiform texts and hieroglyphics. These more ancient languages were also known to emanate frequencies or energies; for example, Egyptian hieroglyphics were known to activate energies in the sacred sites. Also, these languages were written from right to left, as you might expect in people who were more right-brain dominant (and most likely had a left-handed dominance as a result). However, over time, language became more symbolic and abstract and shifted to being written from left to right as people became more left-brain dominant (with an increased propensity for right-handedness).

It is also interesting to note that ancient prehistoric cultures were more lunar in their orientation and intimately connected with the movement of the Moon in the sky (which grows in size from right to left or counterclockwise). In contrast, in our patriarchal solar cultures, we are very attuned to the movement of the Sun rising in the east and setting in the west in a clockwise movement. In this way, the directional orientation of pictorial vs. written languages may reflect these cultural changes.

Along with this shift to left-hemispheric dominance came an increase in linear, analytical, and abstract ways of thinking. This resulted in the development of human law (as opposed to natural law) and an increasing disconnection from nature. In this era, people began to separate themselves from a sense of unity with the natural world and to analyze the world around them in the context of objective thinking or the perspective of self and object. It is also during this period that dualistic thinking became even more prevalent.

Interestingly enough, this is also the age when even our orientation to the movement of the stars in the sky reflected our increasing separation from nature. The modern Western tropical zodiac was fixed in time in the Age of Aries, when the sun was rising in Aries at the spring equinox. In this way, the constellations and signs of the zodiac began to take on separate meanings as the Sun signs became more reflective of the seasonal changes and time of year rather than the actual positions of the stars in the sky. The sidereal zodiac, which more accurately reflects the placement of the planets in the constellations, is now different from the tropical zodiac by 24 degrees due to its factoring in the precessional movement of 1 degree every seventy-two years. In this way, while the meanings of the signs and constellations continue to overlap, the modern tropical zodiac chart and signs also now have a separate identity from the constellations in the sky.

In the Age of Aries (in which the Sun is exalted in traditional astrology), we also see a shift from lunar cultures to solar cultures. There was a transition from a reverence for the Earth to deification of the sky and the sky gods. With right-brain dominance, the experience of the divine was immanent; it was present in all of creation, in all of life. With the shift to left-brain dominance, spirit became separated from nature, and the divine was viewed as transcendent, above us, apart from us. In this way, the experience of the divine was sought through propitiation, through sacrifice, and through guidance and control from external authorities and was no longer an intrinsic part of the human and natural experience. This time was also characterized by a transition from the honoring of the Great Goddess to the image of a male God as the dominant deity. The goddess cultures continued to be destroyed during this period and were replaced by nomadic, herding patriarchal cultures.

A story that is at the heart of the Hebrew and Islamic (and later Christian) traditions arising in this age is that of Abraham, known as the Father of the Israelites through his son Isaac and as the Father of the Arabs through his son Ishmael. Originally known as Abram ("High/Exalted Father/Leader" in Hebrew), he later was named Abraham, meaning "Father/Leader of Many." In the Qur'an (Koran), he is portrayed as a founding prophet. In both the Hebrew Bible and in the Qur'an, Abraham was called to sacrifice his son in obedience to God and was later blessed as the Father of his people and future generations. In the Hebrew Bible, this sacrifice foreshadowed the Christian story of the sacrifice of Jesus, God's son, for the life and salvation of the people. While the historicity of Abraham has not been definitively proven, research places his birth around 1812 BCE within the Jewish traditions or around 2166 BCE by other calculations, either at or near the beginning of this age.

Below is the Hebrew version of this story (from Genesis 22) of God's test of Abraham in asking him to sacrifice his son:

> After these things, God tested Abraham and said to him, "Abraham!" And he said, "Here am I." He [God] said, "Take your son, your only son Isaac, whom you love and go to the land of Moriah and offer him there as a burnt offering upon one of the mountains of which I shall tell you." So, Abraham rose early in the morning . . . and went to the place of which God had told him. . . . And Abraham took the wood of the burnt offering and laid it on Isaac his son; and he took in his hand the fire and the knife. . . . When they came to the place of which God had told him, Abraham built an altar there and laid the wood in order and bound Isaac his son and laid him on the altar upon the wood. Then Abraham put forth his hand and took the knife to slay his son. But the angel of the Lord called to him from heaven, and said, "Abraham . . . Do not lay your hand on the lad . . . for now I know that you fear God, seeing you have not withheld your son, your only son, from me. . . . By myself I have sworn, says the Lord, because you have done this . . . I will indeed bless you, and I will multiply your descendants as the stars of the heavens and as the sand which is on the seashore . . . and by your descendants shall all the nations of the earth bless themselves, because you have obeyed my voice.[3]

Of significance in this story are the themes of obedience to a transcendent Father-God and the importance of sacrifice. Prior to this age, there was a stronger sense of the interconnection of Earth and Sky and of deity as immanent, manifesting in nature and in an embodied manner. The holy places were caves, groves of trees or pools of water that held the energy of the sacred Earth. In this age, there was an increasing shift toward the notion of a sky god who was worshiped on the mountain tops and high places. This story also marks the full transition into patriarchy, where lineage was no longer through the woman (matrilineal) but was now through the father's line (patrilineal). In addition, there is the theme of separation and individuation, as Abraham was called away from his community to face his individual test from God, and he was asked to be willing to sever the commitment to his human son to obey the transcendent Father-God. In the story, God released Abraham from having to slay his son and offered a ram to be sacrificed in his stead, again reflecting the cult of the ram of this age.[4]

With the Israelites, the notion of monotheism emerged. From a lineage of polytheism and the worship of many deities came the idea of one god, Yahweh, to be worshiped above all others. A few thousand years later, it is difficult for us to conceive how radical this belief was at that time and how it led to a separation of the Israelites from the surrounding peoples, who, according to the Judaic tradition, worshiped "false gods." Again, the theme of separation became prominent in this age. It is also significant that the Hebrew Bible describes the command of this Father-God to annihilate the surrounding cultures due to their worship of false gods (or, actually, goddesses). So, the destruction of the goddess-honoring cultures increased during this age.

As separation and individuation came into the collective consciousness, so also did the idea of "sin" or "evil." In the Hebrew Bible, sin originated out of the human consciousness of separation from God as Adam and Eve ate of the Tree of the Knowledge of Good and Evil. In eating the fruit of the tree, Adam and Eve became self-conscious and experienced themselves as separate from God.[5] Evil, then, in this story refers to the sense of separation, of division and duality. Sacrifice became the ritual practice to provide propitiation for that rupture and to allow renewed union between humanity and divinity. The polarity of Aries (the notion of individuality and oneness) and Libra (relationship) are again dominant in these cultural and religious themes. What is significant is that the unity and communion with nature and spirit that were once a given in human experience became increasingly elusive and were now sought after through obedience, sacrifice, and devotion to a transcendent god.

This also was reflected in the shift from a lunar culture to a solar culture. Heinrich Zimmer explained the impact of this shift in India:

> The recurrent phases of the Moon were a visible pledge of eternally renewed rebirth. But this lunar era of the human spirit with its hope of immortality grounded in perpetual alternation, gave way to the solar era, when the unchanging eternity of solar existence was promised to those initiated through "knowledge." The Moon, formerly a symbol of the supreme consolation and visible hope, now came to stand for the nightmarish vicious circle of death and birth, when only an esoteric "knower" could escape into a higher transcendent world.[6]

The Moon was exalted in the Age of Taurus, while in the Age of Aries, the Sun became exalted.

The sub-age of Aries is Libra. In this way, the sign of Libra, ruled by Venus, offered a possible balance to the individualism and assertion of the ego fostered by Aries. Libra, an air sign associated with the longing for balance, harmony, and mutuality in relationship, is able to bring to the Aries emphasis on the self an awareness of the needs and concerns of others. Each age contains its balancing archetypal polarity in the meaning of the opposite sign; however, if the deeper meaning and energy of a sign is not integrated, then the distortions are likely to continue into the sub-age. This seems to be the case with the historical period of the Libra sub-age of Aries. At the end of this age, we see the movement toward the Dark Ages and the nadir of human culture and development with an overemphasis on materialism, individualism, violence, and wars for power, land, and wealth. The out-of-balance Aries energy from the beginning of the age became channeled into interaction with others (Libra) in a destructive manner and in a quest for dominance.

Interestingly, this out-of-balance expression of the Age of Aries is also a disconnection from the deeper archetypal meaning of Mars, the planetary ruler of Aries. Mars is the first planet outside of the orbit of the Earth. In mythology, it represents the hero's journey and the archetypal meaning of the Age of Aries, and this development of the individuated sense of self and of our exploration of our own individual self-expression. Mars, in its hero's journey, moves away from the Sun and is in its own journey of separation and discovery.

However, the transformational moment of the cycle, when Mars is at its brightest in the sky, is when Mars moves into opposition with the Sun. This is the moment of awareness and transformation, when Mars awakens to its relationship with the Sun and Source. This is also when the hero realizes that the quest has led back to the inner knowing, the wisdom that was always within and not outside of the self. Then, the hero realizes that the journey was not about separation but about the exploration of individuation in order to bring this understanding and the gifts from the journey back into relationship—with Source and with others. The integrated expression of the Libra sub-age of the Age of Aries would have symbolized this realization and integration.

As we reflect on these archetypal meanings of Mars and Venus, the two planets associated with the Age of Aries and sub-age of Libra, we realize that with Venus and the principle of the Sacred Feminine, we undergo transformation through our inner process of descent and return and in the context of relationship. This is the path of the journey inward and of reclaiming the lost parts of ourselves that then leads to shifts in our patterns in interaction with others. This is Inanna's journey to the underworld and her return. With the Sacred Feminine, we also experience the touch of Spirit in the body and in all of life around us. This is immanence, embodied spirituality. Venus guides us in the journey of transformation in relationship—with the self, others, and all of life.

With Mars and the principle of the Sacred Masculine, we transform through our search for individuation and transcendence. This is the journey of transformation through our outer experiences, through the quest for self. We then realize we need to dissolve the identification with ego and open to something larger and beyond our individual self. We seek transformation and expansion through the movement outward and upward.

The moment of profound transformation in the Venus journey is when Venus is in its inferior conjunction with the Sun. Venus is at its closest to the Earth and is merged with the light and energy of the Sun. At this time, Venus is invisible. She is in unity with the Sun. She is in the process of transmutation and in the energy of the Sacred Marriage. She is then at her brightest in her cycle as she first emerges as a morning star. This is when Venus has reclaimed a deeper understanding of herself to return into interaction with others. She then continues in her journey as a morning star until she again disappears from view now in her superior conjunction with the Sun (and in opposition with the Earth). This is when Venus reflects on her journey and communes with the stars to then re-emerge as an evening star.

For Mars, the moment of transformation is when Mars is opposite the Sun. This is when Mars is farthest from the Sun yet closest to the Earth and at its brightest. This is when Mars has reached the peak of the hero's adventure and has found the Holy Grail, and yet has realized that the journey was actually not for something beyond the self but within the Self. This is the time of the dissolution of the ego, the reconnection with the soul self, and remembrance of the Oneness of all that is. As the poet David Whyte writes, this is when the pilgrim realizes that the pilgrimage was not about the destination but about the discovery of the Self.[7]

After Mars reaches its opposition to the Sun, it begins its journey back. Mars is now sharing the lessons learned from its quest and is able to act in ways that are of service to others. As Mars returns, moving back toward the Sun, it goes through a crisis of identity or consciousness as it begins to realize the deeper meaning of the journey—that we are not truly alone or separate, but that we each are an expression of the consciousness of the Cosmos. At the end of its cycle, Mars disappears from view as it merges with the Sun for a few months, to review and reflect on the journey, and to return to oneness with Source before birthing a new cycle.

We here on Earth lie between the orbits of Venus and Mars. We are here to learn the lessons and to undergo the transformation available to us by journeying within and by dealing with our deep emotions and relationships with others. Venus reminds us of the journey of relationship and of reconnection. Mars guides us in the journey of learning and growth through separation and individuation. We venture into this incarnation to experience our capacity to act, to make choices, and to be on our own evolutionary quest. But eventually, Mars also realizes that this separation is an illusion, and that we are truly one with and guided by Spirit, by Source. Mars, when it is acting most consciously, is able to be on the journey of exploration while remaining attuned to Source. Then, personal will is aligned with divine will, and we realize that we are here on the earth plane as spiritual beings having a human experience in order to grow and evolve, and, as we realize our true identity, we then become co-creators with Cosmic consciousness and use our unique gifts in service to others.

While the Age of Taurus emphasized the spiritual journey of transformation through relationship and the inner process (Venus) to then bring it out in action in the world (Mars), the Age of Aries guides us in how we can work this outer journey (Mars) to then bring it back into relationship and into harmony and balance with all of life (Venus).

If we reflect on these deeper archetypal themes and learning of this age, it is a reminder to us to integrate the expression of self with a concern for the needs and welfare of others. It is a reminder that the journey is ultimately not about separation and individuation but about the discovery of the soul self and realization of our interconnectedness with each other and all that is. Then, our self-assertion and self-expression become a manifestation of our alignment with our soul selves and come from love and a longing to be of service and to live in harmony with all that is. In integrating the energies of Mars and Venus, we come to understand the balance of the Sacred Masculine and Sacred Feminine and the balance of our uniqueness and individuality with relationship and our sense of community and communion with all of life. In this integration, we also are able to move beyond the polarities of Spirit as immanent (as seen in the more ancient, earth-based goddess cultures) and Spirit as transcendent (as evident in most patriarchal religious belief systems) to an understanding that Spirit is both in all of life and beyond all that is.

However, in that this integration did not occur in our journey through the Age of Aries and the sub-age of Libra, the shadow aspects of this age and of the distorted understanding of Mars and the archetype of the Sacred Masculine continued to dominate. Our spiritual consciousness continued to decline in this period of the Kali Yuga and war, violence, power-over paradigms, and destruction of the Earth continued to increase. These patterns then prevailed as we moved into the Age of Pisces.

CHAPTER 8

# The Age of Pisces

## *(approximately 0–2000 CE)*

In the Age of Pisces, we continue to experience the Kali Yuga period, but we are in the ascending phase of this yuga, and there is an increasing theme of the need for redemption, transformation, and a return to connection with Spirit. The Age of Pisces is symbolized by the constellation of two fish swimming in different directions; the eastern one swims upward, while the western fish aligns with the ecliptic. This is often seen as symbolizing the integration of spiritual transcendence (the fish swimming upward) with how this spiritual nature is embodied and manifested in life on the earth plane (the fish along the ecliptic). Interestingly, according to Bernadette Brady, Pisces and Aries merge in the sky because "there was never a clear distinction between these two constellations, as Pisces is so large, its two Fish reaching through the sky actually encompass the stars of Aries."[1] In this way, the constellation of Pisces is able to absorb the stars of Aries and overcome that age's illusion of separation to bring back the remembrance of unity with the Oneness of all that is.

The symbol of the fish was ancient. It denoted wisdom and was associated with the image of the yoni (womb, source of life). For example, in ancient China, the goddess Kwan-yin was the Great Mother and "Yoni of Yonis" and was seen as a fish goddess.[2] It is not surprising then that classically, this sign has been seen as yin or feminine in its energy.

In astrology, Pisces is a mutable water sign coming at the end of the cycle of the zodiac. Archetypally, its themes pertain to the surrender of the self, of the ego, to some larger vision or purpose. Traditionally ruled by Jupiter, it relates to faith and spiritual beliefs. Many religious ceremonies developed in this age involved the ritual use of water, such as for baptisms and blessings. Later, Neptune became the modern ruler of Pisces and relates to that longing to merge with Oneness, with the sea of Cosmic consciousness, with Source. Neptune also relates to our longing to redeem ourselves, to recover from the sense of separation and restore our relationship with the Divine.

The Age of Pisces was characterized by the rise of the great religions of Christianity, Islam, Buddhism, and Confucianism calling on people to commit themselves to a larger purpose. Buddha was born in 510 BCE, setting the stage for this age, and Jesus was born at the beginning of the age (sometime around 1 CE) at the time of a major conjunction of Jupiter and Saturn. While the core teachings of both Buddha and Jesus relate to a mystical relationship with Spirit, their followers over time institutionalized and codified their teachings, forming the religions of Buddhism and Christianity, respectively. Interestingly, the symbol for Christianity across the past two thousand years has been the fish, and Jesus was referred to as a "fisher of men."

Following the sense of separation and individualization arising during the previous age, the message of Jesus and Buddha and other spiritual teachers of this age was one of mystical communion, of merger with the divine. Throughout this era, there was an emphasis on mysticism and dissolution into a larger sense of service to and identity with Spirit. Perhaps this was a corrective to the separatism of the previous age, but it is noteworthy that the theme was primarily of the individual soul attempting to merge with the divine. The mystical notion of this time is that Spirit or divine love permeates all life and the entire

Universe, and that if the self can dissolve and let go of the boundaries of individuality, there can be a return to that sense of Oneness. This is the dissolving that Pisces offers, the death of the ego that can lead to rebirth into a greater unity and mystical sense of Oneness.

In their origins, all of the great religious traditions arising in the Age of Pisces come from these mystical roots. It is the core message of Christianity, Judaism, Hinduism, Buddhism, Taoism, and the Sufi path of Islam. All hold the awareness that the connection to the divine, to Cosmic consciousness is within us, and that we are all part of the Oneness. Jesus taught that "God is love" and that the "kingdom of God is within you," and in the Vedic tradition, Atman (analogous to the Soul) is Brahman (of divinity). All of these traditions emphasize letting go of the ego to merge with divinity and return to a more immanent sense of spirituality. There is also a reemphasis on the mystery and unknowable nature of the divine. Through our intuition, enlightenment, ecstasy, or the dissolving of our sense of separateness, we can experience (rather than intellectually know or assert) our connection with the divine.

The theme of the redeemer or savior is also significant in this age. This fits with the meaning of the traditional planetary ruler of Pisces, which is Jupiter. Archetypally, this planet is associated with characteristics of the teacher, guru, or spiritual leader. At the advent of the Age of Pisces, there was an "extraordinary proliferation of redeemer cults . . . which spread with a mystical intensity quite unknown to the ancient world at any previous epoch."[3] These cults included those of the early Gnostics and involved competing redeemer/saviors, including Mithras, Orpheus, and Jesus. These cults viewed the Cosmos as a battleground between the powers of darkness and light and between matter and spirit. In their quest for redemption, their practices focused on "a preoccupation with perfectionism, visionary experience, sexual abstinence and martyrdom."[4] Unlike the cults of the Bull and the Ram in which sacrifice was often done to ensure fertility for the land and the people, sacrifice in this age took on an even greater emphasis as a form of propitiation for separation from the divine and an abnegation of the body to bring greater union with the pure realm of spirit. In this way, we see a continuation of the split between spirit and matter that became embedded in the religions of the Age of Aries. However, the mystical roots of spirituality in the Age of Pisces, which were focused on reclaiming an integration of physical and metaphysical reality, took on greater emphasis on the abnegation of the body and the devaluation of material reality as these spiritual traditions became institutionalized in the patriarchal religious systems of the age.

This form of sacrifice is evident in the Christian religious tradition's story of the crucifixion of Jesus. Embodied in this tradition was a sense of the body and the realm of earthly matter as the source of separation and sin. Practices to transcend or release the spirit from the body became the focus, and the duality between the realm of spirit and of flesh was encoded in the religious ideology. This dualism and its concomitant effects characterized the nature of this age. At the outset of the age, the effort to reestablish union with the divine through mystical "knowing" and opening to love and the sense of oneness was emphasized. Then, the religious systems of the Age of Pisces encoded the increasing split between spirit and matter. Later, in the sub-age of Virgo, the realm of spirit began to be denied and devalued, resulting in idealization of the realm of the mind and an obsession with efforts to control the physical world around us.

As distortions from the Age of Aries continued to permeate the Age of Pisces, we retained not only the split between spirit and matter but also the theme of conquest and control. It is in the Age of Pisces that we see an increase in religious wars with the Christian crusades and the expansion of the Islamic empire. The mystical roots of the spiritual traditions at the outset of the age were institutionalized into Buddhism, Christianity, and Islam, which then merged with political power to assert dominance and control. We also see in this age the increasing power of the Roman empire and the significant merger of religion and political power when Emperor Constantine convened the Council of Nicaea (in 325 CE) to unify Christianity and integrate it with the empire. This then led to Christianity becoming the official religion of the Roman empire in 380 CE, resulting in increasing persecution of those who held to the "pagan" beliefs and practices of the past (and of the more earth-based spiritual traditions).

The distortions from the Age of Aries continued into the Age of Pisces and overrode the corrective energies of the deeper archetypes of Pisces and resulted in religion as a form of social control rather than as a path to spiritual enlightenment. Even in our modern times, we see the results of this in the global power of the Vatican in Rome and of Catholicism. This also led to other distortions in the sub-age of Virgo. As Virgo is an earth sign, this sub-age could have been a time of integrating the mystical roots of the Age of Pisces into daily life and into healing from the divisions of the past and finding ways to be in service to others.

Instead, the imbalances of the beginning of the Age of Pisces led to our experiencing the shadow aspects of this sub-age. The sign of Virgo is ruled by the planet Mercury. Its themes relate to discrimination and mental analysis and are evident in the formation of these religious belief systems. Virgo, in its relation to Mercury and analytical thought, led to an increasing emphasis, toward the end of the age, on science, technology, and efforts to comprehend and control our environment and the workings of our body and nature. It involved harvesting natural resources for our own use. As part of the shadow side of this sign, it also led to an increasingly myopic vision (focusing on the "trees" and losing sight of the "forest") on work and day-to-day reality. In reaction to the Piscean emphasis on spirituality and the dissolution of self, Virgo focused on the primacy of the mind and our capacity to manage our bodies and our environment. This is evident in the Copernican revolution of five hundred years ago and our movement into scientific materialism, resulting in our current scientific worldview that emphasizes our intellectual capacities and the human ability to analyze and decipher the nature of the Universe.

Virgo in its highest sense is associated with the ancient Grain Goddess and with the Sacred Feminine and retains a deep connection to Piscean spirituality and Cosmic consciousness. In this way, Virgo discrimination can enable us to integrate our connection with Spirit into daily reality. This fits with the association of Pisces with the feet and the ways in which spiritual expansion could then be embodied and metaphysical reality grounded in physical reality. Virgo is also the sign of the healer, who is able to discern the movement of energy in the body and who understands the complex interaction between body, mind, and spirit.

In addition, Virgo is the sign of the vestal virgin. While this tradition became distorted in patriarchal times, in its more ancient meaning it related to a deep understanding of sexuality as a pathway to the divine. Tantric sexuality at its origin was an intimate knowledge of the way in which sacred sexuality is about union and communion. In entering into the fullness of the body and raising kundalini energy, we move from physical union to a communion with the divine Spirit. Integrating Virgo wisdom with Piscean mysticism might have led to a more fully embodied understanding of spirituality and sacred sexuality, a deeper sense of the sacred in our day-to-day reality, and a richer honoring of the sacredness of the Earth and all of the life around us.

Unfortunately, in the last thousand years, we have seen more of the shadow side of the Virgo archetype in modern Western culture. Virgo in its polarity to Pisces can become a reaction to Spirit and an overemphasis on physical, material reality. If we get caught in fear of the loss of identification with ego and sense of individual boundaries that are a part of the deep Piscean mystical communion with Spirit, Virgo can then become the determination to maintain an illusion of dominance and control. The gifts of discrimination and discernment now morph into obsessive-compulsiveness and the need for control. A capacity for analysis devolves into the deification of the intellect in the "Age of Reason." It is no longer the deeper Virgo longing to know and understand the integration of Spirit in matter but becomes the quest to gain factual information in order to control external resources and events. Instead of wisdom, we focus on gathering data. Instead of communion, we see a fanatical desire for control and power-over. Instead of merger, we become mired in materialism. Sexuality no longer is a pathway to the sacred but becomes an objectification of the other, an addiction, an escape, or a manipulation of others for personal gain.

We live now with the aftermath of the shadow side of the themes of this age. In religious fundamentalism, the mystical notion of the dissolution of self into merger with the divine becomes distorted into notions of martyrdom, sacrifice of self, and the idealization of death as a path to salvation. Drawing on the themes of the previous age, fundamentalists demonstrate an obsession with the one "true" path and the evangelical need to convince others of their rightness. The shadow side of Pisces is victimhood, martyrdom, and the fog of illusion. Rather than mystical awareness leading to greater integration and wholeness, the mystical longing can result in fanaticism, delusion, and destruction.

In addition, the addictions that have become prevalent in Western cultures also relate to the shadow side of the Age of Pisces. When we lose the deep mystical connection with Spirit, we seek it in other ways—through "spirits" (alcohol), drugs, or other substances that give us a sense of altered consciousness. In our longing for that mystical communion, we may seek it through addictions that momentarily give us that experience of loss of self and dissolution into another way of being. Addictions are the shadow side of the archetypal meaning of Neptune, the modern planetary ruler of Pisces. Rather than responding to addictions through an increased effort for control (Virgo), perhaps we need to see in them the deep hunger for Spirit, for nonordinary states of reality, and provide guidance to those caught in addictions in how to come back into that relationship with Spirit in a true rather than illusory way.

Archetypally, the deeper integration of the themes of the Age of Pisces is about integrating mind, body, and spirit to understand that we are a part of the wholeness of life and are in service to the Divine, while honoring the uniqueness of our incarnation and the divinity in everyone and everything around us. The balance of Virgo and Pisces is the integration of being here now in physical form, while celebrating our spiritual nature and the way in which we are ultimately a part of the unity of the Cosmos.

As we come to the end of this age, it is important to reflect on the deeper meaning and purpose of this time and to release the shadow aspects of this age and the ongoing distortions from the Age of Aries. As we leave the Age of Pisces, we are moving out of the Kali Yuga, giving us the opportunity to release these out-of-balance patterns and our descent into disconnection, discord, and chaos, and to remember who we truly are and how to reconnect with our deeper spiritual nature and move into higher consciousness.

CHAPTER 9

# The Age of Aquarius

## *(approximately 2000–4000 CE)*

We are currently moving into the Age of Aquarius. While astrologers debate the exact starting point of this new age, it is clear that we are in transition from the Age of Pisces into the Age of Aquarius. In addition, the stars of this constellation now rise in the sky before sunrise at the time of the spring equinox in the northern hemisphere and at the time of the autumn equinox in the southern hemisphere. The beginning of this age also marks our movement out of the Kali Yuga and into the Dwapara Yuga and a time of ascending consciousness.

Pluto, which is viewed in evolutionary astrology as the planet symbolic of our soul's evolutionary journey individually and collectively, first moved into the sign of Aquarius in March 2023 in the tropical zodiac chart and then moved fully into this sign by the end of November 2024. To me, this signifies a profound threshold point into the Age of Aquarius. It is also significant that Dev Misra sees the Kali Yuga as having ended in March 2025, thus marking our movement into an ascending cycle and higher consciousness.[1] In addition, geobiologist Rory Duff, who has been tracking shifts in the energies of the Earth's ley lines, believes that they all came into a time of harmonic convergence and year-long activation at the end of 2024. It seems clear that in 2025, we moved more fully into the energies of the Age of Aquarius and out of the Kali Yuga, the time of humanity's lowest level of consciousness. However, as we have seen, 2025 was a profound time of accelerating change and global tumult as we witnessed the dissolution of the paradigms and structures of the past as we are called to move into the new patterns of the Aquarian Age. It is also significant that as we move into a new age, there is often a concomitant "backlash" as some try to cling to the patterns of the past, while others are rapidly transforming and creatively moving into the paradigms of the new age—in this case, the Aquarian paradigms of collaboration, truth, justice, equality, and spiritual awakening. This can result in social turmoil, confusion, and polarization, which has been evident.

For thousands of years, cultures around the world have seen the constellation of Aquarius as the Water Bearer, pouring living waters from his urn toward the Earth. In Greek mythology, Aquarius is associated with Ganymede, who was taken by Zeus to become the cupbearer to the gods. The gods lived on nectar and ambrosia, and it was thought that Ganymede poured ambrosia from his cup. This liquid was known in Sanskrit as "amrita," or "the drink of immortality." Aquarius was therefore associated not only with the waters of life but also with the drink of immortality.[2]

In earlier times, in ancient Babylon, Aquarius was linked with the Gilgamesh epic and with Utnapishtim, a character in that myth. As described earlier in the book, Gilgamesh was distraught after the death of his closest friend, Enkidu. In trying to bring him back from the realm of death, Gilgamesh went in search of the herb of immortality. In the process, he passed through various tests or trials, each associated with one of the other fixed signs. First, he faced a bull (Taurus) sent by the Goddess. Then he fought a pride of lions (Leo). Finally, he had to go through a doorway guarded by the scorpion-men (Scorpio). He descended to the underworld to find Utnapishtim, who was the keeper of the herb of immortality (Aquarius).

Utnapishtim was once mortal but was granted immortality because he heeded the divine message that the world would be destroyed by a flood. Like the later biblical story of Noah, Utnapishtim built a boat and survived the destructive flood. The deities then granted him eternal life. Gilgamesh gained the herb of immortality from Utnapishtim but later lost it as he sought to return to the upper world.[3] Again, we see the theme of Aquarius being related to the herb of immortality, a life-giving substance. It is also significant that these myths refer to the memories of the great flood, which was the cataclysm 12,000 years ago in the Age of Leo (the constellation opposite Aquarius). In holding the energies of immortality, Aquarius is guiding us in how we can step out of the repetition of the cataclysmic crises of the ascending and descending cycles of consciousness and reclaim our being a part of infinity and movement into higher consciousness.

It is also significant that the Gilgamesh myth marked the importance of the four fixed signs (Taurus, Leo, Scorpio, and Aquarius). Many ancient pagan rituals and ceremonies marking the inflow of energy from the sky to the Earth were associated with times when the Sun was in one of these constellations. In ancient Europe, the cross-quarter holidays were associated with the fixed signs and marked the midpoints between the solstices and equinoxes. These were the pagan holidays of Beltane, Lammas, Samhain, and Imbolc. In addition, we have seen how these signs also historically marked the times of the greatest Earth changes or crises (at the 12,000-year and 6,000-year periods of the precessional cycle) and also are associated with shifts in the Great Year or Kali Yuga from one phase to the next.

In other understandings of the archetypal meaning of Aquarius, we see that in ancient Egypt, Aquarius rose at sunset when the Nile was flooding. This constellation was associated with the life-giving nature of these waters, which brought fertility to the earth. To the Egyptians, Aquarius was linked with the physical and spiritual waters that renew and fertilize all of life.[4] This also fits with the association of Aquarius in traditional astrology with our circulatory system and the flow of living waters/blood within us.

In going back to the earliest known cultural images related to Aquarius, we find Gula, the ancient Sumerian goddess of healing. Temples to Gula and myths related to her date back to 2000 BCE, but she arose out of an even earlier goddess, Bau, who dated back to 3000 BCE or earlier. Gula (and Bau) were both goddesses of fertility and life-giving power as well as healing. Gula was associated with herbal healers and healers who could free a person from illness. She was known as the "Lady of Birth and the Mother of Dogs"[5] and was often represented by dog figurines. She was also the goddess who wrote down a person's destiny at the time of their birth. In times of illness or crisis, people would beseech Gula for her help, asking her to heal them and extend their lives.

Interestingly, Sirius, our binary star that guides us through the precessional cycle, is also known as the dog star and is currently in the constellation of Canis Major. As we move into the Age of Aquarius, Sirius is now guiding us into the ascending cycle of consciousness, supporting our healing, reconnecting with our soul consciousness, and reclaiming our awareness of our immortality.

As we enter the Age of Aquarius, however, in that we have not worked through the correctives of the past sub-ages and have stayed mired in war and destruction of the Earth, we face a global crisis of ecological imbalance and increasing global turmoil. In order to move into ascending consciousness and the deeper meaning of the Age of Aquarius (reconnecting with the wisdom of the Cosmos and coming back into balance with each other and with all of life), we need to heal and release the out-of-balance paradigms of the past.

The theme of healing, as we saw in the archetype of Gula, is embedded in the deeper understanding of Aquarius. This constellation is guiding us collectively in healing from the trauma of the past to come back into balance. Also, as we move into the Age of Aquarius, there is increasing interest in holistic and more natural ways of healing, such as herbalism, naturopathy, and homeopathy, as well as in energy healing.

The two zig-zag lines, the symbol of Aquarius, are the ancient symbol for water, seen on pottery dating back to Paleolithic times, and they honor the life-giving waters. Archaeologist Marija Gimbutas noted that it is "the earliest symbolic motif recorded."[6] Neanderthals used it as far back as 40,000 BCE. In Magdalenian times and in the Neolithic period, it was often found engraved or painted in association with images of the uterus or vulva, linking the symbol for water with the life-giving fluids of women and of the Goddess. In Old Europe, this symbol was often painted on water containers, often in conjunction with images of the Goddess, further strengthening the association between water and the Goddess. It was often drawn or painted under the breasts of goddesses, signifying their life-giving milk and the generative nature of the mother goddess.[7]

It is significant that recent research, such as the work of Masaru Emoto and Veda Austin, has also revealed that water is not only life-giving but conscious and capable of encoding memories and messages for us. It is also interesting to note that water is becoming an increasingly dominant issue in our collective consciousness, as many scientists and political leaders have predicted that conflicts between nations in the years ahead will focus on water rights, and we will be increasingly affected by diminishing resources of potable water.

It is also significant that scientists now realize that water is widespread through our universe and interstellar space in the form of water vapor, ice, and hydrated minerals. Aquarius is not only associated with physical water but is also seen as the source of the life-giving energies of the Cosmos. This sign is also associated with energy and with the awareness that we live in a Universe pulsing with electromagnetic energy and plasma.

Aquarius is a correction to the theme of separation and individuation that was a hallmark of our experience of the Age of Aries that carried over through the Age of Pisces, and it reminds us of our interdependence and interconnectedness with the life around us and the energies of the Cosmos. As Elisabet Sahtouris stressed in *EarthDance*, we realize in this age that we need to move into a new understanding of ourselves as a species, and move beyond the paradigm of competition and control and into an honoring of our need for collaboration and cooperation with each other and with other life-forms on the planet.[8]

The meaning of Aquarius also signifies a coming back into balance with the energies of the Sacred Masculine and Sacred Feminine. We need to release the paradigms of the patriarchal period and move into new understandings of community, collaboration, and cooperation. Aquarius symbolizes an honoring of unity in the midst of diversity and a coming back into mutual relationship and harmony with each other and with the natural environment. It represents the energies of justice, truth, and compassion and the capacity to co-create a new world together.

Astrologically, Aquarius is ruled by Saturn (as the traditional ruler) and Uranus (as the modern ruler) and is a fixed air sign. We will explore the meaning of Saturn and its relationship with Uranus as corulers of this sign later in the book. For now, we will reflect on the archetypal meaning of Uranus, the modern planetary ruler of Aquarius. The planet was discovered by William Herschel in 1781 around the time of the French and American Revolutions when culturally, much of our world was in upheaval and in a time of change. Uranus is an unusual planet in that it defies the established scientific understanding of planetary orbits and movements. While most planets spin on an axis perpendicular to the plane of the ecliptic, Uranus's axis is almost parallel with the ecliptic. Uranus's south pole points almost directly at the Sun, meaning it absorbs more solar energy, yet its equatorial region is hotter than the poles. Unlike other planets, whose magnetic fields are located in their center, Uranus's magnetic field is 60 degrees from the axis of rotation. Scientists are baffled by these patterns that break known planetary rules.

In this way, Uranus carries the archetypal energy of the rebel who breaks with tradition. Richard Tarnas equates the meaning of Uranus with Prometheus (whose name means "foresight"), the mythic rebel Titan who defied the gods to steal fire for humankind. Prometheus sought to equalize the relationship between humans and the gods by bringing enlightenment to humanity. Uranus therefore holds the energy of freedom from cultural or normative constrictions or traditions and an openness to truth, to diversity, and to unique ways of being.[9]

With Uranus as its modern ruler, Aquarius relates to the ways in which we need to transform our social structures so that they are more authentic, humanitarian, and egalitarian. The energy of Uranus is about shattering illusions and structures that are built on false premises. We can expect that in this coming age, our national boundaries and sectarian identifications will break down as we are called to understand what it means to be a global community.

In addition, archetypally, Uranus is associated with energy, electricity, and innovative technology. In this coming time, we will see a continuing escalation and expansion of our technological understanding and the development of computer technology and artificial intelligence, in particular. However, it is significant that Uranus is seen as the higher octave of Mercury and our capacity to connect with divine mind. In this way, Uranus and the Age of Aquarius are calling us to remember the capacities of our consciousness. As we reclaim our higher consciousness and our multidimensional nature, we will move beyond an idealization of artificial intelligence and machine technology and recover the capacities of our consciousness, which are far more advanced than any materialistic device. We see evidence of this advanced understanding in the architecture and advanced skills of ancient cultures dating back 12,000 years. Their advanced knowledge of mathematics, astronomy, spirituality, and the ability to work with light, sound, and vibration are beyond our current modern understanding.

Also, in Uranus's association with energy, we can anticipate an increasing understanding of the energetic nature of all of life. New forms of medicine will be developed that utilize this understanding, as well as new forms of travel. In addition, new sources for renewable and sustainable energy will be discovered. In connecting with a deeper understanding of energy systems and of the quantum and sub-quantum levels of reality, we will see a resurgence and further development of ancient healing traditions that are based on an understanding of the body as an energy system (such as Ayurvedic medicine, traditional Chinese medicine, and acupuncture as well as many shamanic healing traditions). We will also develop new ways of healing that tap into the regenerative energies of the sub-quantum field as seen in the work of theoretical physicist David Clements.

Another aspect of this deepening understanding of energy will be a return to natural law. Since the Age of Aries, we have been living under human law, which includes our efforts to control nature and to see ourselves as superior to and distinct from the natural world. This has led to the widespread destruction of our earthly home and a distorted view of ourselves and our relationship with the world around us. Uranus shatters our illusions and hubris and brings us back to an awareness of the interconnectedness of all of life and of our being part of this living web. In returning to an understanding of natural law, not only will we have to abandon destructive laws and principles based on hierarchical systems that we have used to construct our modern cultures, but systems of religious thought and practice will also be called into question. Uranus is the lightning bolt that strikes at the heart of institutions and structures that are built not on natural truth but rather on false premises or illusions and are out of balance.

What does it mean to reconnect with natural law? It means that we will need to be more open to cultural diversity, much like the way in which nature finds its resilience and strength in biodiversity. We will also need to be open to variations in sexual expression. Aquarius is associated with androgyny as well as with sexual and gender diversity. It is associated with the understanding that, in nature, sexuality is fluid and often not gender specific and that this is true in humans as well. We will have to let go of our false notions of what is "right" and more fully accept what is, the broad spectrum of ways of being that we find in the world around us.

We will also need to realize that the gender imbalance of patriarchy, viewing maleness as superior, is an illusion based on cultural shifts arising in the Age of Aries. It is, in fact, a recent development in human history and not, as many believe, the way things have always been. It is only in the time of our lowest level of consciousness in the precessional cycle, in the Kali Yuga, that we move into patriarchal and power-over paradigms. In letting go of the illusion that this is our natural way of being, we can recover balance in the relationship between men and women with a deeper understanding of the complementary differences and strengths that we bring to each other. In this way, Aquarius is linked with a renewed sense of balance between the genders and the return of a connection with the Sacred Feminine. In the last few decades, we have seen a resurgence in women's spirituality movements and an increasing emphasis on the Divine Feminine in various religions. The Age of Aquarius will support us in coming back into right harmony and balance between the energies of the Sacred Masculine and Sacred Feminine.

Another facet of natural law is an understanding of balance in nature. When one species becomes dominant or overpopulates an area, nature reasserts itself to bring back balance and harmony. If we do not heed this natural law of balance, we will begin to die off as a species either through the increasing spread of illnesses (cancer, autoimmune disorders, epidemics, etc.) or by our own violence toward each other, or through a cataclysmic reset (as happened 12,000 years ago), so that the Earth can regain a natural balance. The meaning of the sign of Aquarius reminds us that we must develop more sustainable ways of living on this Earth in respect for and in balance with the other life-forms who share our planet. It is calling us to remember the spiritual understanding of the Oneness of all of life.

Aquarius and Uranus also relate to radical transformation, and we are likely to see rapid, sometimes explosive, changes in our culture, technology, politics, and world situation. Uranus is represented by the Tower card in the Tarot. In its shattering of traditional forms and beliefs, Uranus is asking us to let go of what is false or superficial in our lives. It calls us to remember our essential being, our deeper truth. The themes of Aquarius emphasize multilateral relationships and cooperation among nations. It is a call for equality and tolerance of diversity. What is demanded of us is a respect and honoring of people of all races, creeds, and religions. The energies of Aquarius also lead us to honor and explore the ways in which we can be in community in more local ways and establish collaborative and cooperative relationships with each other, sharing our gifts and being of service to allow all to thrive.

However, the shadow side of Aquarius (a fixed air sign) is intellectual detachment and a fear of change. The Virgo sub-age's overemphasis on the intellect and on control in modern Western culture could continue as we move into this age. It is significant that in Chinese medicine, the spleen and stomach, representing the earth element, are at the center of the human body and bridge the heavenly Qi (energy) and earthly Qi. This element is the source of nurturance and of the digesting of energy for the human body. It is a reminder that if we disconnect from the earth element and from our relationship with the Earth, we lose our center. In the process, we risk becoming ungrounded and emotionally and spiritually disengaged. The shadow aspects of Aquarius would then be an increasing idealization of technology, artificial intelligence, and a movement into transhumanism.

From a more hopeful perspective, in moving from the sub-age of Virgo, an earth sign, to Aquarius, we may regain our perspective and detach from the overly materialistic nature of industrialized nations. The sign of Aquarius reminds us of the importance of nonattachment and that what is most important is the energy, the spirit, that resides in all of life. Uranus cuts through our illusions of security and self-sufficiency and reminds us that we are a global community linked by common concerns. In this age, we have the opportunity to move from duality consciousness to a unity consciousness.

In the Age of Aries, there was a shift to left-brain dominance. Now, in the Age of Aquarius, we see an increasing balance in the functioning of our left and right hemispheres. We need to move beyond the eras in which one hemisphere or the other is dominant. In the earliest cultures, from about 40,000 BCE to 1500 BCE, the right hemisphere was dominant. In these cultures, there was a predominance of peaceful, artistic, goddess-honoring cultures with an emphasis on holistic, intuitive, experiential ways of knowing. With the shift into left-brain dominance, patriarchy and analytical, linear thinking increased. Now, in the Age of Aquarius, the challenge is to reintegrate the gifts of both hemispheres, to move beyond duality to a new sense of unity. We need to reweave our holistic, intuitive ways of knowing with our intellectualism, to reintegrate wisdom with knowledge.

Right-brain functioning is more about being, while left-brain functioning is more about doing. The beta brain-wave state is highly valued in Western industrialized cultures emphasizing productivity and linear thought. The alpha and theta brain-wave states are emphasized in cultures that value art, altered states of consciousness, and ways of seeking wisdom from the realm of spirit. As we honor the deeper meaning of the Age of Aquarius, we will regain our capacity to connect with all of these different brain-wave states and remember our ability to open to multiple levels of consciousness.

The sub-age of Aquarius is Leo. This signifies both the need to integrate the emphasis on community (Aquarius) with individual self-expression (Leo), as well as the importance of integrating the mind (Aquarius) with the heart (Leo). Leo signifies living from the heart and, in this way, can guide us in this time of ascending consciousness to reclaim the opening of our hearts and our remembrance of unity consciousness. This then supports our capacity to live in greater balance and harmony with each other as well as to open more fully to the higher levels of spiritual consciousness. It also supports our developing new forms of community and living in justice and acceptance of diversity (Aquarius) while also honoring individual creativity and expression (Leo).

In the Age of Aquarius, we are called into new paradigms of identity and community, new ways of being, and new states of consciousness. As we integrate the energies of Aquarius and Leo, we are guided to move into new forms of creativity and self-expression that are integrated with this deeper spiritual understanding, humanitarian concern, and sense of global community.

As we exit from the Kali Yuga, this is a time of accelerating transition and transformation. Humanity is at a karmic choice point and has the opportunity to awaken and move into higher consciousness or to resist the energies of the Earth and sky guiding us into this new age and into new ways of being and face another cataclysmic reset as we experienced 12,000 years ago.

For hundreds of years, our thinking has been shaped by Descartes's notion of "I think, therefore I am" (arising out of the individualism of the Ages of Aries and the overemphasis on the intellect of the Virgo sub-age of the Age of Pisces). We have been overly focused on our intellectual and analytical abilities. Enamored with our increasing technological understanding, we have become more and more myopic, breaking reality down into smaller and smaller units in our effort to know and master the secrets of the Universe. In our hubris, we divided the atom and created the potential to destroy ourselves and the world around us. In our hunger for information and knowledge, we have lost our sense of meaning and an understanding of our place in the larger whole. Silently, the sky reminds us of who we are, where we are, and calls us back into relationship. "As above, so below." Seeking the wisdom of the stars and planets is not about causation or determinism. The stars do not control our destiny. Instead, they reflect the patterns, the currents of energy, in the Cosmos. They remind us of the interconnectedness of all of life.

We live in a symbolic Universe. The Cosmos is sentient and filled with creative intelligence. Part of the wonder of our human nature is our ability to witness and celebrate that creative intelligence. It is not our consciousness (for all of life has consciousness) but our degree of self-consciousness that sets us apart from other creatures. The extent of our self-consciousness allows us to reflect on our own nature and to see and celebrate the Other in the context of deep relationship. We seek to know and be known. We search for the Divine, and the Divine is in search of us. What we need to remember is that the Cosmos is in communication with us in every moment—in the patterns of the stars, in the movements of nature, and in the stirrings of our own hearts. We are called into relationship by the sight of a bird, the cry of a newborn child, or the pain in the eyes of a stranger. If we are open, we can see that recent Earth changes—severe storms, flooding, and earthquakes—are a call to awaken to our relationship with the Earth. Our responsibility is to see and hear, to listen and respond. We have the choice, moment by moment, to enter into mutual relationship or to separate ourselves. If we close our eyes and our hearts, we sever ourselves from that attunement and from our Source.

The message of Aquarius is a call to remember our Source—to honor the living waters of our connection with the creative intelligence of the Universe and to remember the living waters of our Earth. Uranus, the ruler of Aquarius, is shattering our illusions and our denial. Uranus calls us back into truth and right relationship. Uranus reminds us of the equality of self and other, the value of diversity, and the need for compassion and tolerance. Uranus and the Age of Aquarius are guiding us back into higher consciousness and the reintegration of the Sacred Masculine and Sacred Feminine. We are being called back into the wholeness of who we are and into a remembrance of our place in the Cosmos. As we move into the Dwapara Yuga, we are experiencing an acceleration of our movement into higher consciousness and our remembrance of the nine levels of consciousness. No longer mired in and identified with third-dimensional reality, we regain our awareness of the consciousness of the Earth, the expansiveness of the consciousness of higher dimensions, and the deeper meaning of the energies of light, sound, sacred geometry, and our galactic center. We remember that we are soul selves, beings of infinity, having this human experience.

However, to open to these profound shifts and to move into higher consciousness, we need to heal and recover from the imbalances of the past and release the shadow aspects of the Age of Aries and of Pisces in particular. We can then reclaim the wisdom of each age of the precessional cycle and come into wholeness to co-create a new world together.

CHAPTER 10

# Around the Wheel

We have now journeyed through more than half of the wheel of the zodiac with the precession of astrological ages. We have seen how the archetypal themes of the constellations and their associated archetypes and mythologies shape our human and cultural experience when these stars touch our horizon at the vernal equinox in the northern hemisphere and the autumnal equinox in the southern hemisphere, and how the movement of the stars is mirrored in our lives on Earth.

Interestingly, as we have followed this circuit from the Age of Leo to the Age of Aquarius, the rulers of these ages move outward from the inner part of our solar system. The Age of Leo is ruled by the Sun, the star at the center of our solar system. Then, in order, moving through the zodiac, the rulers are the Moon (Age of Cancer), Mercury (Age of Gemini), Venus (Age of Taurus), and Mars (Age of Aries). In our most recent astrological ages, we have two corulers, one traditional and one modern, to include the outer planets discovered in the past few centuries. So, for the Age of Pisces, we have Jupiter and Neptune as corulers and then Saturn and Uranus for Aquarius. As can be seen, these rulers take us from the center of our solar system out toward the outer planets.

In astrology, the Sun, Moon, and inner planets are viewed as shaping our personal lives, while the outer planets (Uranus, Neptune, and Pluto) are transpersonal planets that affect the themes of our generational periods and guide us to seek a larger spiritual meaning and purpose for our lives. These planets are beyond our vision and move in slower cycles, exerting their influence on us over larger periods of time. Dane Rudhyar, one of the foremost modern Western astrologers and philosophers, described these outer planets as avatars, bringing us the wisdom of the spiritual realm beyond our personal and cultural ways of knowing and being.[1]

As we work with these planetary rulers, we can also honor their associations with the chakras, the energy centers of our bodies. Traditionally, the root chakra is associated with Saturn, helping us to be grounded and in our embodiment. Jupiter is connected with the second chakra, guiding us to have faith in ourselves and in our creativity and to clear the trauma that gets absorbed in our second chakras. Mars rules the third chakra, the solar plexus, and guides us in how we define who we are and express ourselves in the world. Venus is associated with the heart and guides us in how to be in right relationship with ourselves, with others, and with all of life. Mercury rules the throat chakra and supports us in right speech and in our ability to express our true selves. The Sun and Moon are associated with the sixth chakra, the third eye, and with our pineal gland, supporting us in attuning to the guidance and wisdom of Spirit. Uranus is at the crown chakra, connecting our minds with divine mind. Neptune is at the eighth chakra, known as the soul star, supporting us in opening our consciousness to Cosmic consciousness, divine love, and the Oneness of all that is. And finally, Pluto is at the chakra below our feet, known as the Earth star, helping us to connect with the wisdom of the crystal core of the Earth that is connected to the energies and wisdom of the Cosmos and to align our personal will with divine will. In this way, as we work through the ages, we are also working to align our energy centers, our chakras, with these energies from the sky and with Cosmic consciousness.

In terms of the movement through the Yuga cycle, the Sun, the center of our solar system and our star, guides us as we move out of the Golden Age (Satya Yuga) into the Silver Age (Treta Yuga) and begin the descending cycle of consciousness. Then, I think it is significant that as we begin our ascent out of the descending Kali Yuga (our lowest level of consciousness in the cycle), we are guided by the transpersonal planets—Neptune and then Uranus, supporting us in reconnecting to the wisdom from these "avatars."

It is also significant that the ages in the precessional cycle associated with the four fixed signs and four royal stars align with shifts in the Yuga cycle. Leo guides us into the descending Treta Yuga/Silver Age, Taurus into the descending Kali Yuga/Iron Age, Aquarius into the ascending Dwapara Yuga/Bronze Age and Scorpio into the ascending Satya Yuga/Golden Age.

Perhaps we can see these four fixed signs and four royal stars as the pillars or protectors of the four directions and of this stellar medicine wheel. As we honor their energies with the movement of the Sun through the zodiac across the year, perhaps we can attune to their energies and honor how they mark these profound shifts in our precessional cycle. As Leo guides us into the Silver Age, the royal star Regulus, the heart of the lion, supports us in living from our hearts with courage and in honoring the light of the Sun and the ways that we can maintain our connection to the consciousness of the Cosmos as we move into this descending cycle. Aldebaran, the royal star of Taurus and the eye of the bull, supports us in aligning with integrity and honesty in our interactions and in how to see our movement into matter and embodiment here on Earth as a sacred initiation and not as being trapped in a mortal form. Fomalhaut, often associated with the Salmon of Knowledge and of Wisdom, is the royal star associated with Aquarius and guides us in the ascending cycle to remember and reconnect with the living waters and wisdom of the Cosmos being poured to us by the Water Bearer in the sky. Antares, the heart of the scorpion and the royal star of Scorpio, supports us in honoring our process of transformation and the alchemical burning away of what no longer serves us to come into the true gold of who we are as we move into the Golden Age.

It is important to remember that while one aspect of the wheel may be more dominant in a certain age, in every moment we live within the wheel in its entirety. The archetypal themes and myths of the past Ages are a part of our ancestral and incarnational lineage. They shape our lives personally as well as being a part of our history, cultural evolution, and collective consciousness. As the ancients knew, the path toward wholeness is to eventually step off the wheel and come to center, to integrate the meanings and wisdom of the whole rather than living out one part or aspect. As we are surrounded by all of the signs of the zodiac and the wisdom of all of the planetary rulers in our birth charts, so we live every day with the tapestry of stars encircling our Earth. Perhaps in this time of crisis globally and environmentally, it is more important than ever before that we find our way to the center, to integrate the wisdom of the stars and find healing, wholeness, and right relationship with all of life.

As we have followed this journey, we have also seen how the times when the cycle has been governed by the fixed signs have also been times of crisis or cataclysmic change on the planet, especially in the Age of Leo, 12,000 years ago. This cycle of Earth changes and of the major cataclysms has occurred in cycles of approximately 12,000 years. As we are now moving into the Age of Aquarius (opposite Leo in the sky), this is the time for potential recurrence. So many prophecies as well as scientific predictions foretell this as a time of major shift, either through a major solar flare or comet strikes. These times of reset have occurred not in a random way, but due to the ways that humanity has become out of balance and disconnected from our alignment with the Earth and sky and Cosmic consciousness. In that we are co-creators with the Cosmos, this time in the precessional cycle is a critical choice point. We can make an evolutionary leap in consciousness and step off the cyclical karmic wheel, or we can continue to resist reconnecting with the energies and wisdom of the Cosmos and go through another cataclysmic reset. The choice is ours.

In her book *Alchemy of Nine Dimensions*, Barbara Hand Clow describes how, in ancient times, we were able to attune to all nine dimensions of consciousness (as described previously). She asserts that we are now called to reopen and access these dimensions of consciousness. As we do that, we align with our hearts, expand our consciousness, and come back into right relationship with the Earth and sky and Cosmic consciousness. Then, together, we can co-create a new Earth and the new paradigms of the Aquarian Age (of community, collaboration, truth, justice, and harmony with all that is).

The living waters of the wisdom of the Water Bearer/Aquarius are guiding us to remember who we are, what we are capable of, and how to make this evolutionary leap out of our paradigms of imbalance, disconnection, and destruction and into higher consciousness, love, and right relationship. The movements of the stars are guiding us in this.

As we step off the wheel and into the center and reconnect with this expanded consciousness, we are no longer identified with these ages or with linear space and time. We reclaim our awareness that we are soul selves and become beings of love and wisdom. As we heal and transform, we are then able to again become galactic citizens in interaction with other beings in the Universe.[2] This is the path of enlightenment. We are then no longer destined to move through this cycle of forgetting and remembering, of descending and ascending consciousness. This was the deeper message of the Age of Pisces and the teaching of Christ: "the kingdom of God is within you." This was the message of Buddha, that we can be liberated from the wheel of samsara (cyclical change) by following the eight-fold path of right understanding, thought, speech, action, livelihood, effort, mindfulness, and concentration. Hinduism also spells out the path to enlightenment, to moksha, through meditation, aligning with the soul self, through yoga and through acquiring knowledge of the Universe.

The energies of the stars of the zodiac, the constellations that we move through during the year with the processional cycle as well as the precessional cycle, guide us in our spiritual journey and path of enlightenment. We could call this the twelve-fold path. Perhaps we can simplify their themes and lessons as:

ARIES—aligning with right action, exploring individuation, and then coming back into relationship, community, and connection and remembering our oneness with Source, with Cosmic consciousness

TAURUS—transforming through relationship with self, others, and all of life; remembering the meaning of sacred embodiment and that all of life is sacred

GEMINI—honoring right knowing, integrating duality, and moving beyond polarization

CANCER—practicing right feeling, being aware of our emotions but not identifying with them, and being nurturing and compassionate toward others

LEO—living from the heart and higher consciousness, living with courage

VIRGO—being of service and acting with discernment, understanding the importance of healing and of integrating mind, body, and spirit

LIBRA—living in right relationship, right balance, and harmony with all that is

SCORPIO—understanding the meaning of life/death/rebirth; burning away the karma and trauma of the past to transform and live out of the true gold in who we are, living from our soul selves and remembering sacred sexuality and transformation through deep intimacy and communion

SAGITTARIUS—keeping our focus on Source, on Cosmic consciousness, and knowing that we are spiritual selves having a human experience

CAPRICORN—remembering that we are spiritual beings who have

incarnated to grow in love and wisdom and to manifest our gifts here and then return to source

AQUARIUS—aligning with and taking in the living waters/energies and wisdom of Cosmic consciousness and remembering that everything is an expression of that consciousness; remembering our immortality, that we are a part of infinity; honoring the sovereignty of the self in the context of community and in unity with Cosmic consciousness

PISCES—following the path of spirituality and the understanding that the metaphysical and physical are both expressions of the divine; all is part of the Oneness

As we have explored the archetypal meanings of these signs and ages, it is important to remember that in the precessional cycle, we journey through the signs counterclockwise, while in the course of the year, the Sun and planets move through the signs and constellations of the zodiac clockwise. This means that as we move through the annual cycle, we can continue to explore and process the meaning of these energies and integrate the polarities in our day-to-day lives. This then supports us in remembering and reintegrating what we need to heal or resolve in terms of the polarities of the Ages and their sub-ages as we move through the larger cycles of human history and evolution. In this way, the energies of the ages and these energies are constantly calling us to integrate the polarities and come to center. It is in the center of the medicine wheel that we are no longer bound to the wheel of karma and linear time, and we remember our wholeness and align with the Earth and sky and our soul selves and come into enlightenment.

PART THREE

# UNDERSTANDING THIS TIME OF TRANSFORMATION AND MOVEMENT INTO HIGHER CONSCIOUSNESS

## CHAPTER 11

# Liminal Periods

### *Transitions Between Ages and the Movement into Ascending Consciousness*

We now live on the cusp between the Age of Pisces and the Age of Aquarius. As the ancients knew, transitional periods are times of turmoil—globally, culturally, and in terms of Earth changes—but they are also a period for creativity and the initiation of new forms of consciousness. What is critical is how we respond to this time of change and whether we attempt to cling to the patterns of the past or open to new and unfamiliar ways of being. As astrologer Jeffrey Wolf Green has stated, the archetypal meaning of Uranus, the ruler of Aquarius, is "freedom from the known."[1] We now live in a time of uncertainty, when we sense that the ways in which we have been in control and have formed our sense of identity and security, individually and collectively, are dissolving and shattering. Before any new form can emerge, the old way of being needs to die. This is the story of the caterpillar dissolving in the chrysalis to re-emerge as the butterfly and of the phoenix burning in the ashes to resurrect in a new way, and how new stars and galaxies are born. It is the archetypal pattern of death and rebirth. How do we support ourselves in this time of transformation?

It is important that we hold our understanding of this time in the larger framework of the ages historically and astrologically. This allows us to understand the deeper meaning and purpose of this turmoil and change. Attuning to the meaning of this time and to the messages from Earth and Sky allows us to open to the new consciousness and ways of being that we are being called into in our human evolution. It also allows us to more consciously let go of old patterns and old ways of knowing. Rather than attaching to these old forms and resisting change, we can honor the ending of what has been and open to what is being born.

Not only are we moving from the end of one age into a new one, but we are also at the end of one precessional cycle and the beginning of a new cycle and are shifting out of the Kali Yuga into ascending consciousness. In addition, we are at that crucial time in the precessional cycle that occurs every 12,000 years when we experience more profound Earth changes and shifts in consciousness. Through our scientific understanding, we are now aware that at these critical times every 12,000 years, we are moving through the galactic current sheet.

The galactic current sheet is an electric sheet that aligns with the galaxy's plane and is a wavy, disc-shaped region shaped by the rotation and magnetic fields of the galaxy. It contains the galactic magnetic reversal point and is filled with dust, gas, and electric particles. As we move through this part of the galaxy, the magnetic fields of the Sun and our Earth lessen, which increases the intensity of our exposure to solar energies and to energies coming to us from the galactic center. As we navigate this galactic current sheet, it can energize and activate the Sun, leading to a solar micronova, which in turn can activate a pole reversal on the Earth and major Earth changes, including floods, earthquakes, volcanic activity. This time in the precessional cycle is also when we experience increased risk of comet strikes. According to Dev Misra, this risk is strongest for us in 2032 when the Earth will pass through the center of the Taurid Resonant Swarm, which contains a large number of densely packed comets and asteroids.[2]

As we move through this period of intensification and transformation, it is important that we not get caught in fear. As Barbara Hand Clow discusses in *Awakening the Planetary Mind,* we need to be conscious of our past trauma in these cataclysmic times so that this time we can heal and work through this consciously. Otherwise, in our fear and the cellular memories of the past trauma, we are in danger of reenacting the very thing that we fear and continuing on a path of destructiveness as humanity.

As we move through the galactic current sheet, the increased cosmic rays are energizing the Earth's core and the ley lines of our planet and are reactivating the dormant strands of our DNA. They are also triggering changes in our pineal gland and increasing our spiritual consciousness. As the Peruvian Q'ero shamans describe it, we have the opportunity in this time to become homoluminous ones, beings of light. We have the potential to reopen the nine dimensions of consciousness and reclaim our multidimensional nature. If we honor this time of transition and the possibility of spiritual awakening and transformation, then we can reclaim our ability to be galactic citizens again and move off the wheel of samsara, of descending and ascending consciousness, and become "enlightened" ones.

To do this, we need to engage in community and support each other through the transition and transformation. In alignment with the energies of the Age of Aquarius, it is important to find our soul tribe and work together to release the paradigms of the past and together co-create new ways of being. As the Peruvian shamans and other spiritual teachers have expressed, if enough of us can awaken and move into higher spiritual consciousness, that energy in the morphogenic field of our planet can transform the collective consciousness.

We can also support each other through working in ceremonial ways, in that ceremonies support us in moving through transitions in an integrated and holistic way that incorporates mind, body, and spirit. We can symbolically let go of what needs to be released and honor what is dying or changing in our lives. We can do this through ceremonies with any of the elements (fire, water, earth, and air). With fire ceremonies, we are able to burn what is being released, or with water ceremonies, we can allow it to dissolve. Using the element of earth, we may bury something symbolic of that which we are leaving behind. Utilizing meditation practices working with the breath, we can take in new ways of being with our inhalation and release the old patterns with our exhalation. Being in relationship with nature can teach us how to move with this life/death/rebirth cycle and to see it as a process of transformation. In letting go of our linear ways of knowing and returning to an understanding that nature operates in a cyclical or spiral manner, we can trust in these currents of change. We can also honor the energies of the Sun and open to the transformation of the solar rays. We can also honor the "Central Sun," our galactic center and open to the cosmic rays that are coming to us.

As we work with this transition and this rite of passage, it also means holding and honoring the liminal time, the transition time when we feel that intense sense of vulnerability and insecurity as we experience the loss of who we were but do not yet know our new identity or new ways of being. Engaging in individual or group ceremonies to hold this transition in a sacred way is very important in order to stay centered emotionally, physically, and spiritually. Using ways of entering into altered states of consciousness (such as meditation, prayer, drumming, or chanting) allow us to seek guidance for the next steps in the change process, help us attune to Cosmic consciousness, and help us to stay centered and aligned with trust in times of uncertainty and existential anxiety.

In the transition time, there is often an impulse to seek answers and clarity from outside ourselves—through a teacher, a leader, a group, or an institution that claims to provide the certainty that we seek. Teachers are helpful guides in the evolution of our consciousness; however, we need to be careful not to give over our power to another. This is the shadow side of the Age of Pisces and can lead to fanaticism and loss of the sense of self, not to union with Spirit but to passivity and yielding of control to an idealized leader or group or belief system that gives us that illusion of certainty. This can include giving our power away to artificial intelligence. We need to remember that the capacity of our consciousness far exceeds any technology or artificial intelligence that mirrors the knowledge of our minds but does not incorporate the higher consciousness only accessed through our hearts.

The challenge in the Age of Aquarius is to understand the deeper call to personal sovereignty while also honoring diversity and equality in community and to step fully into our own connection with the Divine, with Cosmic consciousness. In doing so, we realize that the energy of life, of Spirit, is in all things. In that larger sense of interconnectedness, we recover a sense of our true identity as part of a larger whole. As we lose the illusion of individuality, we retain our own unique consciousness and experience of being one strand in the larger web of life. In finding our place in this larger whole, we can experience a deep sense of unity, community, and oneness while celebrating our own gifts and uniqueness. Like a drop in the sea, we can feel the wind and currents and move freely, while also knowing that we are ultimately merged with the larger cosmic ocean around us and within us. Therefore, the deeper meaning of Aquarius is the sovereignty of the self in the sanctity of community and in unity with Cosmic consciousness.

In this time of change, we are moving out of the Kali Yuga (also known as the Age of Ignorance, when humans lose the wisdom that they once had known) and into the Dwapara Yuga, a time of increased awareness and enlightenment. The Hindu scriptures (particularly the *Vishnu Purana* and *Mahabharata*) describe the times of decline in our consciousness and the Kali Yuga as being associated with periods when male power assumes dominance. It is significant that it is in the time of patriarchy, over the past five thousand years, that we have experienced the destructive consequences of dualism and polarization—in the separation of Earth and Sky, of male from female, and of humanity from nature and from our once unbroken communion with the Spirit. Perhaps we needed to go through a developmental period of separation and individuation, much like the adolescence process, to further define and develop parts of ourselves neurologically, spiritually, and psychologically. However, to become mired in a false sense of separation can only lead to distortion and destruction of ourselves and of the natural world in which we live. Opening to the energies of the Age of Aquarius supports us in releasing these patriarchal power-over paradigms and reclaiming the wisdom of the Sacred Feminine (and the sacredness of the Earth, of our embodiment, and of our relationships with each other and with all of life). In this way, we can move back into balance and into higher consciousness.

Part of the challenge of this time is to honor the learning, the development that has occurred in these past ages. We have developed our left-brain capacities and learned how to experience the extent of our individual expression and creativity, but now we need to reintegrate those with a more balanced and whole sense of ourselves as part of the web of life. This time of transition is a time of moving beyond a belief system based on polarities to a time of unity consciousness. In modern physics, we now realize that the notions of self and other or self and a separate object of study are illusions. Everything is interconnected. However, we can reclaim that consciousness of interconnection while integrating the self-consciousness that we have fostered and developed across the past five thousand years. Rather than using that self-awareness for a false sense of separateness, control, and exploitation, we can now use it to honor our relationship with all of life and to celebrate that larger unity. In returning to that natural sense of right relationship, we are able to truly honor the lives of the creatures around us and the natural resources of our world, not from a place of fear or survival mentality, but from an attitude of reverence and love, realizing that we are indeed One.

As Elisabet Sahtouris has expressed it, we humans need to wake up and grow up. We need to learn from other species and move from separation into the mature phase of development, which is cooperation and interdependence. As she explained it:

> It's time for humans to reach the mature cooperative phase. We need not the hero's journey myth that brought us to where we are now . . . but a story of cooperation, a story of ecstasy, of forming real community by recognizing our oneness, by focusing on love rather than fear and by making the Earth a sacred place again.[3]

Aquarius as the Water Bearer pouring the living energies of cosmic wisdom to the Earth also reminds us that we are energy beings and supports us in honoring these currents of change guiding us into a new form and a new world. We can remember the Hopi Elders' prophecy about this time:

> There is a river now flowing very fast.
> It is so great and swift that there are those who will be afraid.
> They will try to hold on to the shore.
> They will feel they are being torn apart and will suffer greatly.
> Know that the river has its destination.
> The elders say we must let go of the shore,
> push off into the middle of the river,
> keep our eyes open, and our heads above the water.
> And I say, see who is in there with you and celebrate.
> At this time in history, we are to take nothing personally,
> least of all ourselves.
> For the moment that we do,
> our spiritual growth and journey come to a halt.
> The time of the lone wolf is over.
> Gather yourselves!
> Banish the word struggle from your attitude and your vocabulary.
> All that we do now must be done in a sacred manner
> and in celebration.
> We are the ones we've been waiting for.[4]

CHAPTER 12

# Guidance from the Cosmos

It is significant that as we move through our evolutionary process of consciousness as humanity and through the precessional cycle, new planetary bodies are being discovered that bring us new archetypal energies and guidance. The timing of the discovery of these new planets is significant in that it reflects our readiness to bring these archetypes into our consciousness awareness.

In recent history, several outer planets have been discovered—or rediscovered, in that there is evidence that ancient cultures were aware of some of these planets. The timing of their reemergence into our awareness has coincided with significant shifts in our collective consciousness associated with the archetypal meanings of the planets. These outermost planets, Uranus, Neptune, and Pluto, are known as the transpersonal planets. (Note: While astronomers may have re-labeled Pluto as a dwarf planet in 2006, astrologers still know and understand Pluto as a planet.)

These transpersonal planets guide us into higher levels of consciousness. Uranus is the higher octave of Mercury, Neptune is the higher octave of Venus, and Pluto is the higher octave of Mars. These are powerful planets that guide us individually and collectively into profound transformation. How we work with these energies is our choice, and we can be guided by them into higher consciousness or misuse their energies in ways that are destructive to ourselves or to others. This is another reminder that the energies of the stars and planets are not deterministic but are shaped by our level of consciousness and the choices that we make as we interact with them.

Uranus, with its archetypal energy of creativity and radical change, was discovered in 1781 during the time of the American and French Revolutions. As we have discussed previously, this planet (and ruler of Aquarius) shatters our illusions and guides us into truth, justice, and equality with each other. As the higher octave of Mercury, it guides us to move from identification with our minds to an awareness of our capacity of our consciousness as we connect with divine mind, Cosmic consciousness.

Neptune, with its message of dissolution of the self and of mysticism, was first observed by astronomers in 1846, when spiritualist movements were starting in the United States and Europe and when the use of hypnosis and mesmerism became more prominent. As the ruler of Pisces, it calls us to dissolve our egos and sense of separation and come back into our hearts and connection with Cosmic consciousness and with the Oneness of all that is. As the higher octave of Venus, it calls us to move beyond personal love to remember the power of divine love, the unconditional love of the cosmos.

In 1930, Pluto, the planet of profound transformation (of life/death/rebirth) came into our consciousness following the global turmoil of World War I and preceding World War II with its concomitant massive economic, political, and cultural changes. This is also when Plutonium was discovered, and the atomic bomb was developed. Depth psychology and the understanding of the unconscious (individually and collectively) emerged. Pluto, as the modern ruler of Scorpio, guides us in facing our fear of death and our shadow selves to open us to transformation and higher consciousness and to birth a new sense of self and ways of being. As we connect with Pluto as the higher octave of Mars, we align our personal will with divine will, with the ways and wisdom of Cosmic consciousness.

These planets, in coming into our awareness, were bringing to human consciousness certain archetypal energies needed to guide us in the changes of those times. In consciously working with their meaning rather than resisting them, we further our own development and the evolution of our consciousness.

In recent years, we have also come to understand more deeply the healing energies of the Centaurs, the planetary bodies that orbit primarily between Jupiter and Neptune and bring us their wisdom and healing energies. The primary Centaurs are Chiron, Chariklo, Nessus, and Pholus. These minor planets guide us in holistic healing and in how to heal physically, emotionally, and spiritually, as well as in the healing of ancestral wounds.

We will also explore a few of the newly discovered dwarf planets or Kuiper Belt objects and the messages they are bringing to us in this time. We will explore the meaning of Sedna discovered in 2003. Sedna is a messenger from the farthest outer reaches of our solar system, the Oort cloud. This dwarf planet, in a profound way, is a messenger to us of the great shifts at the midpoint and end of the precessional cycle and a guide to us in how to move into higher consciousness. We will also discuss the dwarf planet Eris, discovered in 2005, and how her orbital pattern and name are guiding us in deepening our understanding of ourselves and the challenges to us in our collective consciousness in this time. And we will also explore one of the newly discovered Kuiper Belt objects, many of which were named after Indigenous creation deities. These newly discovered planetary bodies are supporting us in our evolutionary journey and in seeing more clearly the new paradigms and ways of being that we are being called into in this intense time of transformation and transmutation.

## THE HEALING CENTAURS

The Centaurs are planetary bodies with long elliptical and unstable orbits that move between the orbits of Jupiter and Neptune. They evidence physical features similar to comets and asteroids. These celestial bodies are the bridge between the outer planets and the Kuiper Belt objects and guide us in how we can heal individually and collectively. The primary Centaurs are Chiron, Chariklo, Pholus, and Nessus. These planetary bodies are associated with the centaurs in Greek mythology who are half horse and half human, therefore also bridging our human consciousness with our physical nature. They also signify important rites of passage or experiences in our lives in which we are called into healing and transformation.

The first Centaur discovered was Chiron. Its discovery in 1977 came at a time of innovation and an increasing interest in holistic ways of healing. Chiron has an orbit of fifty years as it moves through the orbits of Saturn and Uranus. In this way, it bridges the energies of these two planets that are the rulers of the Aquarian Age.

In Greek mythology, Chiron was a wise centaur who was both a spiritual teacher and healer. He was accidentally wounded by his student Heracles who shot a poison arrow that lodged in his leg. Chiron, being a demi-god, lived in pain—unable to heal himself yet unable to die. He was finally released from his pain when he exchanged his immortality with Prometheus, allowing Prometheus to be set free from being tortured by Zeus and taking on his mortality in order to die. Chiron then became honored in the stars of Centaurus.

Chiron is therefore symbolic of the Wounded Healer and represents in our astrology charts where we may have experienced a primary wound in our lives. It often represents early emotional trauma that haunts us until we finally face it and heal it. Then, once we work through that wound, Chiron represents our healing gifts. Often, if we have not consciously worked this trauma or emotional issue in our lives, it gets reactivated to come into our awareness for healing at around age fifty when we experience the Chiron return. Those with a strong placement of Chiron in their charts are often themselves Wounded Healers who work as therapists, healers, shamans, or spiritual mentors.

Discovered in 1997, Chariklo is the Centaur with the most stable orbit, and her orbit is between that of Saturn and Uranus. Chariklo was originally a water nymph, but she changed form into a centaur to be with Chiron and was his life partner. Throughout his years of chronic pain, she was a faithful companion, holding him in compassion and supporting him. Although she was unable to heal him physically, her ability to hold sacred space, to hear and see him and hold him in love, was profoundly healing for him. She guides us in this time to be present with and for each other, to hold ourselves and others in compassion and to have the courage to truly see and hear each other.

Pholus was discovered in 1992 and also orbits between Saturn and Uranus. Pholus was known in Greek mythology as the wise centaur who was the keeper of the sacred wine of Dionysus. He was meant to keep this jar of wine unopened for four generations. However, when Heracles visited him in his cave, he opened the jar to offer him a drink. The energies of Dionysian ecstasy drifted through the air with the scent of the wine and attracted the wild centaurs who came and created chaos. Heracles slew them with his poison arrows. Pholus then walked through the field of dead bodies reflecting on the consequences of his choice. Pholus symbolizes those ancestral or generational patterns that we have have inherited that need to heal. According to Melanie Reinhart, the astrologer who has specialized in the study of Chiron and the Centaurs, the theme of Pholus is "the lid comes off."[1] Transits to this Pholus in our charts may trigger this ancestral wound and activate our awareness that this needs to be healed and cleared. This call to heal may often be catalyzed by unexpected events that bring this issue into our consciousness. We are then guided to heal this generational wound in order to not pass this on to others.

Nessus was discovered in 1993, and this Centaur has a larger orbit that extends out, crossing the orbits of Uranus and Neptune. This centaur is different from the others in Greek mythology in that Nessus was not seen as a wise mentor or healer but rather driven by his own desires and impulses. He was a ferryman—half horse, half human—who carried others across the River Evenus. One day Heracles came with his wife Deianira to cross the river. Nessus took Deianira on his back while Heracles watched and waited on the shore for his turn. As he crossed the river, Nessus lusted after Deianira, wanting to rape her. As Heracles saw this unfolding, he shot Nessus across the river with a poison arrow. As Nessus was dying, he told Heracles's wife to take some of his blood as protection and to use it on Heracles if she feared he was going to be unfaithful to her. When months later Deianira saw Heracles lusting after another woman, she spread the blood on his cloak. As Heracles wore the cloak, the blood, which was poisonous (and intended by Nessus to cause Heracles harm as his revenge), burned into his flesh and eventually led to his death.

It is a profound tale of how across time and generations, we can become mired in experiences of abuse of power and trauma patterns of perpetrator and victim. These patterns often repeat in cycles of betrayal and revenge. For Melanie Reinhart, the theme with Nessus is "the buck stops here."[2] This Centaur calls us to heal our ancestral trauma patterns that keep us stuck in this perpetrator/victim dyad and to take responsibility to stop the trauma related to power-over or experiences of victimization and helplessness.

It is significant that these Centaurs came into our awareness at the end of the Age of Pisces and as we move into the Age of Aquarius, ruled by Saturn and Uranus. As we are called into moving into the new Aquarian paradigms of truth, justice, and living in right relationship, we have to heal the trauma of the past that would keep us mired in destructive coping patterns and a repetition of these painful themes in our own lives and in our ancestral lineage. In order to transform and move into new ways of being, we first need to heal individually and collectively and clear the way that these traumas constrict and control us physically, emotionally, and spiritually. This then allows us to open more fully to the wisdom of the Kuiper Belt objects and recently discovered dwarf planets like Sedna and Eris-Xena that guide us into these new ways of being and higher consciousness.

## SEDNA: OORT CLOUD PLANETARY BODY AND THE INUIT GODDESS OF THE SEA

In November 2003, astronomers from California's Palomar Observatory discovered a planet deep in space and named her Sedna, after the Inuit goddess of the sea, due to her location in the dark, cold reaches of outer space. In a meeting of the International Astronomical Union in 2006, there was intense debate as to the definition of a planet and whether Ceres, Pluto, and the planetary body Xena (now Eris) discovered in 2005 would be classified as planets or not. The result was that all three were designated as dwarf planets or planetoids, although there is ongoing conflict in the astronomical community about this decision. Because of this decision, Sedna is also thought to be a dwarf planet; however, she has also been defined as an inner Oort cloud object. Whatever her designation, it was significant that Sedna had been discovered, and that she brought the meaning of this Inuit goddess into the forefront of our consciousness.

Sedna is approximately three-fourths the size of Pluto and is so far from the Sun that, from her surface, you could block out the Sun with the head of a pin, according to astronomer Michael Brown. Sedna consists of ice and rock and is reddish in color. After Mars, it is the second-reddest object in the solar system, according to NASA. Sedna is eight billion miles away and is the first object of the inner Oort cloud to be observed by astronomers. The Oort cloud circles the outermost edge of our solar system and consists of the repository of materials that supply the comets that enter our solar system and streak by the Earth. This debris consists of the remnants of the original nebula that collapsed and formed the Sun and the planets of our solar system over four billion years ago. It is thought that the gravitational pull of Jupiter and the other gas giants tend to keep this debris in the outer reaches of our solar system and cause the cometary material to be scattered into a spherical "cloud" surrounding our solar system. The Oort cloud is also affected by gravitational interaction with other star systems and sometimes overlaps with the Oort clouds of two other nearby stars. In this way, as she moves into her interface with our Oort cloud, Sedna is communing with other star systems and then bringing that wisdom to us.

Sedna has a very long and unusual elliptical orbit. The researchers who hypothesize that we are part of a binary star system believe that Sedna's unique elliptical orbit relates to the gravitational forces of our binary star. If so, then her coming into our consciousness at this time may also be as a messenger about the true nature of our solar system and a reminder that we are, in fact, part of a binary star system.

Sedna comes from the outer edges of our solar system, where it is so cold that the temperatures never rise above negative 400 degrees Fahrenheit. This is one of the reasons that she was named after the Inuit goddess of the deep, frigid Arctic sea. Sedna then travels in to move around our inner solar system before journeying out again to our Oort cloud. She was observed in 2003 as she came close to Earth. She will reach her closest approach to us in 2076 and then begin her journey back out to the farther reaches of our solar system. To complete one full orbit takes Sedna approximately 11,487 years. This means that the last time Sedna was in her current position was at the end of the last ice age on Earth. It also means that her orbit is equivalent to almost half of the period of the precessional cycle.

What meaning does this planet hold for us? What wisdom does she bring us from the outer reaches of our solar system, from the primordial matter of our origins? What messages does she have to share with us from her communion with other star systems? What does her namesake, the Inuit goddess of the sea, have to tell us about ourselves and this time?

To explore this, we must first listen to the story of Sedna, goddess of the deep sea. There are many versions of this Inuit myth. Here is a compilation and synthesis of some of the best-known versions of the story of Sedna:

*Once upon a time there was a young Inuit woman named Sedna. She lived in the far north of Canada and was a rebellious young woman. Her family wanted her to marry to help hunt and fish and provide food for the family. Her father brought many men from the surrounding villages for her to choose a mate, but Sedna refused them all.*

*One day, a mysterious stranger walked into the village. He wore a long, black cloak with a hood pulled up over his head. Without knowing why, Sedna felt a stirring within her. She found herself drawn to him. When he asked her to go with him in his boat, she consented. Together, they left the village and journeyed far, far away to a barren island out in the sea. After they landed on the rocky shore, the mysterious stranger pulled back his hood, and Sedna gasped and saw that he was Raven. With fear and trembling, she knew that she was with the Magician, the Shaman, who knows the ways of the spirit world. Day after day, month after month, she struggled through the cold weather, the icy winds, and the loss of all that she had left behind. There was not much to eat other than the few fish Raven brought back from his hunting. But all the while, Raven taught Sedna the ways of Spirit.*

*After much time had passed, the villagers grew worried for her, not understanding where she had gone and why she never came back to visit her family and her village. Her father became afraid and decided that he must go and rescue her from her fate. He paddled his kayak out and found her on the island. When he arrived, Raven was off hunting for fish, and Sedna sat alone on the shore. Seeing her on this cold, barren island, her father insisted on bringing her home with him. He pulled her toward his boat. "No, father, I cannot go home," Sedna cried. Her father would not listen to her words and carried her into his boat. He paddled rapidly out to sea, heading toward his village. Raven, returning from his hunt, realized that Sedna was gone. He cawed in rage and flew high over the sea to find her. Raven circled over the waves and saw Sedna in the boat with her father. Summoning the spirit of the wind and of the storm, Raven dove down by the boat and touched the tip of his wing to an ocean wave. The wind grew wild, and stormy waves rose and began to break over the sides of the boat.*

*Sedna's father, seeing that it was Raven, became filled with terror. He knew the power of Raven, and he felt the strength of the storm. Fearing for his life, he cried out to Raven, "Take her. Take Sedna. She's yours. Just spare me my life." Then he threw his daughter overboard into the stormy sea. Sedna screamed and called out to her father but to no avail. Frightened, she grabbed the side of the boat, trying to pull herself to safety. Her father took his paddle and hit her hands to keep her from getting back into the boat. Filled with anger and disbelief, Sedna again reached for the edge of the boat. Again and again, her father struck her fingers, until they broke off and sank slowly beneath the surface of the sea. Sedna looked down and saw that her fingers had turned into seals and whales, swimming off beneath the storm-tossed waves.*

*Struggling to catch her breath in the cold sea and raging wind, Sedna looked toward her father's boat as it rocked wildly in the waves. She saw that there was no safety in the boat. She knew that she could not go home again. There was no home for her there. Letting out her breath, feeling her salty tears join the surging sea, she slowly sank beneath the turbulent waters. Deeper, deeper she dove, down, down beneath the waves and wind and storm. Deeper, deeper she sank, and the sea became quiet and dark and still. She began to feel her body dissolve. No longer bound by bones and skin, she felt herself become fluid, moving with the currents of the deep arctic waters. She felt one with the sea, and the sea became one with her. Looking around her, she saw whales and seals and fish calling out to her, calling her by name. And Sedna, the maiden was no more, and Sedna knew the magic and wisdom of the deep, and Sedna became the goddess of the sea.*

*Now, when people from the village set out to fish, they call to Sedna to honor her and ask her for protection. Hunters have great respect for her. Fishermen pour fresh water into the first catch of the day and thank Sedna for gifting the village with food to eat. They realize that as Raven knows the ways of the winds and the magic of the Earth and Sky, Sedna knows the ways of the deep, dark sea. She is the Goddess who can provide them with food and life, and the Goddess who brings storms that can destroy them. To honor and appease her, shamans must swim down to her to comb her long, tangled hair and plead for the people. They understand that Sedna holds the power of life and death. Some of the old villagers, as they sing their songs and repair the nets and wait for the fishermen to return, remember the young maiden who was betrayed by her father and left to die and who has now become the goddess of the sea. And they sigh and shake their heads, and they whisper her name in wonder and give thanks.*

This story comes from the Inuit people who live in the Arctic. The Arctic region extends from eastern Siberia to Greenland and is north of the tree line. The area consists of high mountains, sedimentary plains, bedrock, and lowlands with little or no soil. Because of this, there are few edible plants. It is a cold and harsh environment with long, cold winters and short, cool summers, as well as large seasonal shifts in sunlight. During the winter months, there is little sunlight, while in the summer, there are only a few hours of darkness. Year-round, the ground is frozen. During the winters, many of the sea channels of the Canadian Arctic Archipelago freeze.

Archaeological evidence indicates that this region has been occupied by humans since about 10,000 BCE (in the Age of Leo), about the time that the dwarf planet Sedna was in the position that it is in today in her orbit, in close proximity to our inner solar system. The Inuit people are more recent inhabitants in the Arctic and are distinct from other native populations in the area, according to anthropologists and linguists. They are descendants of the Thule people who migrated from Asia about four and a half thousand years ago. The Inuit are a Mongol-type people, and their name literally means "The Living Ones Who Are Here."[3]

Due to the harsh environment, the Inuit were historically a nomadic people who relied heavily on animal resources for their survival. They developed snow houses, harpoons, and various types of boats and dogsleds to live and hunt for food. They relied on hunting land animals such as caribou, musk ox, arctic fox, and hare and were heavily dependent on marine life, including seal, walrus, whale, polar bear, and arctic char.

"Sedna" is an English translation of the Inuit word "Siarnaq," the goddess of the sea whose body parts gave birth to the sea creatures. She is also known among the Inuit people as Talilajuk and Nuliajuk.[4] She is the creation goddess on whom the people depend for food and for their survival.

There are many versions of the myth. Some describe Sedna as an orphan child who was thrown into the sea. All of the stories hold the theme of Sedna's betrayal by her father and the people of her village, and the Inuit belief that Sedna transmuted into a goddess who was not only the source of their sustenance but also the source of storms and the harsh weather that could lead to their destruction. Therefore, the shaman's task was to appease Sedna, to dive into the depths of the sea to comb her hair and ask for her help in providing food for the people.

This story holds many layers of meaning for us in this time. On one level, it is the story of spiritual initiation. Sedna found herself drawn to the mysterious stranger and chose to follow him, even though this meant leaving behind her village and all that was familiar to her. Similar to Inanna's descent to the underworld, the journey did not unfold as

Sedna might have expected. She found herself on a desolate island with Raven, the powerful teacher and shaman. While her journey was initiated by her will and her own intentions, she soon found herself in a situation beyond her control. All that gave her a sense of identity and community had been stripped away, and she was alone with Raven in a harsh environment. For the Inuit people, isolation from the community often meant death. Those who became shamans had to face death and go off alone for their initiation, much like Sedna in the story.

With the return of Sedna, the dwarf planet, to our inner solar system, we, like Sedna in the Inuit myth, are now in a stormy time of transition, leaving behind the familiar forms of our cultural heritage and moving into the wilderness of the unknown. We, like her, have realized that the paradigms of the patriarchal period have betrayed us and are on the threshold of destroying us. We also realize that this is a time of spiritual crisis and, like Sedna, we need to dissolve our old ways of being and our ego consciousness and reclaim our connection with our source, the sea, and with our soul consciousness.

We, like Sedna, are on a path of spiritual initiation and of reclaiming the wisdom that we once knew. Sedna knew that she could not stay in the cultural context that she had grown up in, and she chose to leave her village and move into a new way of life. Those who were part of her family and community were frightened by her departure and sought to rescue her. Sedna's father set out to find his lost daughter. Once he found her, he was angry and distraught to see her condition and that she was isolated on the barren island with Raven. He wanted to bring her back to the village, to her old way of life; however, once a journey of spiritual initiation has been undertaken, it cannot be reversed. We cannot "go home" again. Once we realize that these old paradigms are no longer viable, we realize that they have no safety or security for us anymore. Sedna, on the island, was in that liminal space between worlds and was unable to go back to her life as she had known it.

Raven, the shaman and teacher, stirred up a terrible storm to prevent the father from taking Sedna away. Sedna's father, in his fear, betrayed Sedna and chose to sacrifice her life to save his own. He threw her overboard and then actively blocked her efforts to climb back into the boat by literally cutting off the fingers of her hands. Sedna died, sinking into the sea, with the anger and pain of this betrayal going with her. As she died, her body parts became whales and seals and the creatures of the sea. Sedna transformed, moving through this death/rebirth experience, and became the goddess of the sea, who held the power of life and death. The people feared her desire for revenge and worked to appease her as well as give her gratitude for providing food from the sea. In this way, the story of Sedna restores the ancient understanding and unity of the Goddess archetype as the Creator and Destroyer, the One who brings both life and death.

Sedna speaks to the meaning of the time that we live in, when the familiar structures and forms that we have known culturally are in transition. Her story reminds us of the shadow side of the patriarchal era and the way in which we have been betrayed by the "fathers." In the story, the father's intentions were good; he set out to save his daughter and to protect his village. Yet, as we see with the shadow side of the sub-age of Virgo in the end of this Piscean Age, the effort for control often results in disconnection and destruction. In his desperation to survive and to cling to the way of life he had known, the father resisted the transformation that Sedna was undergoing and then tried to destroy her to save himself. Does this not resonate with the actions of so many of our global economic and political leaders in recent years, who seek their own wealth and power at the expense of others? They seek to cling to hierarchical and patriarchal paradigms despite the destruction they cause to the Earth and the increasing harm they bring to the majority of humanity.

Sedna reminds us that sometimes we need to let go of everything and leave all that we have known behind, even though we have no idea where this journey may lead us. She also teaches us that the path of

Spirit means the loss of our ego identity and the dissolution of our sense of self. We need to dissolve and become part of the larger whole, at one with the sea and the Cosmos. It is in that unity that we find our deeper purpose and meaning as part of the larger web of life.

In the story of Sedna, we understand the sea as the source of life and sustenance as well as the source of the storms that threaten our existence. Interestingly, a key archetypal theme in the age of Pisces is the lineage of flood stories in which the sea rises and destroys the land and people. Neptune, the modern planetary ruler of the Age of Pisces, is associated with the "god of the sea," although as Liz Greene asserts, while Neptune is named after a male Roman god, Neptune's deeper archetypal meaning is very much that of the "sea goddess."[5] In its deeper meaning, Neptune reminds us of the oceans, which are the source of all life on Earth and the liquid womb from which we emerged at birth. The sea is the source of creation and destruction, our beginning and our end. In the flood myths that come from around the world and trace back into prehistory, the rising of the seas are often the way in which the gods cleanse the Earth of human wrongdoing or insolence. In the Judaic-Christian story of Noah, God sent the flood to punish the sinfulness of humanity. Noah was spared because of his righteousness and told to build an ark, which allowed him to save himself and the seeds of plants and pairs of animals to repopulate the world.

The Hebrew story of Noah is a retelling of a more ancient Sumerian-Babylonian version. As mentioned earlier, this was the story of Utnapishtim, who was spared when Enki warned him of the impending flood and instructed him to build an ark. In all of these stories, the flood involves a cleansing of the Earth due to conflicts between the realms of the divine and of humanity. In the Hebraic version, the flood is sent due to the sinfulness of humans beginning with the "fall," when Adam and Eve went against God's injunction not to eat of the fruit of the Tree of the Knowledge of Good and Evil. In their action, they asserted their independence and gained consciousness but also experienced a rupture from blissful union with the divine. These themes speak to the archetypal energies of separation and individuation in the Age of Aries and the longing in the Age of Pisces for redemption and reunion with the divine.

Interestingly, in the earlier Sumerian-Babylonian version of this myth, the "original sin" is not an act of independence or defiance but rather of blind obedience. In this story, Adapa, the son of Enki, angers the gods when he breaks the wing of the South Wind in a fit of anger. When Anu, the god of heaven, sends for Adapa to reproach him, Enki counsels his son to present himself in a penitent manner. He further instructs his son to refuse when Anu offers him the bread and water of death. Adapa follows his father's advice and comes to Anu in mourning and penance. Anu is pleased by his humility and piety and then offers him the bread and water of life, of immortality. In blind obedience to his father's instructions, Adapa misunderstands the offering and refuses it. In this way, he loses immortality, and the world is thereafter plagued with misfortune, disease, and death as a result.[6] These are perhaps the twin shadow sides of Neptune and the Age of Pisces: blind allegiance to an idealized leader or fierce assertion of separation and individuation. Both result from the illusion of separation and the dilemma of dualism, whether it is the dualism of self and other, spirit and matter, or human and divine.

The flood then becomes the dissolution of the false dualism, bringing us back to connection with source and to unity consciousness. These flood stories from around the globe speak of the historical cataclysmic crisis of the Younger Dryas period and resonate with the ancient prophecies, reminding us that we are now in that recurring time of the 12,000-year cycles of cataclysmic crisis, cleansing, and reset for humanity and for the Earth. Sedna the planet, with her almost 12,000-year orbit, comes into our solar system as the messenger of this time of transition and transformation.

With the arrival of Sedna into our consciousness and the archetypal meaning arising from the Inuit myth, we are reminded of the ancient wisdom of the Sacred Feminine and the powers of the Great Goddess as the Creatrix and Destroyer. While the father in the story attempts to control his and his daughter's fates, through the vehicle of a boat that rides above the waters, Sedna finds herself drowning and dissolving in the waters. Her immersion in the ocean was not retribution or punishment for wrongdoing but rather a path for transformation and reunion with the divine. The story reminds us that the way to divinity and unity is not through transcendence or control but rather through the dissolution of the ego and our sense of separation. The story shows us that we, as humanity, have no control in trying to override these currents of change, and the efforts of those caught in this time in the patriarchal paradigm of striving for power and control are futile.

A crucial moment in the story is when Sedna chooses to let go of the boat and dives deep into the sea. While merging with the sea, with Source, Sedna does not lose her awareness or consciousness. Instead, her form, her way of being, becomes fluid, no longer fixed or separate from source or from other life-forms. She is now one with the sea but also with the creatures of the deep, the seals and whales and fish. She becomes a source of sustenance for the people, an ambassador of the Ocean-Mother-Source, while retaining her memory of her humanity. Sedna teaches us that we are not separate from the divine, but that the divine flows within and through us. She teaches us not to strive to deny our humanity or mortality but to dissolve into the deeper awareness of our ultimate nature, our immortal soul selves and our union with Source and with all of life. She reminds us that in reclaiming our true identity, we reconnect with the sacredness of the life around us and are able to become co-creators with Cosmic consciousness.

This story speaks to our need in this time to no longer attempt to dominate or control nature or our life experience. Instead, we are asked to dive into the mystery, into the unknown, in trust that this transformation will lead to a more fluid, integrated, and whole way of being. This is the dissolution of the primary dualism that has characterized human consciousness for the past five thousand years and that is ultimately an illusion. This was also the message of Neptune in the Age of Pisces—that the very cause of our longing, our sense of separation, is ultimately an illusion, a false premise. The shattering truth of the Age of Aquarius and the lightning bolt awareness of Uranus is that all is One, everything arises from Cosmic consciousness. Form is merely a momentary manifestation of being, a fractal expression of this Cosmic consciousness, and not a fixed reality in time and space. We "foam in and out of being" and then return to Source.[7]

With the awareness that Sedna brings us in this time, perhaps we can understand the deeper integration of Uranus and Saturn as the rulers of this Age of Aquarius. Within Western astrology, Uranus and Saturn have often been viewed as diametrically opposed in their meanings and energies. Uranus is the energy of the reformer, the one who challenges cultural structures and norms. Saturn has been seen as the manifestation and enforcer of societal structures and ideology. Saturn, as the outermost visible planet, has been viewed as the boundary between the infinite and the finite, between spirit and matter.

For the Greeks, Saturn was identified with Kronos, the Father of Time, binding us in our mortality and physical form. In medieval times, Saturn was seen as malefic, associated with age, illness, melancholy, and isolation. The planet was associated with lead, a metal at the opposite end of the spectrum for alchemists from the lightness and purity of gold. As the split between spirit and matter became a primary duality in patriarchal thought, Saturn represented the fall from grace, from immortality and from the purity of spirit unencumbered by form, into mortality and the constraints and entrapment of physical matter. In modern Western astrology, Saturn has been associated with our fears, restrictions, and pain. Yet, the understanding has also been that if we work through these Saturnian issues, this planet leads us to deeper strength and wisdom.

Perhaps, instead of this patriarchal understanding of Saturn colored by the separation between spirit and matter, we might look to an earlier archetype from the mythology of ancient Sumer and Babylon. In Babylonian mythology, Saturn was associated with the god Ninurta and was seen as sacred, because this god was closest to the sacred heavens. Ninurta was the god of agriculture, the plough, and thunderstorms. Ninurta gained power after rescuing the tablets of fate stolen from Enlil by the wind Dragon in league with the powers of chaos. Here we see the way in which Saturn was elevated for its closeness to the sacred heavens and was viewed as the portal, bridging the worlds and opening us to our connection with the divine. Ninurta was also the overseer of fate.

An even more ancient mythological reference for Saturn is Enki, the Sumerian god of wisdom, the androgynous deity who rescued Inanna, the Queen of Heaven, from death, and the one who brought knowledge of the ways of civilization (the sacred "me") to the people. Enki held the wisdom of how to move between the worlds, between the realm of the heavens and Earth, as well as being the one who knew the way of descent to and return from the underworld. In the Sumerian language, "Enki" means "God of the Earth," yet he was also known as the god of the sweet waters, fertilizing the Earth, bringing life and creativity.[8]

While the realm of the heavens and Earth were split apart in the Sumerian cosmology at the threshold of the patriarchal period, Enki belonged to no realm; he moved between the worlds. In Sumerian mythology, he was the Creator of Humankind, the Fertilizer of the Land, and the Organizer of his Creations.[9] Like Raven in the Sedna story, Enki was the shaman, the magician, and the one who knew the ways of the Universe and how to live an embodied life on Earth.

Enki's more fluid way of being and his identity as the mediator between the realm of heaven and Earth and the gods and humans is more consistent with the astronomical nature of the planet Saturn. This planet bridges the realm of the invisible and visible for us, as it is the outermost visible planet in our sky. Yet, unlike its medieval associations with lead and the weight of form, it is a gaseous planet and the only one in our solar system that is less dense than water. It is almost entirely gas and liquid and consists mostly of hydrogen, the life force of the Universe. Astronomers now question whether it has a solid rock core or, more likely, a molten/liquid core. In its essence, Saturn is fluid and bridges the worlds. Saturn has a hot interior and radiates more energy into space than it receives from the Sun. It is surrounded by beautiful rings of ice and space debris that it has shaped into form with its gravitational field. These ever-changing rings speak to us of the possibilities of living in a more fluid and ever-changing manner. Amazingly, it has a hexagonal pattern at its north pole, due to a storm system that swirls there. In sacred geometry and in ancient cultures, the hexagon is seen as a symbol of harmony and balance. It is the shape of life, as in the honeycombs of bees and the shape of snowflakes. As a six-sided figure, it resonates with the number six, which in numerology and in the Tarot is symbolic of love and union.

We are now in a time where we must face the challenge of integrating spirit and matter and no longer live in the destructive illusion of duality. We need to move into a new cosmology in which we realize that there is no separation between Earth and Sky, flesh and spirit. As hydrogen moves through the Universe as a river of energy, fueling the stars and planets, so Spirit moves through all of life. Like Enki and Saturn, when we are embodied, our form is not fixed. We do not belong to one realm or the other. We are fluid, like Sedna, manifesting for this moment in this shape and incarnation, which, rather than being a separation from spirit, is a celebration of Spirit's endless possibilities of manifestation. We are each a fractal expression of Cosmic consciousness. Unless we truly embrace this awareness and let go of the illusion of separation and dualism, we are destined to engage in an endless struggle between our spiritual and natural selves and between ourselves and the Earth, the planet where we reside.

In this way, we now may view the planetary rulers of this new Age of Aquarius, Saturn and Uranus, not as antagonists but as allies. Uranus shatters the illusions, the forms that bind us from our true essence, and reminds us of our essential, energetic being. Saturn allows us to find ways to integrate that awareness and essence in form, holding the manifestation lightly, knowing that it is fluid and never fixed. Saturn guides us in reclaiming what it means to honor our interconnectedness and to come back into balance and harmony with all of life. Saturn teaches us how to live in the mystery and wonder of the shamanic art of shape-shifting, the wisdom that all is Spirit, all is energy, that we can partake of form in celebration rather than in a sense of confinement, and that we can be open to change and live in the enormity of the possibilities of the Universe. If we could but embrace that truth, that consciousness, the world could transform in the blink of an eye.

## ERIS/XENA: DWARF PLANET GUIDING US INTO NEW WAYS OF BEING

Another guide in this time of change is the recently discovered dwarf planet Eris or "Xena." Discovered in 2005 (from images taken in 2003) by astronomers Michael Brown (Caltech), Chad Trujillo (formerly of Gemini Observatory), and David Rabinowitz (Yale University), she is the largest dwarf planet known. When first identified, her discoverers and NASA declared her to be our solar system's tenth planet, due to her size (which has been determined to be about 4 percent larger than Pluto). Eris is a trans-Neptunian body and is part of the Kuiper Belt. This belt consists of asteroids and cometary matter that were scattered outward into the farthest reaches of our solar system at its birth. Sedna, whose orbit is much larger than that of Eris, is another trans-Neptunian object (TNO), but she is now considered an inner Oort cloud planetary body.

What is unique about Eris is that her orbit is eccentric and very different from those of other planets in our solar system; her orbit is tilted off the path of the ecliptic by 44 degrees. This is why she was not discovered until 2005, when astronomers began to search the sky beyond the path of the ecliptic. It takes 556.7 years for her to complete an orbit, and she is now at her farthest distance from the Sun (almost ten billion miles, even farther out than Sedna at this time and three times more distant than Pluto). She currently is moving through the constellation Cetus. Interestingly, she was in the stars of Phoenix from 1840 to 1875, then she moved through the constellation of Sculptor until 1929, and she will now be in Cetus until she enters the stars of Pisces in 2036. She rarely moves through the constellations of our zodiac due to her highly inclined orbit, which is off the path of the ecliptic.

Her discovery generated debate at the August 2006 meeting of the International Astronomical Union (IAU) as to whether she should be classified as a planet or not. In the ensuing conflict among astronomers, she was designated as a dwarf planet, and Pluto was demoted to this status as well, along with Ceres, which is the largest planetary body in the asteroid belt. Due to their size, Eris, Pluto, and Ceres all had to either be classified as planets or designated as dwarf planets. In the contentious debate, the resulting definition of a planet was defined as needing the following criteria: it was necessary for the planetary body to be in orbit around the Sun, have sufficient mass so as to be nearly round in shape, and to have "cleared the neighborhood around its orbit." It is this last qualification that excluded Pluto, Ceres, and Eris from planetary status due to the fact that all of them share their orbits with other planetary bodies. Pluto shares its orbit with its large moon, Charon, and intersects with the orbit of Neptune for part of the time. Interestingly, this did not exclude Neptune from planetary status. Ceres and Eris share space with surrounding asteroid belts and do not "clear their orbits" to become the primary entity in their orbital field; instead, they are, in essence, part of a larger community.

From a philosophical perspective, the IAU's recently established definition of a planet is significant. It creates a definition of importance that is defined by isolation and individualism. To be a planet, it is important to be large and to dominate your own field of movement, such that you are the only primary body in that area of space. Pluto is in essence a double planet, with its moon Charon almost its same size, and is able to move in and out of orbit with Neptune. Ceres is part of the main asteroid belt between Mars and Jupiter, while Eris moves among the Kuiper Belt objects. Sedna is an inner Oort cloud object whose elongated orbit takes her out to the outer edges of our solar system. These planetary bodies perhaps bring into our collective consciousness a corrective to the idealization of individuation and a new perspective about connection and community. It is interesting that these planets are calling us out of our overemphasis on individualism and isolationism as we are rediscovering that our solar system may be part of a binary star system and as we move into the Age of Aquarius with its emphasis on community.

The contentious debate and ongoing conflicts about the new definition of a planet and the resulting designations led astronomers to name the planetoid Eris, after the Greek goddess of strife, and Eris's moon Dysnomia, after the demoness of lawlessness who was one of the Greek goddess's children. Eris is most well-known in Greek mythology for her role in triggering the Trojan War by stirring up conflict among the Olympian goddesses. When she was not invited to a wedding party, Eris arrived unannounced and tossed into the crowd a golden apple that was inscribed with the word, "Kallisti," meaning "for the fairest one." This resulted in the goddesses Hera, Athena, and Aphrodite all vying for the prize, with each trying to bribe the judge, Paris, the prince of Troy, who was chosen by Zeus to resolve the conflict. When Aphrodite offered Helen, wife of the king of Sparta, to Paris if she was chosen, Paris consented. This led to the Trojan War and resulted in the destruction of the city of Troy. This tale shows the dangers of competition, abuse of power, and strife. In the end, the need to be the best, the one chosen from the field of competitors, led to the downfall of all involved.

In selecting this name for the new planetary body, the IAU may have consciously or unconsciously signaled its own shortsightedness. The effort to restrict the definition of a planet was an effort to cling to the chosen few who have "cleared their neighborhoods" and seemingly shown their power and prowess in the process. This is an idealization of the "colonizers," echoing conquests by modern Western nations in taking over the territories of other cultures. The astronomers themselves, in their need to avoid the expanding community of planets that would result from a more liberal definition, may have set themselves up for ongoing strife, competition, and conflict and certainly were mirroring this shadow aspect of our modern patriarchal cultural paradigms.

In contrast, let us consider what we know of the nature of this new planetary body, which for two years prior to this debate was known as Xena. Astronomer Michael Brown, a fan of the popular television series *Xena: Warrior Princess* (aired September 1995–May 2001), named her after this heroine. He named her moon Gabrielle, for Xena's companion and closest friend. The setting for the television show was ancient Greece, and it drew liberally on ancient mythologies from around the world. The primary storyline was about Xena's transformation from a violent warlord to a spiritual warrior on a quest for justice and healing for all.

The character Xena had initially become a warlord bent on revenge after being traumatized and enraged as a child by seeing her village destroyed by warriors. After years of seeking revenge on those who had destroyed her village and family, she underwent a profound transformation, realizing that she had become the enemy that she hated. She then took a radically different path and set out on a quest to become a warrior for peace and justice, to right the wrongs of her previous crimes and try to end the cycle of violence. Instead of seeking revenge and conquest, she became an agent of healing, emanating compassion and respect for diversity, and fostering right relationship.

In the series, Xena moved through many adventures, with other characters from assorted historical periods and cultures making their appearance on the show. Time, history, and culture were fluid as they wove through the narratives. Xena refused to ally with any group, though many tried to gain her allegiance. She was a warrioress of the people, of those in need and of those who were in danger or unjustly treated. She intervened to bring peace, love, and justice and then moved on. Her quest was not for fame, power, or material advantage but to set wrongs right. She moved through many relationships with friends and many sexual encounters, including a brief erotic interlude with her female companion. Her sexuality was her own, and she engaged in a diversity of relationships, truly an Aquarian trait.

At the end of the series, Xena's daughter, Eve, born out of wedlock, was decreed to be the one who would bring about the death of the Olympian gods. It was interesting that she was named Eve, who is the biblical character blamed for original sin and the downfall of humanity. Now, the deeper wisdom of Eve as an archetype of the Sacred Feminine was reclaimed, and she was destined to become a savior of humanity rather than the source of its destruction and banishment from paradise. In an effort to thwart her and to preserve their prowess, the gods attempted many preemptive strikes to kill Eve in order to retain their power. During this time, Xena and Gabrielle went through their own death/rebirth experience. After a period of twenty-five years, Eve accepted her purpose and her fate and stepped into her part in the profound transformation of the culture around her, leading to the end of the religion of that era and fostering an increasing context of compassion, acceptance of diversity, and collaboration in community.

The Olympian pantheon came into prominence in Greece in the Age of Aries at the end of the first millennium BCE and continued into the time of the Hellenistic period in the early centuries of the current era, at the beginning of the Age of Pisces. Xena, a character created in our culture at the end of the Age of Pisces, was depicted in the storyline of the series as instrumental in the transition out of the earlier Age of Aries.

Our current Western civilizations have been profoundly shaped by Greek cosmology arising in the Age of Aries and, in particular, by the Platonic notion of the ideal as separate from material reality and reflecting the separation of spirit from matter. The ancient Greek culture also idealized the mental capacities and forms of logic that so permeate our Western ways of thinking and knowing. The character Xena, in her effort to set things back into balance, into right relationship, perhaps hints to us of a return to a more natural form of law, a more integrated notion of spirit and matter, and an honoring of the Sacred Feminine and the sacredness of all of life.

Unlike Eris, Xena was dedicated to undoing the damage of strife and warfare. Perhaps even now, Xena teaches us how to follow her example and radically transform our lives and step out of the cultural paradigms and collective consciousness of our time. Through her deep inner and outer exploration, Xena became aware of and freed herself from her unconscious reactivity and cultural conditioning and stepped into a new way of being at the threshold of a new age. She dared to be her authentic self even if it meant breaking cultural constructs or not meeting others' expectations. She embarked on a journey with no clear destination whose only purpose was to live in truth, to act from the heart, and to serve justice. Her companion in the series, Gabrielle, in contrast to Dysnomia, the demoness of lawlessness, was known for her sensitivity and compassion, her love of mythology, and the way in which she understood how stories weave meaning and connections in our lives.

The character of Xena is much more in attunement with this new planetary body whose orbit is so eccentric and off the beaten path of the ecliptic than the name that the astronomical community assigned to her. This dwarf planet, like the character Xena, follows her own path, circling in close to the Sun and the other planets of our solar system and then off into the outer edges of the Kuiper Belt. She moves in harmony, not disharmony, with the planetary bodies around her but dares to be unique in her orbit. She has no need to "clear her neighborhood," to prove her dominance, or to strive for hierarchical advantage. She was content to move unseen in our midst for millennia and was not noticed until astronomers dared to look at the sky with a new perspective. She is now guiding us to heal the out-of-balance paradigms of the Age of Aries to reclaim the gifts of the Age of Pisces (compassion, peace, love, spirituality, and an honoring of our Oneness).

True to her original name, she shows us how to step out of our cultural conditioning and engrained patterns of thinking and acting. From an astrological perspective, she defies our efforts to place her on the ecliptic, because her very nature is about her disengagement from this "traditional" or normative path. At this time, at the end of the Age of Pisces and the beginning of a new age, she teaches us how to change our lives and how to step out of old paradigms, patterns, and habitual ways of knowing, doing, and being. She asks us to dare to be our true selves and to follow our own unique creative paths. She encourages us to have the courage to embark on a journey into the unknown and to live in compassion and in right relationship with all of life around us.

How significant that this planetary body evoked conflict in the astronomical community and a subsequent effort to demote her from planetary status to a "dwarf planet" and to name her after the Greek goddess of strife. Perhaps this reflects our fear of or reaction to her unique character and her audacity in stepping off the ecliptic and out of a traditional orbit and way of being. Her original name, Xena, seems to correspond more closely to her true nature, and is it not significant that in this age of technology, one myth for our time may come from our modern media? In this time of transition and global change, the debate about her may reflect the tumult between the call to new forms of consciousness and new ways of being and the rigid, regressive efforts to cling to old forms and the patriarchal paradigms.

The dwarf planet, which I now refer to as Eris-Xena to acknowledge her official name while honoring her true nature, currently travels through the constellation Cetus, one of the constellations (along with Aquarius, Pisces, and Eridanus) in the southern sky, in the region known as the Waters. The ecliptic touches the edge of this constellation, but for the most part, Cetus lies below it and is associated in Greek mythology with the gateway to the underworld. In Greek and Roman mythology, Cetus was seen as the whale, which reminds us of the mythology of Sedna, the goddess of the deep sea who has whales and seals as her companions. The Arabs, along with the ancient Hebrews and Greeks, viewed this constellation as a serpentine sea creature.

In Mesopotamia, the stars of Cetus were associated with Tiamat, the primordial Mother of all life in Sumerian and Babylonian mythology. While imagined in Greek and more modern interpretations as a "sea-monster," Tiamat was not depicted this way in the ancient stories. Instead, she was associated with the deep sea, with the primordial waters from which all life comes. She gave birth to the dragons and serpents that were the earliest images of the Sacred Feminine and of the divine, both in the sky and on Earth. She was the supreme goddess of the sea and of the source, the chaos of creation. In the Babylonian epic the Enuma Elish, she is the holder of the Tablets of Destiny who was later slain when the gods feared her powers of creation and destruction, and she was sliced in half to form the heavens and the Earth.

As our new planet Eris-Xena passes through this constellation, she reminds us of the depths, of the source of all of life, of the power of chaos, the cauldron of creation and destruction. She heralds the return of the Sacred Feminine and the transformation and dissolution of our current patriarchal belief systems. She calls us into the truth of who we are, our attunement with our soul selves, and to trust in following our own unique paths. She encourages us to let go of our personal stories and cultural conditioning and to dive deep and return to right relationship with Source and with all of life.

## QUAOAR: KUIPER BELT OBJECT AND CREATION DEITY

Quaoar was discovered in 2002 and is a large ringed dwarf planet in the Kuiper Belt about half the size of Pluto. It has one moon, Weywot. It has a circular orbit of 288 years and moves just outside the orbit of Pluto. This planet, like some other recently discovered Kuiper Belt objects, was named after an Indigenous creation deity. Others include Haumea (the ancient Hawaiian goddess of fertility) and Makemake (the creation deity of the ancient Rapa Nui culture of Easter Island). Quaoar was the creation deity of the Gabrielino/Tongva people who resided in the area that is now the Los Angeles basin in the United States and date their culture back to 6000 BCE. Quaoar was their androgynous creation deity, integrating the energies of the Sacred Feminine and Sacred Masculine. Quaoar's son was Weywot, god of the sky. Quaoar sang creation into being and then called all that was created into this song until all of creation was singing in harmony and balance with the song of the spheres. In many ways, the archetype of Quaoar resonates with the ancient principle or "neter" of ancient Egypt, Ma'at, who symbolizes all of life living in right harmony and right balance.

In a profound way, this Kuiper Belt planetary body is reminding us how we need to move out of the disharmony and discordance of this time and back into balance with each other and with the life around us. It is also a reminder of the higher levels of consciousness and of the sacredness of sound and the way in which everything in our Cosmos has frequency and vibration.

While some astrologers refer to the Kuiper Belt objects as being the higher octave of the outer (transpersonal) planets, I see them as resonating with the wisdom of the Earth's core and telluric realm (the first and second dimensions in Barbara Hand Clow's nine dimensions of consciousness) as well as with the higher dimensions of sound, vibration, and light (the sixth and seventh dimensions).[10] For example, another

Kuiper Belt planetary body, Salacia, named after the Roman goddess of the sea and the sun on the waters, reminds us of the dance of light and of the oceans as the source of life on the Earth.

These dwarf planets help us remember our origins and the interconnectedness of all of life. In their association with creation deities and ancient mythology, they help us reconnect with the wisdom of our ancestors and the ancient cultures of the past who lived in greater balance with the Earth and who exhibited the higher-level spiritual consciousness of past ages. They also carry the wisdom of many of our current Indigenous cultures who have retained their connection with these ancient lineages and with the remembrance of the sacredness of all of life.

There are thousands of objects in the Kuiper Belt, which is a donut-shaped ring of icy objects that orbit outside of Neptune. The Kuiper Belt now includes Pluto and Eris/Xena and other newly discovered dwarf planets, but, as of now, only two hundred have been named and catalogued to date. The icy debris of this belt consists of remnants from the origins of our solar system. It surrounds and encloses our solar system.

As we explore the planetary bodies of our solar system, we know that all of the planets circle the Sun, our star, which is in its own orbit with its binary star, and together they move in a large 225,000,000- to 250,000,000-year orbit around the galactic center, our source. Within our solar system, as we move out from the Sun, we experience the planets that speak to the archetypes of our nature as humanity: Mercury, our ways of communicating and thinking; Venus, our relationships and journey of transformation in the context of our relationship with self and others; Mars, our hero's journey of discovery and exploration; Jupiter, our faith and beliefs; and Saturn, how we define ourselves and form the structures of our society. Then we journey to the outer (transpersonal) planets: Uranus, how we balance individuation and belonging and integrate the archetypes of truth and justice; Neptune, how we integrate our spiritual awareness, divine love, and the realization of the Oneness of all that is; and Pluto, our soul's journey of evolution and transformation and our experience of life/death/rebirth. These transpersonal planets are the higher octaves of Mercury, Venus, and Mars (our more personal ways of thinking, feeling, and being), and they hold the energies of aligning our minds with divine mind (Uranus), loving with divine love and compassion (Neptune), and aligning personal will with divine will (Pluto).

Within our inner solar system and between the orbits of Mars and Jupiter, we have the asteroid belt that is most likely the debris of an exploded planet. The primary asteroids within this belt are named after goddess archetypes, and within our patriarchal period, they have supported us in reclaiming the lost remnants of the energies of the Sacred Feminine. Then, we have the belt of the Centaurs who orbit primarily between Jupiter and Neptune. The most well-known Centaurs are Chiron, Chariklo, Pholus, and Nessus, and they hold the archetypal energies of healers. They guide us in finding our path of healing to come back into wholeness within ourselves and into right relationship with others.

Further out beyond Neptune's orbit is the Kuiper Belt, surrounding our solar system and reminding us of our origins. This belt also protects us from incoming comets and provides a protective boundary for our solar system. At the farthest reaches of our solar system is the Oort cloud. This sphere of icy debris surrounds our solar system and holds the fragments of our origins and early development as a solar system billions of years ago. So, as we move farther out in our solar system, we are reminded of our origins and of our relationship with the Cosmos. We remember that we are in the Orion arm of our Milky Way galaxy that swirls around our center, Sagittarius A*, the black womb of our galaxy. In this way, these Kuiper Belt planetary bodies remind us of the oneness of all of life and the vastness of the Cosmos. At the same time, they remind us that our Earth and all of the life around us are sacred expressions of Cosmic consciousness. They remind us that the sacred is within us and is immanent as well as transcendent. They help us to come back home to ourselves and to the sacredness of our planet, and they are a corrective to the patriarchal idealization of spirituality as transcendent and of the quest for what is beyond us rather than honoring the sacredness of the land beneath our feet and the presence of the divine within us.

As we connect with the Centaurs and Kuiper Belt objects and these recently named dwarf planets, they remind us of our place in the Cosmos and of our being part of the web of life. They teach us that as we heal and remember our origins, we can become co-creators with Cosmic consciousness and once again bring our own voices into the song of creation and back into harmony with the music of the spheres.

# CHAPTER 13

# Our Galactic Center

We have moved around the wheel of the precessional cycle, and we need to now explore more fully the galactic center that has birthed us, that shapes our evolutionary process and is guiding us in this time of transition. What is the galactic center? What is this birthplace, this source, the cosmic womb that has given birth to all life?

In ancient texts, this dark rift in the Milky Way, our Source, has often been referred to as the "Central Sun" or the ultimate source of divine light, life, and spiritual consciousness. There are references to this Central Sun or hidden Sun in many cultures, such as in ancient India, Egypt, and Greece as well as in the hermetic text of the *Corpus Hermeticum*, in which it is referred to as the source of all creation. These ancient texts reflect both a profound understanding of the galactic center as the source of all life in our galaxy and solar system and an awareness of how its energy affects us physically, emotionally, and spiritually. It is now becoming clearer from a scientific perspective that the powerful electromagnetic energies of the galactic center affect our DNA and our physical health and activate our pineal glands, increasing our spiritual consciousness. The descriptions of this "black hole" as the Central Sun may also relate to times when the galactic center is fully active in its AGN (active galactic nucleus) phase and then emits a light brighter than our own Sun. In this way, the galactic center is the hidden, central Sun or source that guides our own evolution of consciousness and births, shapes, and guides the evolution of our galaxy.

Across the past century, physicists and astronomers have been struggling to grasp the scientific nature of the energies of our Universe and of the galactic center. Their findings have revolutionized our understanding of reality. Einstein's explorations of the forces moving through the Cosmos led to the theory of relativity and the revision of Newtonian physics, which has shaped our understanding of the Cosmos for the past five hundred years. Recent research using the Hubble telescope and examinations of the galactic center through radio and gamma ray technologies have led us to a deeper understanding of the nature of the center of our galaxy.

As we noted at the beginning of our journey through the zodiac, across human history, we have searched for the path to the center. The medicine wheel, the mandala, and the circle as symbols for wholeness and the search for Source permeate all cultures and all religions. Ancient cultures oriented their land and located the seat of power and of sacred sites at the center of their region. We have searched for the center in the sky, from the ancient focus on the celestial pole as a source of stillness in the swirling landscape of stars to the ancient cultural view of the Milky Way as the source of life where the World Tree attaches and holds the Universe intact.

As we look for the center, our origin as humanity, we first must honor our location on our Earth, our home. Then, we journey to the center of our solar system, our Sun. Then, we remember that our Sun is one star among the 300 billion stars in our Milky Way galaxy and is in a binary star system with Sirius, revolving around a central point. Finally, we look to the center of our galaxy, our ultimate source. This is what Sedna is guiding us toward as she moves from the primordial matter of our solar system, the Oort cloud, and experiences the energies of the surrounding star systems and then brings that awareness back into our inner solar system.

## Our Galactic Center

Our Earth resides in the Milky Way galaxy, a spiral galaxy consisting of billions of stars and with a diameter of about 100,000 light years. Our galaxy is the second largest in a group of over thirty galaxies comprising what is called the Local Group.[1] Our nearest galaxy is Andromeda, which is 2.4 million light years away. Our solar system is on the Orion arm of our Milky Way galaxy about two-thirds of the way out, or about 26,000 to 27,000 light years from the center. We orbit around this galactic center at about 514,000 miles per hour, taking approximately 250,000,000 years to complete one cycle. Our Sun was formed roughly 4.6 billion years ago, so the elements that make up our bodies have orbited the center of our galaxy approximately twenty times.[2]

Recent research has shown that we live in a Universe of which only 4 percent is visible matter as we know it; 96 percent is dark matter and dark energy of which we only have the beginning glimmers of understanding. Of the 4 percent that is visible matter, astronomers have seen and researched only 1 percent of that. We live in a Universe filled with mystery far beyond our comprehension and in a spiral galaxy filled with wonder.

Only in recent years have scientists come to understand more fully the location and nature of our galactic center. Prior to the use of radio telescopes, our most powerful optic telescopes were unable to glimpse this amazing site due to the cloud of space dust obscuring our vision. Through radio astronomy, we are now able to move beyond this veil to glimpse the amazing source of our galaxy. What we now know is that if the galactic center was unobscured, its size and brightness would be comparable to the full Moon or another bright Sun, lighting up our night sky.[3] Instead, as it is now only starting to reactivate and move into AGN, it still moves in darkness, veiled from our eyes. Surrounding the galactic center is a concentration of stars, drawn by the powerful gravitational pull of this source. It is from this center that our galaxy was formed almost fourteen billion years ago in a cosmic explosion, or, as Jude Currivan would say, in a cosmic out breath.[4] As we noted earlier, this dark region of the galactic center is pointed to by the constellation of Sagittarius, the archer whose arrow points into the galactic center.

What is the nature of this cosmic source? Our radio telescope views of this amazing site have given us some sense of the composition of this region. What we find are a concentration of stars and three spiraling arms of hot gas, known as Sagittarius A West, emanating from the source and moving in a counterclockwise manner, a triskelion of sorts. There is also an enormous bubble of hot gas, known as Sagittarius A East, that is most likely the result of a star that ventured too close to the center and exploded, yielding the power of fifty to one hundred supernovas.[5] At the center of all of this pulsing, moving heat and energy is Sagittarius A*, what we now know to be a massive black hole with the power of 2.6 million Suns emanating from its source and with a diameter about the size of the orbit of our planet Mars.[6] While stars close to this center move at amazing speed (up to 3.1 million miles per hour) due to its phenomenal gravitational pull, and the triple spiraling arms of hot gas that dance in graceful movement around it, Sagittarius A*, the galactic center, does not move. This powerful source is truly the still point in our galaxy.

Our galactic center, Sagittarius A*, is a supermassive black hole largely composed of "dark" matter and plasma. The dark matter causes its gravitational pull to be so great that it absorbs all matter and light. Physicists since Einstein and the development of the theory of relativity now realize that gravity affects both light and time. Strong gravitational energy can bend light and slow down time. The compressed energy of the black hole at the center of our galaxy is so great that no light can escape from it, and time stops. It becomes a world onto itself from which nothing can escape, surrounded by a virtual membrane, the event horizon. This powerful center is the source of all life in our galaxy and the place of its ending; it is the Creatrix and the Destroyer. It is the dark womb that has given birth to all of the stars in our galaxy and it is the tomb, drawing them in to die. Within this compressed source of power is a mystery beyond our wildest imagining and a realm that we can never fully comprehend. Brian Swimme refers to this amazing Source as the "all-nourishing abyss." Dev Misra refers to our galactic center as "the central, creative and organizing consciousness of our galaxy."[8]

The powerful gravitational field of the galactic center heats the surrounding gas, creating a turbulent, dense, hot plasma. As this interacts with the black hole, enormous amounts of energy and powerful jets or plasma outflows are released that are capable of extending far beyond the galactic plane and influence star formation. The plasma at the galactic center is also the source of cosmic rays that travel at close to light speed and impact us here on Earth.[9]

According to Robert Temple, who has summarized the latest research on plasma in his book *A New Science of Heaven*, our Universe is actually over 99 percent plasma. He describes how the dusty complex plasma in our Universe interacts with electromagnetic fields and is able to evolve into such complexity that it can be seen as "alive." In addition, his research indicates that the Kordylewski clouds, plasma clouds located close to our Earth, are intelligent and may contain the memories of all of life on Earth, much like the Akashic records. In fact, we ourselves have a plasma body that shapes and sustains our physical body and may be the soul self that never dies and that holds our consciousness beyond death.[10] So, in fact, this recent plasma research confirms that we live in a sentient Universe and that this consciousness of the Cosmos births, surrounds, and sustains us, is within us, and informs all that is.

What is also amazing to comprehend is that we live in an expanding Universe. Einstein's mathematical formulations, which shocked even him, indicate that the galaxies are moving away from each other at a velocity related to the space between them.[11] In other words, the greater the distance between them, the faster they are moving apart. At the birth of our Universe, there was an explosion or expansion that we can still monitor in terms of the movement of photons across the galaxies. Yet, amazingly, this fiery birth was also the beginning of our notions of space and time. There was no space or time before this creation. From this galactic center and from the consciousness of the Cosmos, came all of life.

As Edwin Hubble discovered, as we measure the galactic expansion, we discover that we are at the center with everything moving away from us. In other words, every point used to measure this expansion becomes the center. In his book *The Hidden Heart of the Cosmos*, Brian Swimme explores this amazing paradox. What we find is that we live in a complex, omnicentric evolutionary Universe with a cosmic expansion or out breath as our birth, yet, at the same time, a "developing reality which from the beginning is centered upon itself at each place of its existence."[12]

What does this mean? It means that our Newtonian notions of space and time are inaccurate and inadequate. For centuries, we have held a view of ourselves as fixed in space and time, consisting of solid form. We now know that is an illusion. We initially began to come to this awareness through the discovery that we consist of atoms, tiny invisible molecules of matter, existing in an expanse of space. We are mostly space, the expansiveness between these molecules. Yet, our scientific understanding has now taken us even deeper into the realization that even this concept is false. In reality, we now know that the elementary particles of life, photons, the light energy that forms into matter, arise out of the vacuum itself. They do not move in space or stay in a fixed state; they "foam" into and out of existence. Physicists refer to this ground of being as "space-time foam."[13]

As Swimme describes it:

> . . . the elementary particles and atoms are not permanently existing objects but are events that are vibrating at extremely rapid rates. Even the word "vibrate" is not exact, for it connotes a solid object that moves rapidly back and forth in space. . . . [W]e know in fact that it is not true to think of particles moving back and forth in space. Rather, as has been celebrated and discussed throughout most of the twentieth century, particles exist in one location and then exist

> in another location without traversing the space in between. So, as bewildering as it might sound to us, it is more accurate scientifically to say that the particles and atoms are flashing into existence, surging into existence, and then just as suddenly they are dissolving from their place to surge forth in a nearby location. . . .[14]

Beyond the reach of our eyes, and almost beyond the capabilities of our imagining, the particles of life foam into being and then dissolve again, everywhere throughout the Universe. This birthing of our Universe from the galactic center is thus mirrored throughout time and space. We and all of life arise out of the fertile void, the womb of the Universe, the Great Goddess of Creation and Destruction, and move through cycles of birth/death and rebirth. This galactic center is our birthplace, our true center, and yet the center is also within each of us at each moment. We dance into being and then dissolve back into the sea of all being, of all potentiality. We are each fractal expressions of Cosmic consciousness and are all part of this cosmic hologram.

As we realize that the center is within us and not outside of us, that everything mirrors everything else as a fractal expression of that cosmic hologram, we open more fully to this wonder and mystery and remember that it is within our hearts (our true center) that we are connected with the unified field and the Oneness of all that is. We then no longer seek the center outside of ourselves but find it within. We realize that our hearts are the portal to opening to the love and wisdom of the Cosmos, to the unified field of Cosmic consciousness. We then become one with the Central Sun as we honor that light and love within us. Then, as we honor our hearts and our oneness with the galactic center, we are able to become co-creators with Cosmic consciousness and join our unique voice with the harmony and song of the spheres. We move off the wheel of time and space, of ascending and descending consciousness, and remember our multidimensional nature and remerge with the consciousness of the Cosmos.

CHAPTER 14

# Navigating the Shifts

We are now at the end of one precessional cycle and the beginning of a new one. This is marked by the alignment of the winter solstice sun in the northern hemisphere and summer solstice sun in the southern hemisphere with the galactic center and the intersection of the wheel of karma, the ecliptic, with our Source. This is a profound time of transition and a portal to step into higher consciousness, to remember and reclaim the lessons of the full cycle and align ourselves with the center of our galaxy and the center within us that remembers our connection with the unified field, the Oneness of all that is.

Our awareness of Sedna also speaks to these larger cycles in that Sedna's orbit is 11,487 years. The last time she was in the place in the sky where she is now was at the end of the last ice age, a time of enormous Earth changes. Graham Hancock, in his book *Underworld*, has researched that period of time and describes the massive earthquakes, floods, and volcanic eruptions that occurred as the ice melted across the continents. He also conjectures that civilization as it was at that time disappeared as the advanced cultures residing along the coastlines were flooded by the rise in sea levels. The enormous upheaval and flooding of that time may have led to worldwide myths about the Great Flood. Archaeologists are now searching beneath the waters along the coasts of Mexico, India, and other countries for the remains of these lost civilizations.

Sedna returns to our inner solar system in these times of global and environmental tumult. We are currently experiencing a record number of severe storms, hurricanes, tsunamis, earthquakes, and floods related to climate change and to the melting of the Arctic ice cap and the glaciers in Antarctica. Until we wake up and remember that we are intimately connected with the land, sea, and air around us, these conditions will only worsen.

The healing Centaurs, of which three of the four primary ones orbit between Saturn and Uranus, the rulers of this Age of Aquarius, support us in healing and releasing our collective trauma related to these past cataclysms. They also support us individually in healing and in stepping out of destructive coping patterns and into more true, whole ways of being and into right relationship with ourselves and others.

Our recently discovered dwarf planet Eris-Xena then guides us in how to move out of the violence and power-over paradigms of our past five thousand years. She demonstrates how to step off the ecliptic, out of our engrained patterns of knowing and being, and how to move into new ways of being. She helps us to let go of our personal and collective fixed beliefs and teaches us that we can transform our lives. She guides us in reclaiming our true selves and following a path of creativity. She shows us that we can move from our past patterns of violence and domination to those of compassion, peace, and right relationship. We can open to diversity, to the interconnectedness of all of life, and live in a more present and fluid manner.

Eris-Xena is part of the Kuiper Belt, and we have recently discovered many other dwarf planets or Kuiper Belt objects such as Quaoar. It is significant that most of these have been named after Indigenous creation deities. This is because the Kuiper Belt contains the remnants of the formation of our solar system, our origins. In bringing these deities/archetypes back into our consciousness, they are guiding us to step out of our patriarchal paradigms and treatment of the Earth as an object to be exploited and back into the remembrance of the sacredness of all of life. We have seen how Quaoar supports us in remembering our soul songs and how to come back into harmony with the song of the spheres.

Sedna, as the one who journeys to the far reaches of our solar system, the Oort cloud, communes with the other star systems and reminds us that we are galactic citizens. She also reminds us of these larger epochs, the larger cycles of our human evolution, and beyond that, she guides us to a galactic consciousness that takes us beyond our ego identities and even beyond our identification with the Earth and our solar system. With her vast orbit, bringing her into contact with the primordial matter of our Universe, she is a messenger from the sky reminding us of our cosmic and galactic origins. Sedna teaches us how to dissolve our identification with form and ego consciousness and to remember that we are a part of the Oneness of Cosmic consciousness. She guides us to remember our source in the oceans of this planet and that we are fractal expressions of the sea of Cosmic consciousness. If we listen, she whispers to us to move beyond fear and our limited notions of death and allow ourselves to dissolve into and merge with our soul selves that are a part of the sea of infinity.

We realize, as we have journeyed through the astrological ages and have opened to the wisdom and guidance of these recently discovered planetary guides, that the movements of the sky are mirrored in events on the Earth ("as above, so below"), and that we can find meaning in the stars and planets that surround us. We have searched for the center and found it in the heart of the galaxy and within our own hearts. But what does this mean for our day-to-day lives?

Given we are in profound transition astrologically, globally, and environmentally, we need to realize that we are in a time of letting go and yet not knowing what new forms or ways of being will emerge. This is similar to the monthly lunar cycle when, at the time of the dark of the Moon, the old cycle has ended but the new Moon has not yet become visible in the sky. We now live in a time of mystery, of liminality, and need to honor being in the dark, without knowing what will be born on the other side of this profound change. We know from ancient prophecies and modern science that this is a time of intense change, when either we need to change our ways of thinking and being or we are likely to self-destruct as a species. But what the change means, what we are meant to become, what the new forms of consciousness are—that we cannot fully know. So, part of the challenge of our time is to honor that process of releasing, of dying to what has been, without knowing the shape or form of what is to come.

This process of letting go and of honoring the liminal time (the in-between space) is a critical phase of any rite of passage, and this is the message of Neptune and of Sedna. Rather than fighting to cling to the past and to what is familiar, we need to let those old ways of being dissolve. This is the lesson of nonattachment and the ancient wisdom of dying to ourselves (and our former ways of being) so that we might be reborn. We can honor this letting go through individual and group rituals and rites of passage, as we have discussed.

We also can live that daily in breaking old habits and patterns that keep us locked into an illusion of security and familiarity. This does not mean becoming chaotic or impulsive in our behavior, but rather it means bringing that deeper galactic consciousness to our day-to-day lives in realizing that what we view as fixed and determined and stable in our lives is really an illusion. It is as if the forms and structures of our lives and our world are fractals that have appeared from the sea of chaos and potentiality and must dissolve back into that source for some new form and structure to emerge. If we can view all of matter, systems, and structure in this way, we can live in a more fluid manner and not attach our identity or security to particular patterns, structures, or forms.

On a practical level, this means that we need to simplify our lives. In living more simply, we can begin to honor a more sustainable way of being. In decluttering our external environment, we can begin to pay attention to what is truly necessary and authentic to our lives at a deeper level. It is also important to reduce the clutter and chatter in our internal lives by taking time away from the overstimulation of the world around us so that we can begin to meditate, listen to Spirit and our inner knowing, and take time to attune to the natural world again.

Being open to these changes also means being open to the unknown and to the new ways of being that will emerge. Culturally, it is as if, in modern times and with scientific materialism, we have viewed reality only as that 4 percent of visible matter in our Universe. Yet, 96 percent of our Universe is mysterious dark energy and unseen dark matter. We live in a reality that we cannot fully understand. Our lives are embedded in mystery. We float in the sea of Cosmic consciousness that holds us but is beyond our control or comprehension. As we realize that we are truly a part of this unfathomable Universe and are shaped by larger cosmic patterns and cycles, we can find our security in that mystery and in our awe of the Source of our being.

It is an amazing synchronicity that 4 percent of the Universe is visible matter and scientists have discovered that only 4 percent of our DNA accounts for our visible form. The other 96 percent has been labeled "junk DNA" with no known function, due to our blindness to what is beyond the visible realm. Many spiritual teachers and shamans tell us that this remaining DNA is what holds the star wisdom and our connection to the wisdom from across time and space. Some believe that the cosmic rays that are now bombarding our planet are activating and awakening that DNA.

By engaging in meditation or shamanic journeys or through experiences of altered consciousness, we can activate this DNA and our higher consciousness and open to the wisdom within our bodies that connects us with the stars and with the matrix of Creation and the Universe. Modern scientific knowledge, achieved through our observations, is only able to help us access a limited amount of information, just as we have been able to observe and research only 1 percent of the

Universe (one-quarter of the visible matter). Utilizing more ancient and shamanic ways of knowing can allow us to more directly access wisdom and guidance from the Universe. These more intuitive right-brain ways of knowing provide an important balance and complement our left-brain analytical ways of learning. Also, there is increasing evidence that it is through our hearts and not our minds that we can access the knowledge and wisdom of the Cosmos.

In this time of profound change, we are called to open more fully to the visible and invisible realms and let go of old belief systems and ways of being. The changes in the world around us call us into transition and transformation. We are bombarded daily by news of global chaos, terrorism, and war. We hear how our global economy and modern lifestyles will drastically change across the coming years. We watch as the weather patterns and ocean currents shift in dramatic ways, and we are in the midst of the sixth mass extinction. Our world as we have known it is radically changing.

Many of us react to these changes with fear, despair, or denial. We feel helpless in the face of the magnitude of the challenges that surround us. Some of us work hard through activism to call attention to the current global crises and to help us reorient our lives to make meaningful changes. This is evident in the work of many scientists and environmentalists concerned with climate change and with the efforts of the peace activists who see our need to unite and collaborate as a global community. Others try to deal with the challenges by exerting even more effort to be in control and to cling to the old power-over paradigms. Yet, these efforts will eventually and inevitably fail. We are called in this time to awaken, reclaim our sovereignty, and to move into higher consciousness. If we don't choose that path, the Cosmos will guide us through a reset to support the healing of our planet and the end of these out-of-balance paradigms. As Sedna realized, there is no safety in the "boat" or the ways of the past.

Rather than clinging to the past, following Sedna's example, we need to dare to have the courage to step out of cultural norms, as Sedna followed Raven into the wilderness, into the unknown, setting her life on a new course. We do not know where this path of transformation may lead, but we have to trust that we are held by larger powers and forces that are beyond our comprehension. While making conscious choices and taking the steps that we can in positive ways to address our current issues, we also need to be open to new ways of consciousness and radically new ways of being.

The solar and galactic energies now bombarding our Earth are activating our pineal glands and supporting us in expanding our consciousness and re-awakening our multidimensional nature. As we honor more and more fully the capacity of our consciousness that is far beyond our materialistic technology, we will begin to open to higher consciousness and to remember the ancient wisdom and more advanced ways of technology known by our ancestors from the Golden and Silver Ages.

Being in this time of transition also means preparing ourselves for the changes occurring on a global level—environmentally, economically, politically, and socially. It is important that we do not expect the old forms and systems of government and business to continue as they have across the past few hundred years. What we have relied on as our external sources of security have been bound to a way of being that has exploited the resources of our world and led us to the brink of disaster. We need to allow ourselves to divest from our attachment to and dependence on that way of life.

How do we follow this path? As Pluto speaks to us of the death of old ways of being and knowing, we realize that our guidance will not come through the religious forms or beliefs of the past or through the dictates of political or even spiritual leaders. It will not come from outside of us or from some power over us or external authority. We will not find our way by exerting even more control and dominance over others or over the natural environment. The ancient wisdom of the past and the findings of modern quantum physics tell us that everything is interconnected, and that the path to healing is through going within and finding the center within ourselves and in recognizing the consciousness in all of life and the source, the unity, from which we all come.

What we have realized from our journey through time and across space is that the Universe is sentient. We may call this Spirit or Cosmic consciousness. This consciousness of the Cosmos is speaking to us through the patterns of the sky and Earth in each moment. This means we need to learn the way of deep listening and intuition, attuning to the whisper of Spirit and the wisdom of our own bodies. It means finding the center within, the divinity that resides in each one of us. It means learning to discern truth from illusion and continually refining our ability to see and hear what is all around us. This truth and sense of meaning resides in the patterns of the stars, the shape of a flower, the flight of a bird, and they live in our own hearts. The center, the source, and this deep knowing is within us as well as in all of life.

If we begin to live in compassion, from the heart, the path to that knowing will deepen, and we will begin to understand the truth of our interconnectedness and oneness with all of life. As Thomas Berry asserts, this is the challenge of moving into the new Ecozoic Age in which we remember that we live in communion with all of life rather than relating to the world around us as objects to be exploited. To do this, we have to come back into deeper connection with our hearts.

Recent research by the Heartmath Institute has shown that our heart actually has neurotransmitters, much like our brains. These researchers have found that we tap into our intuition and most effective decision-making abilities not by linear analysis with our minds but by attuning to our hearts. In this way, the brain is entrained by the heart and knows how to respond, rather than the mind dominating and entraining the heart, which results in confusion, stress, and illness as well as disconnection from the body and the natural world.

By learning to listen to our inner knowing and our heart's awareness (living from our center attuned to the center of the Universe), we will learn what it means to be in right relationship with ourselves and with all of life. It is through the heart that we move out of polarity (fostered by the mind) and into unity consciousness.

The Sedna story is a wisdom tale about the importance of honoring this dissolving of the ego and the mind and opening to the heart. It is a story of spiritual initiation, of trusting our inner knowing and daring to step into the mystery and trust that we are guided by the energies of the Cosmos. As we have seen, it also is a myth about being in right relationship, and it speaks deeply of Inuit and Indigenous awareness that to live and thrive, we need to honor and be in right relationship with the land and sea around us. The myth describes how the Inuit honored their relationship with their land and with the Arctic sea, their source of life and sustenance, not as a resource to be managed or exploited but as an entity, a being, to honor and respect. This was manifested in the act of gratitude and reverence after the first catch of a fish, when the fisherman would spill drops of fresh water into the mouth of the fish and give thanks to Sedna, the Mother of the Sea Creatures.

The story also emphasized that Sedna observed how the fish and sea creatures were treated after being killed for the people's food and clothing. If they were treated with respect, she would be pleased. If not, the people could expect her punishment through deprivation of fish or through storms. The meaning of this story is clear: We experience direct consequences in relation to how we treat the natural world around us and its creatures. We see that now in the consequences of climate change and the diseases resulting from toxins in the environment. So, a deep part of the message of the Earth and the sky in this time is our need to return to right relationship with each other and with the world around us.

What does that mean? How do we live in right relationship?

Imagine living as if everything around you was alive and sentient. Think how differently you might live. If we lived this way, we would no longer view our natural environment or others or even our own bodies as objects to be controlled and used. Instead, we would learn to live in reverence, respect, and gratitude. We would begin to truly see and listen again. Everything around us would be seen and known as a celebration and manifestation of Spirit, the energy that is in all of life, in all that exists. With this orientation, when we sit down to a meal, we would feel deep gratitude for the animals and plants that gave of themselves for our sustenance. When we walk outside, we would be aware of how our actions bring life or harm to the creatures and environment around us. Imagine what it would be like to live in right relationship with all that we encounter, acting out of gratitude and wonder rather than out of disconnection, fear, exploitation, or abuse. The message of the Earth and sky to us in this time is that we can no longer afford to live a life of disconnection, dominance, and denial. We must let go of our past patterns or we will bear the consequences of that and face a cataclysmic reset.

Another way to come back into connection with the natural world is to begin to pay more attention to our bodies. Our physical bodies are our link to the natural world. Also, how we treat our bodies parallels how we treat the Earth. If we are burning ourselves out, disregarding our own health and overriding our bodies' messages, we are doing to ourselves what we have been doing to our environment. If we pay attention to our own bodies and begin to honor them as sacred, we will already be on the path to coming back into right relationship with the natural world. Our bodies are often profound messengers, showing us where we are out of balance or not being true to ourselves and how to come back into balance, harmony, and alignment with our inner knowing.

Another step that we can take is to begin to let go of patriarchal and hierarchical ways of thinking and being. Since the time of Aries, these underlying assumptions and the patterns based on them have pervaded our lives. What if we treated each person with the respect that we long for ourselves? What if we treated each person as well as each lifeform that we encounter in that way? Imagine how different our world would become. We can begin that process by living with more awareness of how we step into or out of these hierarchical patterns or power dynamics in our day-to-day lives and whether we are moving more into mutuality and right relationship with each other and all that is.

As we work with what it means to be in right relationship, we come to a deeper sense of respect and compassion for the world around us. As we integrate the archetypal energies of the Age of Aquarius, we discover the wonder and joy of being in community in a collaborative, mutual, and co-creative way. We can then explore new forms, new ways of being that we develop together that allow all in the community to thrive. We are seeing transition towns and communities being developed around the world that are exploring these new Aquarian paradigms and the understanding of acceptance of diversity, mutuality in community, and the capacity to co-create new paradigms, new economies, and new ways of being together.

At the same time, we can also begin to integrate the difference between rules and human laws and right action and natural law. Our current cultural context gives us regulations and laws that we must obey, or we will face punishment. We need human laws to provide guidelines and protections for us within our human societies, yet we need to honor natural law to guide us in living in relationship with the conscious, living world around us and to be aware of the consequences that occur when we violate those natural laws.

What if we lived in a way that honored natural law as much as human law? What if we tuned in to the consequences of our actions and their effects on the world in which we reside? We would, for example, not pollute our yards with pesticides, not because there might be a regulation against it, but because we would understand the natural consequence of poisoning our environment and the plants and animals around us as well as our own illnesses that would result. We would not pollute our lakes and rivers and oceans, because we would see these as sentient and sources of life. This means living with an awareness of the interconnectedness of all of life. Living in right action, then, means having a spectrum of choices before us and living with consciousness rather than operating out of fear, hatred, or blind allegiance to external authority. It means living and acting from the heart and with full awareness of the consequences of our actions and the interconnectedness of our lives with all that is around us, even with those who might be different from us or those who might wish us harm. We are all part of the whole. This is the deeper message of Sedna.

Sedna dissolved into her unity with the sea and the sea creatures. She was human and fish, seal and seaweed. We are not separate. We are all a part of the web of life, and our form, our current incarnation, is fleeting and fluid. We live in a holographic reality, and as we come to understand this, we become co-creators with the Earth, Cosmos, and each other to form a new world. If we live in that awareness and sense of unity, it changes every moment of our lives, every decision we make, and every action we take.

Another message of Sedna and of the Age of Aquarius is that everything is energy, vibration, and ever-changing; we live in a fluid, plasma Universe. Dualism is an illusion. There is no separate self or other, male or female, up or down, in or out. All are parts of the larger whole. This is the meaning of modern physics' understanding that matter is not fixed, that all life "foams" in and out of being. If we could begin to live that awareness, our need for external tangible security and a fixed sense of identity would dissipate, and our fear of death would dissolve. Differences in belief systems, religions, nationalities, ethnic background, sexual orientation, gender, or socioeconomic status would continue to exist but as differing manifestations of an underlying unity rather than as a basis for division, separation, hatred, fear, and polarity. This is the message of Uranus and the Aquarian Age calling us into a true understanding of community and egalitarian relationships and the common energy that permeates all of life.

In moving beyond polarity, we also come to realize that the sacred, the numinous, Spirit, is not transcendent or immanent. It is not outside us or only within us. It is both/and. To fully step into our divinity, to dissolve into that sense of the sacred in all life, is to move into humility and to honor what is divine in everything. It is to realize that we are 30,000 light years from the Source and center of our galaxy that has birthed us and formed us, and the center is also within each one of us and in each object and creature that shares our Universe.

In moving beyond polarity, it also means no longer engaging in the dialectic between a masculine god and a female goddess or one god and a multiplicity of deities. It means embracing the Sacred Feminine that teaches us that Spirit is embodied and is in all of life and that we are born from the womb of a woman and the cosmic fertile womb of the Universe. We live in the mystery of the sacred dark energy of the Universe and are surrounded by the wisdom of the darkness and the potentiality of the fertile void. At the same time, we also reach for the light and the Sky god, the deity beyond the realm of the tangible, and we seek enlightenment and honor the energy of action and manifestation. We honor the Sacred that is incarnate and transcendent, yin and yang, fire and water, earth and air, within and without. Spirit is in all yet beyond all. This is unity consciousness.

The Earth and sky are speaking to us and calling us back to this deeper wisdom and awareness. If we listen, perhaps we will come back into right relationship, find our center, and begin to live out of a galactic and embodied consciousness beyond anything we have ever known.

CHAPTER 15

# Honoring the Journey and Stepping off the Wheel

The ancient art and science of astrology is a source of wisdom and guidance for our lives, individually and collectively, as we have seen in moving through the ages and finding our way to the center. The discoveries of the Centaurs, new dwarf planets, and Kuiper Belt objects signal a new awareness emerging in our consciousness and guiding us in our human evolution. If we tune in to the cycles of the planets, they also give us more detailed guidance for the phases and cycles of our lives, individually and generationally. As we have noted, the outer planets, in particular, bring us their transpersonal wisdom and guidance.

In light of this awareness, it should not surprise us to find that since 1981 all three of the outer transpersonal planets in our solar system have come into alignment with the galactic center. As noted earlier, the galactic center, Sagittarius A*, is located at 4 degrees of Sagittarius in the sidereal zodiac or 27 degrees of Sagittarius in the tropical zodiac. First, Neptune moved back and forth over this point in the sky from February 1981 through October 1984. Then, from January 1987 to November 1988, Uranus was in alignment with the galactic center. Finally, Pluto came into alignment from December 2005 to October 2008.

If we view this period in our human history as a time of intensification and purification, a call to a radical shift in consciousness, as stated in the ancient prophecies of the Maya, Hopi, Hindus, and others, then it is truly a profound synchronicity that the outer planets all came into alignment with the galactic center within these past few decades. Tuning back in to the core archetypal meaning of the outer planets, we might speculate that Neptune's alignment was calling on us to dissolve our attachments to our former ways of thinking and being, to integrate the gifts of the Age of Pisces—spiritual and mystical awareness and compassion, and release its shadow aspects—addiction, escapism, illusion, and delusion. Uranus was channeling new ways of thinking to us and new paradigms based on our understanding of energy and natural law and was calling us into truth, clarity, justice, and new forms of community. Pluto, planet of alchemy, was radically transforming us and calling us back into connection with our soul selves. Pluto has been guiding us to die to our past ways of life and out-of-balance ways of being and open to a radical rebirth, into a new consciousness and new Earth.

Beginning in 1998, we also had the critical period of the Sun's alignment with the galactic center at winter solstice here in the northern hemisphere and summer solstice in the southern hemisphere. Then, we had the ending of the Mayan Calendar in 2012 (fig. 15.1).

In 2024, we had the rare appearance of a comet lingering in the sky for a few weeks, first in the southern hemisphere and then in the northern hemisphere. This was the Tsuchinshan-ATLAS comet (discovered in 2023). This comet came from the Oort cloud and has an orbit of approximately 80,000 years. It came into view in late September to mid-October 2024. It was a important messenger to us, not only because it made us aware that this is a profound phase in our precessional cycle when we are more vulnerable to comet impacts, but also because of its placement in the sky. The comet was calling our attention to the constellation it was moving through—Ophiuchus, the great healer and the Serpent Bearer, who symbolizes the integration of the Sacred Feminine and Sacred Masculine. This constellation is also located just above the galactic center and reminds us that, in this

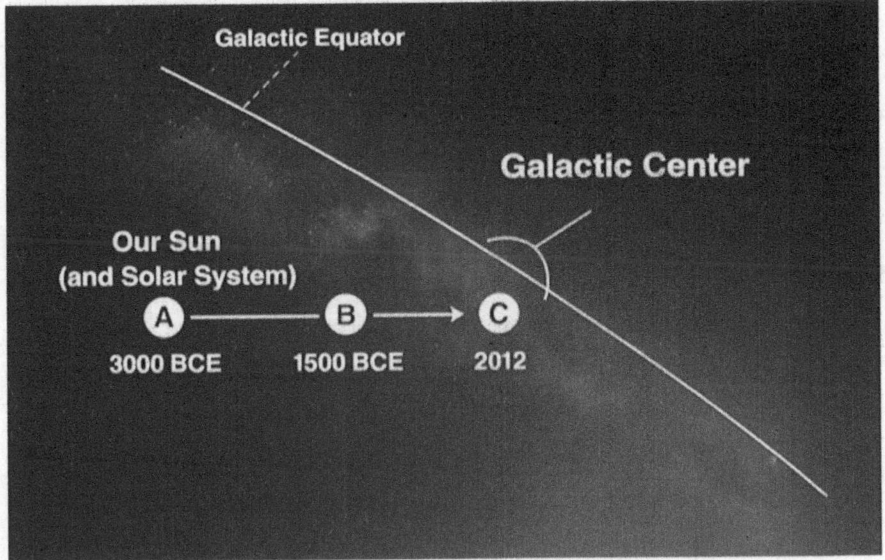


Fig. 15.1. The Sun/Milky Way alignment (beginning in 1998 and still in alignment at the end of the Mayan Calendar in 2012).

critical time, we need to heal and come back into relationship with Source, with Cosmic consciousness. It is also the constellation that is dominant in the time of the Golden Age and was reminding us that we can, at this critical moment in the precessional cycle, awaken, heal, and undergo an evolutionary leap into higher consciousness.

On March 20, 2025, we came to the end of the Kali Yuga. On March 30, 2025, Neptune moved into Aries in the tropical zodiac chart. The meaning of the first degree of Aries in the Sabian symbols (that encode the archetypal meaning of each degree of the zodiac) is "a woman rises out of the water; a seal rises and embraces her."[1] This marks a movement into a new spiritual consciousness. Perhaps this is symbolic of our integration of the wisdom of Sedna and our capacity to move into unity consciousness. It also signifies the return of the Sacred Feminine and our remembrance of the sacredness of all of life.

If we look at the actual placements of the planets in the stars on March 30, 2025, it is significant that the Sun, the Moon, Mercury,

Venus, Saturn, and Neptune were all in the stars of Pisces. They were showing us that we are dissolving our old forms and opening to the mystical and expanded spiritual consciousness of Pisces, guiding us into these new ways of being.

It is also significant that at the end of March 2025, Venus emerged as a morning star, coming out of her inferior conjunction with the Sun and her time of transformation and death/rebirth. She symbolizes our own journey of transformation as well as the importance of the emergence of the Sacred Feminine wisdom as we move out of the Kali Yuga period into higher consciousness. In that she emerged in the sign of Pisces, she was also guiding us to remember that Neptune, the ruler of Pisces, is the higher octave of Venus and symbolizes our capacity to open to and align with divine love, the love that permeates the Cosmos.

In May through August 2025, Neptune was in a close conjunction with Saturn, and in February 2026, they came into exact conjunction at 0 degrees of Aries in the tropical zodiac and, in their actual placement in the sky, were in the stars of Pisces. This conjunction symbolizes the dissolution (Neptune) of old patterns and our collective systems and structures (Saturn) that need to die in order to birth new paradigms and new forms as we move into the Aquarian Age.

In June 2031, Jupiter will be in alignment with the galactic center. This is the planet associated with Christ consciousness and is defined in other spiritual traditions as the "guru" or spiritual teacher. Jupiter is supporting us in the alignment with Source and our expanded consciousness.

Finally, I think it is highly significant that in June 2032, Uranus will be in conjunction with Saturn (in the sign of Gemini in the tropical zodiac chart). Uranus and Saturn have a forty-four-year synodic cycle. The last cycle began with their conjunction in 1988 in alignment with the galactic center. Their synodic cycle symbolizes the activation of new forms and ways of being in our collective consciousness. At that time, they were guiding us to remember our connection with Source

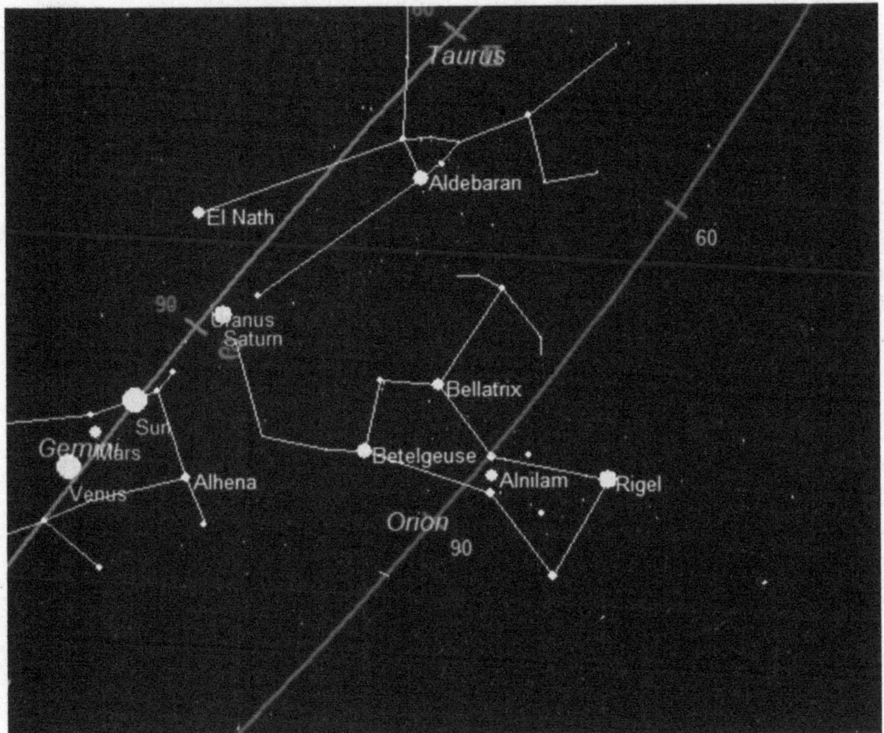


Fig. 15.2. The conjunction of Uranus and Saturn in June 2032.

and come back to center beginning in 1988, just after the time of the Harmonic Convergence in 1987. As they move into their new cycle beginning June 2032, Uranus and Saturn will be conjunct in the sky at the upraised arm of Orion (fig. 15.2). This is symbolic of order arising out of chaos, of resurrection, and of rebirth. Opposite Orion in the sky is the constellation Ophiuchus, showing us that now we can also heal, reweave our connection to the integration of the Sacred Masculine and Sacred Feminine, and come into wholeness. This symbolizes a time of spiritual awakening, our movement into higher consciousness, and our capacity to co-create a new world together.

The energies of these planets and stars are reminding us that like Osiris, Isis/Sirius is guiding us to heal, to reclaim the lost parts of ourselves, to be resurrected and move into being homoluminous ones, beings of light and higher consciousness. As in the story of Osiris, we do not need to stay bound on the wheel of time and chaos (Set), continually moving through times of cataclysmic crisis, only to be revived again and again. We can step off the wheel, come to center, join in sacred relationship with Sirius, and birth ourselves into wholeness and higher consciousness.

As we have explored the movement around the wheel of precession, we are able to see and experience the larger arc of our evolutionary journey as humanity. As we integrate the precessional cycle with the Yuga cycle, we see our journey of ascending and descending consciousness. We understand more fully that as we move through the descending cycle, we move into a more limited consciousness. However, as we move more fully into the density and intensity of third-dimensional reality and consciousness, we are also more fully in a time in which there is the capacity for profound transformation and transmutation. This is the time in the cycle when we move through the constellations and the signs of the ages that are furthest from the galactic center. This is when we are at our farthest distance from our binary star. As we saw in the Mars cycle, this is also when we can realize what the true meaning of this journey has been about and come back into connection with Source and return to our right relationship with the sacredness of all of life. This is when we can awaken, heal, transform. and move into higher consciousness. This is the time of death/rebirth, of resurrection. This is when Osiris is released from the control of Set, is healed by Isis and brought back to life and into wholeness. This is when the constellation Orion rises (and reaches his highest point in the sky) and shows us the path of ascension.

At any time in this spiral of evolutionary process, this cycle of precession, we can reclaim our true nature, our soul consciousness, and move into higher levels of spiritual awareness, into unity consciousness, and live from the heart, from love, and in balance and harmony with all of life. We need not be controlled by this karmic wheel of change and of time. This is the message of Christ consciousness, that the kingdom of the divine is within us. This is the message of spiritual teachers from around the globe and from the ancient wisdom traditions and from the Indigenous people on Earth who have not forgotten this ancient wisdom.

The most intense crisis points in the precessional cycle, with pole shifts, Earth changes, and cataclysm, occur every 12,000 years and come as we begin the descending cycle and then again at the end of the Kali Yuga phase in the cycle. These correlate with the beginning of the Age of Leo and the beginning of the Age of Aquarius. There are also less extreme crisis points, with Earth changes every 6,000 years correlating with the Ages of Taurus and Scorpio.

It is highly significant that these four fixed signs are the signs of the zodiac that align with shifts in the Yuga cycle. In this way, these four signs are the pillars of our journey of consciousness as we move through the cycle. They hold the keys to unlocking us from being bound on the wheel of time and ascending and descending consciousness. As we honor the lessons and initiations that they bring to us, we can integrate the wisdom of this journey and come to the center in the wheel of consciousness. Leo guides us to live from our hearts and to honor the Sun and light of consciousness. Taurus teaches us to honor the sacredness of the life around us and the beauty and sacredness of our embodiment. Aquarius guides us in aligning with the currents and wisdom of the Cosmos and remembering that everything is interconnected and that we are part of infinity. And Scorpio supports us in the alchemical process of burning away what no longer serves us to be in the true gold of who we are and in alignment with our soul selves.

As we move now into the Age of Aquarius, we can reclaim the wisdom of these four pillars. As we enter this age, we realize what a critical time this is in our human evolution and how important it is that we step into higher consciousness. We see a resurgence of the ancient prophecies about this period. There is increasing scientific research validating the

12,000-year cycle and that this is the time that our solar system moves through the galactic current sheet, activating a lessening of our magnetic field and a pole shift on the planet. It is also the time when our Sun moves through the sheet and is activated by a magnetic reversal in the galactic sheet and in the galactic dust, activating the possibility of a major solar flare or micronova that then becomes the catalyst for the Earth's pole shift, cataclysmic reset, loss of life, and extinction of many species.[2] It is also a time when we are more vulnerable to comet strikes that also can activate a global cataclysmic reset. Many humans survive these times of cataclysm, but they are a profound period of Earth change and global reorganization.

How are we to not be caught in fear as we examine the scientific evidence and see the signs of this playing out on the Earth—with the already rapidly shifting movement of the magnetic poles and the increasing intensity of storms, earthquake activity, and cultural turmoil? We see evidence of the conscious or unconscious awareness of this critical transition time playing out in our world with films and books about apocalypse and with the increasing fear, reactivity, violence, and global tumult. The fear of death and the destruction of the planet is increasing in our collective consciousness.

However, it is important to remember the root meaning of "apocalypse." It means "the uncovering, the revealing." What is being revealed is that all of this is our journey of consciousness and evolution as humanity. What we also are facing, as we awaken and reflect on this journey, is that these times of cataclysm are not random. This is when the Earth and humanity go through cleansing and purification, to clear and release what is out of balance. We as humanity are co-creators of our destiny. When we disconnect from Source and from alignment with the consciousness of the Cosmos and allow ourselves to be bound in time and chaos and become controlled by ego, greed, and corruption, then we are called back into purification in order to awaken. We go through the cataclysmic reset. This occurred when ego consciousness began to dominate in the Age of Leo, and it is occurring now as we have allowed ourselves to explore and become identified with the worst shadow aspects of our humanity. It is time for us to awaken, heal, transform, and remember who we truly are and what we are capable of as we open to higher consciousness.

When we realize that we are not separate, when we awaken and come back into awareness of our interconnectedness with all that is, when we remember that we are co-creators of our destiny, then we have the capacity to step off the wheel of time and repeating cycles. We can come to center, integrate the wisdom of the full wheel and the meaning of these profound four pillars. Then, we are able to face this karmic choice point and ascend into higher consciousness. Then, we can co-create a new world and a new Earth with each other and with Cosmic consciousness.

This is the message of the Indigenous peoples, of the Hopi: we are the ones that we have been waiting for. We are meant to let go of the shore, be in the river, let the currents carry us through this time of change. The Hopi have also prophesied that the way to move through this time is "to reconnect with our inner Self and return to a life of simplicity, led in harmony and balance with the Earth and all its creatures, with love for the Creator and one another."[3] This is the also message of the Q'ero in Peru who speak of this time as the time of Pachakuti, the turning over of the world, the time of turning the ways of the past upside down to open to new ways of being. This is what has been foretold in the prophecies of ancient and Indigenous cultures from around the globe. This is also in the prophecies of more recent psychics and spiritual teachers. The time is now.

We can remember who we are, why we are here, and the profound meaning of this journey of spiritual transformation and evolution across the ages. We can step out of this third-dimensional reality of materiality and time and duality, and we can reclaim our alignment with fifth-dimensional reality, with unity consciousness, with living from the heart and in oneness with all that is. This capacity to come back into the heart and into fifth-dimensional awareness then activates our capacity to open to all the other higher levels of consciousness.[4]

In this critical transition time, this is the karmic choice point for all of us individually and collectively. What will unfold in this third-dimensional reality will be shaped by our level of consciousness. If enough of us awaken and move into higher consciousness, this will create a morphogenic field of awakening that will shift the collective consciousness on the planet. If, however, this does not occur, then I truly believe that we will see a dimensional divide in which those who have awakened and moved into higher consciousness will move into the fifth dimension and co-create a new world and a new Earth together. Those who choose not to heal and awaken will stay on the wheel of karma and the wheel of samsara and go through the cataclysmic reset.

The Earth herself is awakening, healing, and transforming. We can heal and transform with her or be taken by her into a time of accounting and into a period of cleansing, purification, and reset. The meaning of our journeys here on the earth plane is to grow in love and wisdom, to reclaim and regain our full capacity for spiritual consciousness, and to choose to live in unity, harmony, and right relationship with all that is. We can choose to continue to journey through the ascending and descending cycle, the periods of remembering and forgetting, the times of death/rebirth, or we can choose the path of higher consciousness and full alignment with our soul selves and with the consciousness of the Cosmos. We can step off the wheel and no longer be bound by time and karma. We can align with the center of the wheel and the center within us, our hearts. We can remember our true nature, that we are infinite soul selves having a human experience, and we can reclaim our true potential to be beings of higher consciousness, choosing to come into form as a creative, fractal expression of Cosmic consciousness and to experience and celebrate the sacredness of embodiment and our capacity to co-create with the Oneness of all that is. Then, we can rejoin our place in the community of other galactic beings who live in higher states of consciousness. We can move in and out of space and time as we reclaim the capacities of our full consciousness in all nine dimensions, and we can join in the dance of love and wisdom of the Cosmos and sing in harmony with the song of the spheres.

*Circles within circles*
*A breathing, swirling spiral,*
*This galaxy, our home.*
*In the center,*
*Pulses a black hole,*
*The dark womb,*
*Birthing stars.*
*All life arises from the*
*Sea of chaos and darkness.*
*We come from the fertile void,*
*Stardust singing in our bones.*
*We are of the Sky and of the Earth,*
*The pulse of the Universe*
*Courses through our veins.*
*The energy of creation*
*Weaves a web that holds the stars and planets*
*And moves in the cells of our bodies.*

*When we no longer hear the song of the Universe*
*And the drumbeat of Mother Earth*
*We sever our connections with the Earth and Sky*
*And cut our umbilical cord to Source.*
*We drift in time and space*
*And lose our way*

*And our sense of who we are*
*And who we have been.*

*It is time to remember*
*To reweave the web*
*To hear anew the singing of the stars*
*And the heartbeat of the Earth.*
*It is time to open once again*
*To the wisdom of the Earth and Sky.*
*Following the path of the labyrinth,*
*We find our center, our Source,*
*The womb of the Earth and of the Sky,*
*And are birthed anew*
*And once again join in the song of the spheres.*

# Acknowledgments

I am deeply indebted to all who helped me to birth this book in its original version published in 2009. I am grateful to Vicki Noble for inspiring me to study astrology. Joseph Crane and Dorian Greenbaum were instrumental in my astrological training. I am grateful to Bernadette Brady for her profound wisdom about the stars that helped to deepen my relationship with the sky. I am indebted to Demetra George for her seminal work reweaving an understanding of the Sacred Feminine with astrology and mythology. Jeffrey Wolf Green has had a profound impact on my life and on my exploration of the spiritual dimensions of astrology. I am also grateful to all of the friends, students, and clients who have all touched my life and heart so deeply and helped me to grow in love and wisdom.

As I revised this book, I wanted to acknowledge the invaluable support and input of Barbara Hand Clow, who I greatly respect and whose friendship I deeply value. I am also grateful to Bibhu Dev Misra for his profound research and his support with my artwork. I am also thankful for my friendships with other astrologers, especially Pam Gregory and Melanie Reinhart, along with many others who have been supportive of me and my work. I am deeply grateful for my friendship with Elisabet Sahtouris, who courageously worked across her life to support our coming back into right relationship with the Earth and all of life. I am also grateful to the dear friends who have supported me in my work.

There are too many to name, but in particular, I am grateful to Ke'oni Hanalei, Jane Gleeson-White, and Dawn Baumann Brunke.

I also want to thank my other soul sisters and brothers and all of those who are serving humanity in this profound time of change. In addition, my spiritual community (through my YouTube channel) and their support for my work have allowed me to bring this out into the world. I am deeply grateful for being a part of this global spiritual community. Finally, I am most profoundly grateful for my partner, Kristina, for her love, for believing in me, and for supporting me in being in alignment with my soul's path and purpose.

The support that I have received for this book goes beyond the human realm. My ever-deepening path with Spirit has led me in this exploration of the meaning of the Universe and of this profound time in the precessional cycle. I have also been forever changed by the mystery, wonder, and energies of the stars and planets as well as by the amazing complexity of life on this planet, Earth. I am honored to be in deep relationship with the Earth and Sky and am filled with gratitude for their wisdom, guidance, and transformative and healing energies. I am deeply committed to being in alignment with my soul song and singing in harmony with the music of the spheres and of all of life, and attuning to the heartbeat of Mother Earth and the rhythms of the Cosmos.

# Notes

## CHAPTER 1.
## LIVING IN A TIME OF TRANSITION

1. Grant, "One Is the Only Constant."
2. Cruttenden, "Precession of the Equinox: The Ancient Truth Behind Celestial Motion," Binary Research Institute website.
3. Reedijk, *Sirius, the Star of the Maltese Temples.*
4. Cruttenden, *Lost Star of Myth and Time,* 159.
5. Cruttenden, "Lost Knowledge," Graham Hancock website, June 6, 2024.
6. Yukteswar, *The Holy Science,* 6.
7. Cruttenden, "Lost Knowledge," Graham Hancock website, June 6, 2024.
8. Evans, "The Origin of Time and the Great Sirius Observatory".
9. Hancock, *Underworld,* 271.
10. Davidson, *Earth Disaster Cycle,* 48.
11. Dev Misra, *Yuga Shift,* 15.
12. Dev Misra, *Yuga Shift,* 6–7.
13. Clow, *Alchemy of Nine Dimensions,* 3.
14. Clow, *Alchemy of Nine Dimensions,* 10.
15. Clow, *Alchemy of Nine Dimensions,* 10.
16. Tarnas, *Cosmos and Psyche,* 13.
17. Jung, *The Archetypes and the Collective Unconscious,* 42–43.
18. Van Gennep, *The Rites of Passage,* 182.
19. Van Gennep, *The Rites of Passage,* 189–90.

## CHAPTER 2. SEEKING THE WISDOM OF THE PAST

1. Brady, comment in a class.
2. Brady, *Brady's Book of Fixed Stars,* 47.
3. Carlson, "The Milky Way's Supermassive Black Hole Erupted with a Violent Flare a Few Million Years Ago."
4. Brady, *Brady's Book of Fixed Stars*, 134.
5. Brady, *Brady's Book of Fixed Stars*, 134.
6. Evans, "The Origin of Time and the Great Sirius Observatory".

## OVERVIEW OF THE AGES ACROSS THE PAST 12,000 YEARS

1. Hand, "The History of Astrology: Another View."
2. Hand, "The History of Astrology: Another View."
3. Green, comment in a class.

## CHAPTER 3. THE AGE OF LEO

1. Young, "The Younger Dryas Impact Hypothesis: A Guide for the Perplexed," Graham Hancock website.
2. Collins and Hale, "Göbekli Tepe and the Rebirth of Sirius," Andrew Collins website.
3. Vidler, *The Star Mirror,* 204.
4. Hancock, *Underworld,* 53.
5. Hancock, *Underworld,* 65–69.
6. Hancock, *Underworld,* 65–69.
7. Brady, *Brady's Book of Fixed Stars,* 259.
8. Hancock, *Fingerprints of the Gods*, 423.
9. Hancock and Bauval, *The Message of the Sphinx,* 17.
10. Bauval and Gilbert, *The Orion Mystery,* 135.
11. Grant, comment in a conversation at a summit, "Ancient Mysteries and Water" webinar, March 16, 2024 (offered by Veda Austin).
12. Hancock and Bauval, *The Message of the Sphinx*, 81.
13. Kreisberg, *Lost Knowledge of the Ancients,* 88–101.

14. Kreisberg, *Lost Knowledge of the Ancients,* 98.
15. Creighton, "The Orion Key," Graham Hancock's website.
16. Hancock and Bauval, *The Message of the Sphinx*, 81.
17. Sahtouris, personal conversation, Oct. 4, 2024.
18. Vidler, *The Star Mirror,* 62.
19. Brady, *Brady's Book of Fixed Stars,* 259.

## CHAPTER 4. THE AGE OF CANCER

1. Samorini, "The Oldest Archeological Data Evidencing the Relationship of *Homo sapiens* with Psychoactive Plants: A Worldwide View," 2.
2. George, *Mysteries of the Dark Moon,* 87.
3. Gimbutas, *The Language of the Goddess*, 31.
4. Gimbutas, *The Language of the Goddess*, 19.
5. Gimbutas, *The Language of the Goddess*, 19.
6. Cashford, *The Moon: Myth and Image*, 68.
7. Karim, "Biogeometry: A New Science to Understand Ancient Sacred Sites."
8. Brady, *Brady's Book of Fixed Stars*, 253.
9. Brady, *Brady's Book of Fixed Stars*, 253.
10. Brady, *Brady's Book of Fixed Stars*, 253.
11. Baring and Cashford, *The Myth of the Goddess*, 17.
12. Owen, *Her Blood Is Gold.*
13. Baring and Cashford, *The Myth of the Goddess*, 512.
14. Baring and Cashford, *The Myth of the Goddess*, 512.

## CHAPTER 5. THE AGE OF GEMINI

1. Brady, *Brady's Book of Fixed Stars*, 243.
2. Gimbutas, *The Language of the Goddess*, 171.

## CHAPTER 6. THE AGE OF TAURUS

1. Grasse, *Signs of the Times*, 10.
2. Brady, *Brady's Book of Fixed Stars*, 229.
3. Gimbutas, *Civilization of the Goddess*, 352.
4. Baillie, *Exodus to Arthur*, 148.

5. Peiser, "Comets and Disaster in the Bronze Age," 6.
6. Peiser, "Comets and Disaster in the Bronze Age," 6.
7. Peiser, "Comets and Disaster in the Bronze Age," 7.
8. Baillie, *Exodus to Arthur*, 115–16.
9. Baillie, *Exodus to Arthur*, 131–35.
10. Kramer, *Sumerian Mythology*, 41.
11. Wolkstein and Kramer, *Inanna, Queen of Heaven and Earth*, 4–5.
12. Wolkstein and Kramer, *Inanna, Queen of Heaven and Earth*, 5.
13. Wolkstein and Kramer, *Inanna, Queen of Heaven and Earth*, 6.
14. Wolkstein and Kramer, *Inanna, Queen of Heaven and Earth*, 37.
15. Wolkstein and Kramer, *Inanna, Queen of Heaven and Earth*, 32.
16. Wolkstein and Kramer, *Inanna, Queen of Heaven and Earth*, 32–33.
17. Wolkstein and Kramer, *Inanna, Queen of Heaven and Earth*, 60.
18. Dalley, *Myths from Mesopotamia: Creation, the Flood, Gilgamesh and Others*, 56.
19. De Santillana and von Dechen, *Hamlet's Mill*, 293.
20. De Santillana and von Dechen, *Hamlet's Mill*, 295.
21. De Santillana and von Dechen, *Hamlet's Mill*, 300.

## CHAPTER 7. THE AGE OF ARIES

1. Grasse, *Signs of the Times*, 11.
2. Grasse, *Signs of the Times*, 11.
3. Genesis 22:1–18 (Revised Standard Version).
4. Genesis 22:13 (RSV).
5. Genesis 3:7–8 (RSV).
6. Zimmer, "Death and Rebirth in the Light of India," 348.
7. Whyte, "Santiago," in *Pilgrim*.

## CHAPTER 8. THE AGE OF PISCES

1. Brady, *Brady's Book of Fixed Stars*, 311.
2. Brady, *Brady's Book of Fixed Stars*, 311.
3. Greene, *The Astrological Neptune*, 71.
4. Greene, *The Astrological Neptune*, 71.

## CHAPTER 9. THE AGE OF AQUARIUS

1. Dev Misra, *Yuga Shift*, 72.
2. Guttman and Johnson, *Mythic Astrology*, 347.
3. Guttman and Johnson, *Mythic Astrology*, 346.
4. Guttman and Johnson, *Mythic Astrology*, 345.
5. Walker, *The Woman's Encyclopedia of Myths and Secrets*, 358.
6. Gimbutas, *The Language of the Goddess*, 19.
7. Gimbutas, *The Language of the Goddess*, 22.
8. Sahtouris and Lovelock, *EarthDance: Living Systems in Evolution*.
9. Tarnas, *Prometheus the Awakener*, 13.

## CHAPTER 10. AROUND THE WHEEL

1. Rudhyar, *The Astrology of Transformation: A Multilevel Approach*.
2. Clow, *Alchemy of Nine Dimensions*, 179.

## CHAPTER 11. LIMINAL PERIODS: TRANSITIONS BETWEEN AGES AND THE MOVEMENT INTO ASCENDING CONSCIOUSNESS

1. Green, *Uranus: Freedom from the Known*.
2. Dev Misra. "Four Signs the Yuga Shift Is Already Underway."
3. Sahtouris, "The Secret to Human Coexisting," posted April 20, 2016, by Big Speakers Bureau, YouTube.
4. The Elders, Hopi Nation, Oraibi, Arizona, prophecy, June 8, 2000.

## CHAPTER 12. GUIDANCE FROM THE COSMOS

1. Tompkins and Reinhart, "Chiron and the Centaurs."
2. Tompkins and Reinhart, "Chiron and the Centaurs."
3. Qitsualik, "Nunani: Esquimaux."
4. Qitsualik, "The Problem with Sedna: Part One of Three."
5. Greene, *The Astrological Neptune*, xiv.
6. Greene, *The Astrological Neptune*, 37–38.

7. Swimme, *The Universe Is a Green Dragon.*
8. Greene, *The Astrological Neptune,* 37–38.
9. Wolkstein and Kramer, *Inanna, Queen of Heaven and Earth,* 147.
10. Clow, *Alchemy of Nine Dimensions,* 10.

## CHAPTER 13. OUR GALACTIC CENTER

1. Melia, *The Black Hole at the Center of Our Galaxy,* 3.
2. Melia, *The Black Hole at the Center of Our Galaxy,* 8.
3. Melia, *The Black Hole at the Center of Our Galaxy,* 8.
4. Currivan, *The Cosmic Hologram,* 39.
5. Melia, *The Black Hole at the Center of Our Galaxy,* 15.
6. Melia, *The Black Hole at the Center of Our Galaxy,* 40.
7. Swimme, *The Hidden Heart of the Cosmos,* 100.
8. Dev Misra, "Supermassive Black Hole or Galactic Consciousness?"
9. "Galactic Center," image-article, NASA website, July 23, 2019 (accessed October 17, 2024). Image credit: X-Ray:NASA/CXC/UMass/D. Wang et al.; Radio:NRF/SARAO/MeerKAT.
10. Temple, *The Sirius Mystery,* 319.
11. Swimme, *The Hidden Heart of the Cosmos,* 75.
12. Swimme, *The Hidden Heart of the Cosmos,* 85.
13. Swimme, *The Hidden Heart of the Cosmos,* 93.
14. Swimme, *The Hidden Heart of the Cosmos,* 102.

## CHAPTER 15. HONORING THE JOURNEY AND STEPPING OFF THE WHEEL

1. Rudhyar, *An Astrological Mandala.*
2. Davidson, *Earth Disaster Cycle,* 44.
3. Dev Misra, *Yuga Shift,* 317.
4. Clow, comment in interview with author, October 18, 2024.

# Bibliography

Anne Baring, and Cashford, Jules. *The Myth of the Goddess: Evolution of an Image.* London: Viking Arkana, 1991.

Austin, Veda. *The Living Language of Water.* Published by the author, 2024.

Baigent, Michael. *From the Omens of Babylon: Astrology and Ancient Mesopotamia.* London: Penguin, 1994.

Baillie, Mike. *Exodus to Arthur: Catastrophic Encounters with Comets.* London: B. T. Batsford, 2000.

Bauval, Robert, and Adrian Gilbert. *The Orion Mystery: Unlocking the Secrets of the Pyramids.* New York: Three Rivers Press,1994.

Berry, Thomas. *The Dream of the Earth.* San Francisco: Sierra Club Books, 1988.

Brady, Bernadette. *Brady's Book of Fixed Stars.* York Beach, ME: Samuel Weiser, 1998.

Burt, Kathleen. *Archetypes of the Zodiac.* St. Paul, MN: Llewellyn Publications, 1993.

Capra, Fritjof. *The Web of Life: A New Scientific Understanding of Living Systems.* New York: Anchor Books, 1996.

Carlson, Erika. "The Milky Way's Supermassive Black Hole Erupted with a Violent Flare a Few Million Years Ago," *Discover* magazine, October 9, 2019.

Casey, Carolyn. *Making the Gods Work for You: The Astrological Language of the Psyche.* Easton, PA: Harmony, 1998.

Cashford, Jules. *The Moon: Myth and Image.* New York: Four Walls Eight Windows, 2003.

Childre, Doc Lew, and Howard Martin. *The Heartmath Solution.* San Francisco: HarperOne, 2000.

Clow, Barbara. *Alchemy of Nine Dimensions: Activating the Full Spectrum of Consciousness.* Rochester, VT: Bear & Company, 2024. Twentieth anniversary edition.

Clow, Barbara. *Awakening the Planetary Mind: Beyond the Trauma of the Past to a New Era of Creativity.* Rochester, VT: Bear & Company, 2011.

Clube, Victor, and Bill Napier. *The Cosmic Serpent: A Catastrophist View of Earth History.* New York: Universe Books, 1982.

Collins, Andrew. *The Cygnus Mystery: Unlocking the Ancient Secret of Life's Origins in the Cosmos.* London: Watkins Media, 2007.

Collins, Andrew, and Rodney Hale. "Göbekli Tepe and the Rebirth of Sirius." Andrew Collins website.

Creighton, Scott. "The Orion Key: Unlocking the Mystery of Giza." Graham Hancock website, June 1, 2010.

Cruttenden, Walter. "Lost Knowledge." Author of the Month (blog). Graham Hancock website, June 6, 2024.

Cruttenden, Walter. *Lost Star of Myth and Time.* Pittsburgh: St. Lynn's Press, 2005.

Cruttenden, Walter. "Precession of the Equinox: The Ancient Truth Behind Celestial Motion." Binary Research Institute website.

Currivan, Jude. *The Cosmic Hologram.* Rochester, VT: Inner Traditions, 2017.

Currivan, Jude. *The Story of Gaia.* Rochester, VT: Inner Traditions, 2022.

Dalley, Stephanie. *Myths from Mesopotamia: Creation, the Flood, Gilgamesh and Others.* Oxford, UK: Oxford University Press, 1998 (revised 2000).

Dames, Michael. *Mythic Ireland.* London: Thames and Hudson, 1992.

Davidson, Ben. *Earth Disaster Cycle.* Colorado Springs: Ben Davidson and Space Weather, News, LLC, 2023 (Observer Ranch Podia website).

de Santillana, Giorgio, and Hertha von Dechend. *Hamlet's Mill.* Boston: David R. Godine, 1977.

Dev Misra, Bibhu. "Four Signs that the Yuga Shift Is Already Underway." Ancient Inquiries, March 19, 2025.

Dev Misra, Bibhu. "Supermassive Black Hole or Galactic Consciousness?," Mysterious Universe website, September 29, 2025.

Dev Misra, Bibhu. *Yuga Shift: The End of the Kali Yuga and the Impending Planetary Transformation.* Chandigarh, India: White Falcon Publishing, 2023.

Evans, Hugh. *The Origin of Time.* Published by the author, 2024.

Evans, Hugh. "The Origin of Time and the Great Sirius Observatory." Presentation at Megalithomania Conference 2024, Glastonbury, UK, May 5, 2024. Posted September 12, 2024, by MegalithomaniaUK, YouTube, 59 min., 02 sec.

Evans, Hugh. *The Origin of the Zodiac: Cadair Idris and the Star Maps of Gwynedd.* Published by the author, 2021.

Firestone, Richard, Allen West, and Simon Warwick-Smith. *The Cycle of Cosmic Catastrophes.* Rochester, VT: Bear and Company, 2006.

Friedel, David, Linda Schele, and Joy Parker. *Maya Cosmos: Three Thousand Years on the Shaman's Path.* New York: William Morrow, 1993.

George, Demetra. *Mysteries of the Dark Moon.* San Francisco: Harper San Francisco, 1992.

Gimbutas, Marija. *The Civilization of the Goddess.* San Francisco: HarperSanFrancisco, 1991.

Gimbutas, Marija. *The Language of the Goddess.* New York: Harper & Row, 1989.

Gleadow, Rupert. *The Origin of the Zodiac.* New York: Castle Books, 1968.

Grant, Robert Edward. "One Is the Only Constant." Presentation at Resonance Retreat, Scotts Valley, California, July 29–August 3, 2019. Resonance Talks, posted April 3, 2021, by Resonance Science Foundation, YouTube, 33 min., 49 sec.

Grasse, Ray. *Signs of the Times: Unlocking the Symbolic Language of World Events.* Charlottesville, VA: Hampton Roads, 2002.

Green, Jeff. *Pluto: The Evolutionary Journey of the Soul: Volume I.* St. Paul, MN: Llewellyn Publications, 1996.

Green, Jeffrey Wolf. *Pluto: The Soul's Evolution Through Relationships: Volume II.* St. Paul, MN: Llewellyn Publications, 1997.

Green, Jeffrey Wolf. *Uranus: Freedom from the Known.* St. Paul, MN: Llewellyn Publications, 1989.

Greene, Liz. *The Astrological Neptune and the Quest for Redemption.* York Beach, ME: Samuel Weiser, 1996.

Guttman, Ariel, and Kenneth Johnson. *Mythic Astrology: Internalizing the Planetary Powers.* St. Paul, MN: Llewellyn Publications, 1993.

Hancock, Graham. *Fingerprints of the Gods.* London: William Heinemann, 1996.

Hancock, Graham. *Magicians of the Gods.* London: Coronet, 2015.

Hancock, Graham. *Supernatural: Meetings with the Ancient Teachers of Mankind.* United Kingdom: Arrow Books, 2006.

Hancock, Graham. *Underworld: The Mysterious Origins of Civilization.* New York: Three Rivers Press, 2002.

Hancock, Graham, and Robert Bauval. *The Message of the Sphinx: A Quest for the Hidden Legacy of Mankind.* New York: Crown Publishing Group, 1997.

Hand, Robert. "The History of Astrology: Another View." Astro.com website, 1996.

*Holy Bible* (New International Version). Grand Rapids, MI: Zondervan, 1978.

Jacobsen, Thorkild. *The Treasures of Darkness: A History of Mesopotamian Religion.* New Haven and London: Yale University Press, 1976.

Jenkins, John Major. *Galactic Alignment: The Transformation of Consciousness According to Mayan, Egyptian, and Vedic Traditions.* Rochester, VT: Bear & Co, 2002.

Jenkins, John Major. *Maya Cosmogenesis 2012.* Rochester, VT: Bear & Co., 1998.

Jung, C. G. *The Archetypes and the Collective Unconscious.* Translated by R. F. C. Hull. Princeton, NJ: Princeton Univ. Press, 1969.

Karim, Doreya. "Biogeometry: A New Science to Understand Ancient Sacred Sites." *Face the Current,* January 23, 2021.

Kramer, Samuel Noah. *Sumerian Mythology: A Study of Spiritual and Literary Achievement in the Third Millennium B.C.* Rev. ed. Philadelphia: Univ. of Pennsylvania Press, 1961.

Kreisberg, Glenn, ed. *Lost Knowledge of the Ancients: A Graham Hancock Reader.* Rochester, VT: Bear & Company, 2010.

Krupp, E. C., ed. *In Search of Ancient Astronomies.* Garden City, NY: Doubleday, 1978.

Lash, John. *Quest for the Zodiac: The Cosmic Code Beyond Astrology.* Loughborough, UK: Thoth Publications, 1999.

Marshack, Alexander. *The Roots of Civilization.* London: Weidenfeld & Nicolson, 1972.

Melia, Fulvio. *The Black Hole at the Center of Our Galaxy.* Princeton and Oxford: Princeton University Press, 2003.

Michell, John. *At the Center of the World: Polar Symbolism Discovered in Celtic, Norse, and Other Ritualized Landscapes.* London: Thames and Hudson, 1994.

Neumann, Erich. *The Origins and History of Consciousness.* Translated by R. F. C. Hull. Princeton, NJ: Princeton University Press, 1954.

Noble, Vicki. *The Double Goddess: Women Sharing Power.* Rochester, VT: Bear & Company, 2003.

Owen, Lara. *Her Blood Is Gold: Awakening to the Wisdom of Menstruation.* 3rd ed. Archive Publishing, 2016.

Peiser, Benny. "Comets and Disaster in the Bronze Age." *British Archaeology,* no. 30 (Dec. 1997).

Perera, Sylvia Brinton. *Descent to the Goddess: A Way of Initiation for Women.* Toronto: Inner City Books, 1981.

Pink, Daniel. *A Whole New Mind: Moving from the Information Age to the Conceptual Age.* New York: Riverhead, 2005.

Qitsualik, Rachel. "Nunani: Esquimaux." *Nunatsiaq News*, June 28, 2003 (accessed November 11, 2024).

Qitsualik, Rachel. "The Problem with Sedna: Part One of Three." *Nunatsiaq News*, March 5, 1999 (accessed November 11, 2024).

Reedijk, Lenie. *Sirius, the Star of the Maltese Temples.* Malet Books, 2018.

Rudhyar, Dane. *An Astrological Mandala: The Cycle of Transformations and Its 360 Symbolic Phases.* New York: Vintage Books Edition, 1974.

Rudhyar, Dane. *The Astrology of Transformation: A Multilevel Approach.* Santa Fe, NM: Aurora Press, 1980.

Ruggles, Clive. *Ancient Astronomy: An Encyclopedia of Cosmologies and Myth.* Santa Barbara, CA: ABC-CLIO, 2005.

Sahtouris, Elisabet. *EarthDance: Living Systems in Evolution.* Lincoln, NE: IUniversity Press, 2000.

Samorini, Giorgio. "The Oldest Archeological Data Evidencing the Relationship of *Homo sapiens* with Psychoactive Plants: A Worldwide View." *Journal of Psychedelic Studies* 3, no. 2 (March 2019).

Schore, Allan N. *Affect Regulation and the Origin of the Self.* Hillsdale, NY: Lawrence Erlbaum Associates, 1994.

Shlain, Leonard. *The Alphabet Versus the Goddess.* New York: Penguin Compass, 1999.

Swimme, Brian. *The Hidden Heart of the Cosmos: Humanity and the New Story.* Maryknoll, NY: Orbis Books, 1996.

Swimme, Brian. *The Universe Is a Green Dragon: A Cosmic Creation Story.* Santa Fe, NM: Bear & Company, 1984.

Swimme, Brian, and Thomas Berry. *The Universe Story.* San Francisco: HarperSanFrancisco, 1992.

Tarnas, Richard. *Cosmos and Psyche: Intimations of a New World View.* New York: Viking, 2006.

Tarnas, Richard. *Prometheus the Awakener.* Putnam, CT: Spring Publications, 1995.

Temple, Robert. *The Sirius Mystery.* Rochester, VT: Destiny Books, 1998.

Tomkins, Sue, and Melanie Reinhart. "Chiron and the Centaurs." Melanie Reinhart website.

van Gennep, Arnold. *The Rites of Passage.* Chicago: University of Chicago Press, 1960.

Vidler, Mark. *The Star Mirror.* London: Thorsons, 1998.

Villoldo, Alberto. *Shaman, Healer, Sage.* New York: Harmony Books, 2000.

Walker, Barbara. *The Woman's Encyclopedia of Myths and Secrets.* San Francisco: HarperSanFrancisco, 1983.

Whyte, David. *Pilgrim.* Many Rivers Press, 2014.

Wolkstein, Diane, and Samuel Noah Kramer. *Inanna, Queen of Heaven and Earth: Her Stories and Hymns from Sumer.* San Francisco: HarperSanFrancisco, 1983.

Young, Marc. "The Younger Dryas Impact Hypothesis: A Guide for the Perplexed." Graham Hancock website, April 15, 2024, accessed October 2024.

Yukteswar, Swami Sri. *The Holy Science.* Rev. ed. Los Angeles: Self-Realization Fellowship, 1990.

Zimmer, Heinrich. "Death and Rebirth in the Light of India." In *Man and Transformation: Papers from the Eranos Yearbooks,* Eranos 5: *Man and Transformation*. Edited by Joseph Campbell. Princeton, NJ: Princeton University Press, 1964.

# Index

Index